MW01712390

The best of Mrs Beeton's Household Tips

The best of Mrs Beeton's Household Tips

RIGEL

First published in Canada in 2005 for Indigo Books by Rigel Publications,
a division of the Orion Publishing Group Ltd
5 Upper St Martin's Lane
London
WC2H 9EA

Designed by seagulls
Index prepared by Indexing Specialists (UK) Ltd
Produced by Omnipress Ltd, Eastbourne
Printed in Spain

Contents

D.I.Y. and Home Maintenance

Becoming a confident home handyperson takes years of practice and experience – this chapter sets out to explain some of the basic facts about the way your home works.

It is important to understand the way in which the services and fabric of your home function so that minor emergencies can be dealt with efficiently and with a certain amount of confidence. Also, when you are commissioning specialists to carry out work, having a basic appreciation of what may be involved is invaluable both for obtaining the right advice and avoiding being misled by unscrupulous individuals.

FINDING OUT ABOUT YOUR HOME

The details of building construction may not interest you but it is important to know a few facts about the way in which your home is put together and, more importantly, the services supplied to it. If you live in a flat or in rented accommodation, some of the following notes will not apply; however, whether you own or rent you should note information which is likely to be helpful in the event of an emergency.

When you first move into a new property, take a thorough look at all areas – the attic is often neglected, yet it can contain a vital network of wiring and plumbing. Dust, dirt and debris should be cleared away from the attic, cellars, store rooms, cupboards and garages adjoining the house. You should be able to gain access to all main attic areas. Once these areas are cleaned, look around at the general condition of pipework, wires and woodwork and make a note of any likely problems.

KEY POINTS TO REMEMBER

Find the main supply points for services entering the house and make sure you know how to cut off the supply.

Electricity The supply is brought into the house through a heavy black cable to a service box, meter and fuse box. A main switch for turning off all power to the house will be somewhere near the service box or fuse box; locate this and remember where it is. Make sure all adult members of the household know where it is; responsible older children should also be aware of the main switch. This is the point at which the electricity should be turned off in case of emergency (such as a burst water pipe which may flood wiring) or whenever any electrical repairs are carried out.

It is also important to know where the fuse box is. The fuses protect every electric circuit in the house, each performing a function according to the 'load' which it can take. If the circuit is overloaded, or if a fault occurs anywhere on the circuit, the fuse will 'blow' as the wire which runs across it breaks, or the circuit-breaker device operates.

Gas The gas supply is brought into a meter and the main gas tap is usually found in the pipe near the meter. By closing this tap, the gas supply to the house is cut off. The tap should be turned off if you smell an unexplained odour of gas anywhere in the house, or in emergencies.

Water The main cold water pipe comes in to the house underground and usually surfaces in the kitchen or under the stairs, although this may vary. Somewhere near the point where the water pipe enters the house you will find a stopcock or stop valve. You should be aware of where this is and it should be kept clear for access at all times so that you can turn off the main water supply to the house in case of an emergency.

In addition, it is sensible to locate stopcocks near the cold and hot water tanks as well as at other key points in the plumbing system. By investigating the plumbing you will find stopcocks to cut off the supply to individual taps and toilets.

It is also worth remembering that there is a stopcock located underground near the point at which the water pipe enters the premises. Usually, an inspection cover is found near the front gate or door. It should not be necessary to use this under normal circumstances, but it can be useful when access cannot be gained to the house or if the main entrance stopcock has failed.

Separate plumbing systems service the central heating and there are stopcocks and drain valves located at key points. By tracing pipes from radiators and the boiler you will become familiar with the pipework in the house.

Drainage Systems The drainage system takes away all water from sinks, baths, showers and so on. Lavatory waste is also drained via different pipes to the same drainage system, and rainwater from gutters also runs down into the drains.

Look around the house to find drain covers, the points at which washing water and rain water exit, and a larger soil pipe or soil stack which may be inside or outside the house and leads from the lavatories directly out.

Locate the inspection chamber which will be covered by a manhole cover. All pipes from inside the house will eventually come out via the inspection chamber. Rainwater from gutters may run in to a soakaway which does not enter the sewerage system. If there are any blockages, or foul smells, then lifting the inspection cover (by using a sturdy lever) can give some indication of the level of the problem. The pipework should be clear of waste, except when in use. With the cover off, run water or flush different toilets to see if the waste water runs away quickly and efficiently.

Some older properties, mainly in rural areas, still have septic tanks rather than being linked to the main sewerage system.

Central Heating Boiler Lastly, make sure you find instructions to go with the central heating boiler on your tour of inspection. If you do not have written instructions, give the boiler a thorough inspection for integral lighting instructions. Taking the trouble to acquaint yourself with the pilot light and the ignition button is far easier when there is not a problem than at 6 am on a freezing morning when something is amiss. The same applies to water heaters and boilers.

TOOL KIT

A tool kit grows and develops over a number of years of experience, but there are a few essentials for every home which should be kept together in a convenient place.

Screwdrivers Choose either a good-quality tool with interchangeable heads or a few different tools for large and small screws, some with cross heads (sometimes referred to as Phillips) and some with straight heads. Avoid inexpensive, flimsy interchangeable kits which are too weak to be of much use in the long run. A re-chargeable electric screwdriver is an excellent buy.

Hammer If you only buy one hammer, choose a medium-sized tool but, ideally, have a small one for hitting tacks and a large one for jobs which need a firmer knock.

Pliers A pair of sturdy pliers is useful for many household jobs, including pulling out old nails and retrieving nails which have been bent. Some pliers have wire-strippers included which can be useful.

Adjustable Spanner Ideally, buy two of these: a very large one, which is useful for coping with large compression joints in plumbing systems, and a smaller one.

Spanner Set A good-quality set of spanners is not expensive and will prove useful for many tasks.

Electric Drill This is invaluable for making holes to hang pictures (in some walls), for fixing mounting wood for curtain rails or shelves and for many other tasks. Also, remember a set of bits in assorted sizes, for wood and for drilling brickwork.

Saw There are many types: small ones or hack-saws with removable blades, coarse saws with double-edged blades for cutting floor boards, fine saws for moulding, picture framing and so on, and a panel-saw which will deal with most jobs. A hack-saw is useful for cutting metals (with the appropriate blade).

Sandpaper Keep a selection of different grades for jobs such as smoothing, finishing, cleaning off old paint and cleaning pipes.

Fuse Wire and Fuses Keep a selection to repair or replace broken fuses.

Wire Cutters These may be included in the pliers but it is best to have a separate pair.

Knife A strong knife with a retractable blade is useful for tough cutting jobs and for slitting the coverings on electric wires before stripping them back to wire a plug.

Selection of Screws, Nails, Tacks and Washers It is handy to have these at the ready for instant repairs.

Small Indoor Repairs

ELECTRICAL REPAIRS

REPLACING A FUSE

A fuse is the weakest part of an electric circuit. If there is a fault, the fuse will blow first to avoid damaging the whole circuit or, more importantly, to avoid any fault on an appliance causing shock or accident.

The important point about a fuse is that it must be replaced with another of the correct rating for the appliance, or the wire in a circuit fuse must be replaced with the same strength wire. If the strength of the fuse is increased it will not fulfil its role as a protector as it will not fail at the appropriate rating limit.

FUSE BOX OR CONSUMER UNIT FUSE RATINGS

- Lighting circuits – 5 amp
- Power circuits (sockets) – 30 amp
- Immersion heater – 15 amp
- Cooker or similar large heating appliance – 45 amp

PLUG FUSES

- Lamp, radio, television – 3 amp
- Power tools, hair dryer, electric heaters – 13 amp

REPAIRING A HOUSE CIRCUIT FUSE

When one of the fuses fails in one house circuit, all lights and electrical appliances connected to that circuit will fail to work. The instructions below detail the procedures for repairing the various types of house circuit fuses.

Traditional Fuses

1 Switch off electricity at the main switch.

2 Pull the fuses out one by one to check which has broken – the wire will be severed.
3 Undo both small screws at the ends of the fuse and remove any old wire. Cut a length of new wire of the same rating.
4 Thread the wire across the fuse, winding the ends around the screws and screwing them up firmly.
5 Check that the screws are firmly in place and trim any excess wire, then replace the fuse and turn the electricity back on.

Cartridge Fuses

1 Switch off electricity at the main switch.
2 Pull out the fuse holders in turn. The failed fuse will be blackened.
3 Unscrew the cartridge holder and lever out the old fuse. Replace it with a new one and screw the cartridge holder back together.
4 Replace the cartridge, then switch on the electricity.

Circuit-breakers These do not have to be replaced, but they have to be reset. A red button pops out when the circuit is broken; this has to be pushed in again in order to repair the circuit. Turn off the electricity at the mains switch before resetting the circuit-breaker, then turn it back on again afterwards.

FITTING A PLUG

1 Unscrew the plug cover and the cord grip. Loosen the small screws or pins which hold the wires in place.
2 Check that the wire from the appliance is in good condition – not frayed or worn. Cut the end off neatly, then slit the outer covering by about 3.5 cm/ 1½ inches to reveal the two or three thinner wires inside. Take care not to damage the coverings on the inner wires.
3 Carefully strip the insulation from each of the inner wires to reveal about 1 cm/½ inch of the bare wire. Make sure you do not cut through the bare wire or make it ragged. Press the wire neatly together.
4 Thread the wire under the core clamp, or place it in position. Take each of the core wires to their respective terminals, pins or small screws in the plug, according to the colour coding:

    Brown – live (linked with the fuse)
    Blue – neutral
    Green/yellow – earth

The terminals should be marked in the socket casing, with an L (live), N (neutral) and E (earth).

5 Make sure the ends of the wires are neat, then thread each one in turn through the small hole under the screw or pin, making sure it has gone right through the hole. Screw the pin down securely. Repeat until all the wires are firmly attached.

6 Press the core wires neatly in place in the plug, then screw down the cord grip or clamp to hold the outer sheath or covering on the wire firmly in place. The clamp must be screwed down firmly as the attachments to the terminals are not strong enough to hold the wire in place. Accidents can result if the wire is loosened by pulling.

7 Replace the plug cover.

Note Some small appliances are not earthed, meaning that they do not have an earth wire, only live and neutral; in this case, leave the earth terminal empty.

CHANGING LIGHT BULBS

1 Switch off the light or unplug a lamp. If the light has a two-way switch, or if you cannot remember whether the light is on or off, turn the electricity off at the mains.

2 Allow the old bulb to cool. Use a clean dry cloth to protect your hand if the bulb is still hot. Never use a damp cloth to hold a hot bulb as it may explode.

3 Insert the new bulb. For a bayonet bulb, locate the two pins in the slots and twist clockwise into the fitting. Screw-in bulbs should be firmly in place. Never force a bulb in place or screw it too tightly.

4 Turn the electricity back on.

FLUORESCENT TUBE

If the tube flickers, it may be the starter which is at fault, not the whole tube. The starter is a small enclosed component which plugs into the fitting. Buy a replacement starter first, then you will know what you are looking for. Make sure the electricity supply is switched off before removing the starter; it will either unscrew or pull out. If the starter is not at fault, replace the whole tube as follows:

1 Switch off the electricity.

2 Pull off the spring-loaded bracket at one end of the tube and this will release the mechanism which holds the tube in place.
3 Once one end of the tube is free, pull it out to release the other end.
4 Fit the new tube by reversing the above steps.
5 Turn the electricity back on.

PLUMBING AND DRAINAGE

UNBLOCKING A SINK DRAIN

Hair, fat and small pieces of food or vegetable matter typically cause blocked drains. For example, pouring a large quantity of fatty water down the drain can quickly cause a blockage when the fat cools and hardens. If you must pour fatty liquid down the drain, then add plenty of detergent and very hot water. Many blockages build up over a long period; small amounts of food debris and fat from the sink can slowly build up, and hair collecting in the drain from a wash basin will eventually block. Be aware of a sink, shower, bath or basin which drains slowly and attack the problem before it becomes a major blockage. The following hints may be helpful.

- Clear away hair or other debris from the drain guard in the plug-hole – use an old toothbrush or skewer.
- Try one of the proprietary products for cleaning drains.
- Boiling water and washing soda, used on several occasions, can clear a build-up of matter.
- Caustic soda can be used to clear a severe build-up. It is very powerful and must be used with care; a very strong solution, left for too long, can melt plastic U-bends. Always use caustic soda in solution and add the soda crystals to water; never water to the soda (the latter method initially produces a very strong solution which can spit).
- Use a plunger. Block the overflow with a cloth, then place the plunger over the plughole to cover it completely. Pump up and down about a dozen times.
- If the sink is blocked and part full of water, bail out as much liquid as possible, then try one of the above methods. If these fail it is time to remove the trap under the plug-hole.

REMOVING WATER TRAPS

Firstly, place a bowl or bucket under the trap and then proceed as outlined below, according to the type of trap you are working on.

Bottle Trap This has a rounded base which unscrews. Once open, remove the blockage and make sure the pipe inside is clear. Screw the base of the trap back in position.

U-Trap These are old, metal and often corroded. Right at the bottom of the 'U' there is a nut which can be unscrewed. Once the nut has been removed, use a piece of hooked, firm wire to clean out the pipe, then screw the nut back into place.

P- or S- Traps These are the plastic traps which are fitted in most modern drains. Plastic nuts located on either side of the bend release the whole section which can be cleaned out with a wire. When removing sections, make sure you keep the washers and replace them before securing the nuts.

Bath Trap Like a P- Trap but shallow, this is removed by unscrewing the two nuts. Bath traps tend to be awkward to get at and messy to remove, with little room for a bucket underneath. An old roasting tin or large dish will catch some water and a few old cloths on the floor ease the mopping-up process.

Once the trap has been replaced, run plenty of water through to clear the drain.

CLEARING A BLOCKED TOILET

The blockage is usually in the trap which leads out of the pan. Special large plungers are available for covering the outlet in the pan. Pump up and down several times to free the blockage, then flush the cistern several times.

CLEARING A BLOCKED MAIN DRAIN

If all traps, pipes and outside drains from the house have been checked and a blockage still exists, the next stop is the first manhole cover on the main drain.

Lift the manhole cover to reveal the inspection chamber. Pipework from the various household drains leads out into this chamber and clearing a blockage is an unpleasant task. If the inspection chamber is full- or part-blocked, the blockage is further down the system; if it is empty, the blockage is further back between chamber and house. If the chamber is filled or overflowing, it may be necessary to move on to the next chamber and work from that point.

Again, being aware of any unpleasant odours which may indicate that the drain is not working efficiently can signify that the main drain requires attention in advance of a major blockage occurring. Cleaning out with a hose pipe and caustic soda, and flushing water through as many drains as possible from the house may be helpful if the drain is not working as efficiently as it might. Once the drain is blocked, specialist tools are required.

Drain-clearing rods can be hired from hire shops and the larger d.i.y. chains. The flexible rods are inserted into the blocked pipe and twisted in a clockwise direction as they are pushed towards the blockage. Additional lengths of rod are screwed on as necessary. The rods must not be twisted in an anti-clockwise direction as some of the connections between the rods can loosen and the rods will become stuck in the pipe.

It is often more practical to call out a specialist drain-clearing firm (check the telephone directory) or to ring the local council who also provide a drain-cleaning service, and may be cheaper than a private firm. Professional drain-clearing companies have power tools which simplify the process.

RUNNING CISTERN OVERFLOW

Overflows run from toilet cisterns and from the cold water tank in the attic. A running overflow is usually caused by a faulty ball valve.

Take the top off the cistern. If the ball (or float) has deflated, then it needs replacing – a simple job of unscrewing the old one and screwing on a new one.

More commonly, the problem is with either a washer or diaphragm in the mechanism at the opposite end of the arm from the ball.

Turn off the water supply under the cistern or, in the case of a cold water tank, on the main cold water pipe coming into the house.

Portsmouth Valve, with Washer Unscrew the round cap on the end of the valve. Pull out the split pin which slides through the float arm, then remove the arm. Push a screwdriver blade into the slot at the bottom of the float arm and lever out the plug, or piston from inside.

Unscrew the cap on the end of the plug or piston and remove the washer from inside. Place a new washer in position and screw the valve back together.

Piston Washer Removal

1 Unscrew cap on valve end.
2 Use a screwdriver to lever out the piston.
3 Unscrew the piston (see note, below).
4 Remove and replace washer.

Note In some new valves, the piston is a plastic cartridge. This either unscrews or the washer may be prised out and replaced possibly eliminating the need to follow steps 3 and 4 above.

Diaphragm Valve Remove the float arm, cap and plunger as above. Use a screwdriver to push out the diaphragm found inside the valve. Put a new diaphragm into the valve and reassemble.

REPLACING TAP WASHERS

A dripping tap is usually caused by a worn washer. There are two main types of tap: the pillar tap and the supatap. A pillar tap is the traditional shape, the supatap is the chunkier, contemporary model. Whichever you are working on, put the plug in the sink or bath to avoid dropping anything down the plug-hole.

Pillar Tap

1 Turn off the water supply at the nearest point and open the tap to drain away water before putting the plug in the drain.
2 Loosen the screw which secures the tap handle, either on top or on the side of the tap, then lift off the handle.
3 Use an adjustable spanner to loosen the tap cover (protect the cover by placing a piece of cloth over it), then undo the large nut inside the tap.
4 Lift out the tap mechanism. There is a spindle inside the mechanism and this has a washer on its end. The washer is usually held in place by a small nut. Remove the nut, then replace the washer. Reassemble the tap.

Supatap Changing the washer on this type is far easier as the water does not have to be turned off and the tap does not have to be dismantled completely.

1 Loosen the retaining nut on the tap, using an adjustable spanner. Hold the nut with one hand and unscrew the tap nozzle . Water will gush out until the nozzle is completely removed.

2 Hit the nozzle firmly and the jumper or anti-splash device will drop out. Prise out the jumper and washer unit and replace the washer, then reassemble the tap.

LAGGING PIPES AND TANKS

All pipes should be lagged to prevent loss of heat from the hot water system and to prevent exposed cold pipes from freezing during extreme winter weather. In particular, check pipework in the attic, in unheated utility rooms, outside toilets, outside walls of unheated cloakrooms and any other areas that can become very cold in freezing weather. Tubular pipe lagging, available in various diameters to fit different pipes, is ready-slit lengthways and easily fitted. Alternatively, bandage-type lagging is suitable for wrapping around pipes. Lagging materials and sheets are also available for use on cold water tanks.

If obtaining purpose-made lagging is a problem, then thick pads of newspaper can be tied around pipes as a short-term measure. Insulated packing material (bubble wrap) can also be used to help keep out the cold. If the pipes are outside or in damp conditions, the paper should be overwrapped with polythene (carrier bags will do) to prevent it becoming wet. Corrugated cardboard can be used for short-term tank lagging. Aim to substitute purpose-made lagging as soon as possible.

Sprinkling salt into toilet cisterns and pans at night can help to prevent them freezing.

Hot Water Tank Many hot water tanks now come complete with a layer of insulation to prevent heat loss. Alternatively, lagging jackets may be purchased to fit around the tank. It is important to make sure the tank is completely covered and that the lagging is firmly secured in place. A well-lagged hot water tank prevents heat loss and reduces fuel consumption. It also keeps the stored water hot for longer periods after the boiler is turned off.

FROZEN PIPES

Firstly, try to locate the point at which the water is frozen in the pipework. If most of the water system is working, with just one tap not receiving any water, it is usually fairly easy to find the frozen area, particularly if there is a section of pipe on an exposed external wall in an unheated area.

If the pipes are frozen near the cold water tank, then the supply to the bath, wash basin and so on will cease. Remember that the kitchen sink and toilet are usually fed directly from the main cold water entering the house and, since the water is under greater pressure in the main pipe, it rarely freezes.

When you have found the likely area, check, as far as possible, for any damage. Water expands when it freezes, therefore ice can crack pipes (particularly old, fragile ones) or push the pipes out of the connecting joints and fittings.

If you do find any cracks or fittings which have been pushed off or moved, place buckets under them to catch water as the ice thaws. Also, turn the water off at the mains or at the nearest point to prevent the flow.

If the flow of water to a central heating boiler or main tank is frozen, do not use the boiler. Similarly, any other water-heating appliance must not be operated if its water supply is not functioning. If pipes to an unheated boiler or heater have frozen, do not light the boiler to thaw them.

Warm the area as near as possible to the frozen section. Hot water bottles, a fan heater or hair dryer are all useful. Do not apply fierce heat directly on a section of pipe (for example by using a blow torch or placing an infra-red heating element very close to it), as this may cause damage.

BURST PIPES

Leaking water running through the house can be highly dangerous if it comes in contact with electric wiring, which is likely when a pipe has burst in the attic or an upstairs room.

1. Turn off the electricity at the mains.
2. Turn off any water heaters or boiler.
3. Turn off the water supply at the main stopcock.
4. Turn off the supply from the cold tank. If you cannot locate the stopcock, then tie the ball float arm to a piece of wood laid across the top of the tank to prevent the water running in. Block the outlet hole in the tank as best you can – a broom handle and pad of cloth (such as a tea-towel) will reduce the flow, if not cut it off completely.
5. Empty the water system as far as possible by running any free taps – the less water in the system, the less there is to flood the house.
6. If a plumber is not available to replace the section of pipe, emergency, short-term repairs can be attempted. Wrapping a paint-soaked rag around the split, rubbing soap into the split and wrapping plastic tape or sticking plaster

around can all help. Special pipe-mending tape is available, or resin may be smeared into a cleaned crack, rubbed with sandpaper and dried as far as possible. Any good do-it-yourself shop or, preferably, a local plumbers' merchant will offer useful advice.

INSULATION AND DRAUGHT EXCLUSION

Reducing heat loss into the roof space, through glass and through poorly fitting windows and doors, makes good economic sense. However, the importance of ventilation must be stressed and ventilation bricks or points in the structure of the house should not be blocked. Similarly, internal doors should not be sealed, although heat loss from one area to another can be reduced by hanging a heavy curtain to draw across a doorway.

Attic or Loft Apart from pipe and tank insulation, the attic or loft should be insulated. The only difficulty arises when there is inadequate access to the loft, as in some older properties, which means cutting a new hole in the ceiling or enlarging an existing entrance. The latter is often impossible if the entrance is in a cupboard.

Before laying insulation, the spaces between the timbers must be cleaned. A soft brush and dustpan may be adequate but many years' build-up of filth or, worse, dust and dirt from building work makes hiring an industrial vacuum cleaner essential.

When handling insulation materials, particularly in an enclosed space, wear protective clothing to avoid contact with glass fibre and a disposable mask to avoid breathing in dust and dirt.

Work carefully, using a strong piece of flooring-weight chipboard laid across the timbers. Slipping off rafters through a ceiling is both dangerous and expensive.

When insulating the loft or attic, as well as using rolls of material between rafters, check and insulate all pipework and other plumbing. Check all electric wiring, noting any brittle or damaged wires and have them replaced by a professional electrician. If you have any doubts about the standard of the electric wiring, call in the local electricity board to inspect the whole house.

Windows and Doors External doors and windows can have large gaps around their edges, allowing fierce draughts to blow in. Stick-on draught excluder is inexpensive and efficient, and easy to fix around frames which should be thoroughly cleaned and dried first.

Sealed, double-glazed window units are the most effective form of insulation. Secondary glazing kits can be fitted to most windows by fixing an internal frame within the window space. The glazing unit can fit permanently into this frame, usually to be opened by sliding separate panes. Alternatively, on smaller windows, the secondary glazing pane is clipped in place and must be completely removed if the window is to be opened.

A cheap, short-term way of insulating windows is to apply a covering of plastic film; ordinary kitchen film will do. First, thoroughly clean the window frame with hot water and detergent, then dry it. Working from the top downwards, stretch lengths of film across the window, overlapping the frame at the top, sides and bottom. Continue fixing film, overlapping it (it will cling firmly to itself if stretched), until the whole of the space is covered. Use masking tape or sticky tape to seal the edges of the film and keep it in place.

Curtains and Blinds Lined curtains help to prevent cold air from replacing room heat. A large door curtain is useful between a lounge and a cold hallway or across an external door. Hinged, rising curtain tracks can be purchased especially for fitting to the top of doors.

EXTERNAL MAINTENANCE

Make the effort to inspect and repair the outside of the house annually; good external maintenance can help to avoid major work becoming necessary. Make a habit of looking at the roof, checking for any missing tiles or any that are sitting at a jaunty angle, and have them fixed before several slide off. Similarly, notice the condition of rendering (the outer cement covering), looking for cracks or damage, and examine the pointing between bricks. Any chimney pots or covers balancing at a precarious angle, or plants (or trees) growing out of chimney brickwork, should be dealt with. The following areas should also receive attention.

Gutters These should be cleared occasionally as leaves and other debris clog them, causing them to overflow. Look for any cracks or loose connecting sections and fill or stick them with a suitable sealing compound or adhesive.

Woodwork Flaking paint should be cleaned and replaced. Rotten sections of wood should be removed and replaced. Any slight damage or deterioration can be repaired by careful cleaning and the application of a suitable base-coat before painting.

Brittle Putty The putty around window panes on old windows often becomes brittle and breaks away. The old putty should be scraped off, surrounding woodwork cleaned, then new putty applied all around the frame. The putty should be allowed to harden before it is painted.

Damp-proof Course and Ventilation Bricks Check around the base of the house walls to make sure that the damp-proof course is still above ground level. Building work, paths, soil or other material which links the wall above the course with the ground can provide a path for damp to enter the fabric of the house.

Check that ventilation bricks and areas are free from debris or obstruction.

Fencing An occasional application of protective fluid will prevent a wooden fence from drying, cracking or rotting. Mend slatted fences by replacing any broken sections promptly and check supporting posts to ensure they are not allowed to rot.

If you are not sure who owns fencing, check the deeds of the property or any formal information in a rental agreement. As a guide, the support posts are usually positioned (and should be positioned) on the side of the fence-owner.

REPAIRS: PLANNING, PROBLEMS AND ASSISTANCE

Maintaining a house can be expensive and/or a constant drain on spare time. This chapter began by introducing the idea of getting to know your own property – advice which cannot be overstressed as, all too often, discoveries about the building in which we live are made when coping with emergencies or problems. Many problems are eased and emergencies avoided by forethought and planning. Being aware of potential problems, and occasionally giving some attention to maintenance, are the answers to avoiding repair bills that come as an expensive surprise.

- Keep a seasonal check on different areas of the house and make a list of jobs that need doing.
- Promptly tackle urgent jobs or situations that are likely to deteriorate into major tasks.
- Draw up a plan of work to complete minor repairs, taking into account the time and money available.
- Budget for any major work that is likely to need doing over the following two to five years.
- If there is a potential problem which you cannot afford to repair immediately, take professional advice on measures to prevent the area from deteriorating.
- Large do-it-yourself centres may be useful for a broad range of goods, but remember that smaller, local companies can provide specialist equipment, unusual or old fittings and invaluable advice drawn from years of experience. A local supplier whom you visit regularly can be a real friend when disaster strikes.
- Local councils and authorities often provide advice and assistance with household problems, from guidance on home improvements to financial help.
- Keep a list of recommended builders, electricians, gas fitters and plumbers in case of emergencies. Personal recommendations from trusted friends and acquaintances are far better than advertisements in the local paper.
- When commissioning work, use recommended craftsmen and companies if possible. Take several quotes before deciding whom to employ.
- Distinguish between a quotation which forms a contract to supply and provide a service for a price, and an estimate of the cost for work.
- Be wary of a vague estimate or quote which does not provide details of the work to be done and the materials involved.
- Find out about professional bodies representing builders, plumbers and so on, and look for companies recommended by them. Local consumer advice centres, libraries and some local authorities provide relevant information.
- Before commissioning major work, always ask for references or to see examples of other work completed locally.
- Never pay a fee before work is completed to your satisfaction. There are some exceptions, in the case of major work in which stage payments are agreed and satisfactory progress is being made.
- If in doubt, confront a contractor with your concerns and, if the response is less than satisfactory, seek consumer advice.

Home Safety

A great number of accidents occur in and around the home every year: this chapter points to some of the causes and notes the pitfalls to avoid. In addition to the many hazardous jobs carried out in the home, the average house will contain many dangerous pieces of equipment and substances. Since home is the place where we all relax, where children play and the elderly spend the majority of their time, being aware of the potential dangers makes good sense.

GENERAL HOME SAFETY

Here are a few general points to observe in order to avoid minor accidents, the possibility of serious injury or the danger of fire.

Flooring Avoid slippery flooring or loose rugs or matting on slippery surfaces. This applies particularly to hall, kitchen, bathroom and any other area that is frequently used.

Lighting Hall, stairs, bathroom, kitchen and any other work area or area through which people walk must be well lit. Awkward steps, either inside or outside, or landings which may be the cause of a fall should be lit with a spotlight.

Storage Untidy or overfilled cupboards are dangerous, as items can be difficult to find or reach and can fall out unexpectedly. Heavy items or others that are used frequently should always be stored in places where they are easy to reach.

Ladders and Steps These should be in good condition, sturdy and easy to lift and handle. Steps and ladders must be used on a level surface; never climb on chairs or furniture instead of using steps. Steps of an appropriate size should be stored in places where they are used frequently and ladders should be kept where they are readily available to the owner but locked away from intruders.

Electricity Never overload the electric circuits in the house. An adapter to take several plugs may be useful, but do not link several adapters and do not plug several appliances into one socket.

Old or faulty wiring in the house or on appliances must be changed as it can easily cause a fire.

Extension leads are handy for short-term use but they are not designed for permanent installations. They must be fully unwound before use, particularly if you are using a high-rated appliance, as the leads can overheat when coiled or curled.

Do not leave flexes trailing across the floor for someone to trip over, and plugs should not be left lying about with pins uppermost in case someone treads on them and injures their foot.

Tidiness and Overcrowding General tidiness is vital to safety. Papers, magazines and objects lying around on the floor are a hazard, particularly toys and pins or needles. Items left stacked on stairs are especially dangerous. Rooms and hallways which are overcrowded with furniture are dangerous as it is easy to trip, or to bump against a corner when walking through or moving around. When something is being carried, for example a sharp object or a pot of hot liquid, the accident can be more serious than a fall or bump.

Dangerous or Poisonous Substances If there are children in the house, all cleaning agents, medicines, decorating materials such as paints and strippers and any other substances that are dangerous when ingested or rubbed into sensitive skin must be kept out of reach. Household cleaning products have child-proof closures but these are not always effective, so it is also a good idea to keep toddlers away from the cupboard under the sink where most cleaners are stored, and to keep sprays and other fluids in higher cupboards.

BATHROOM SAFETY

- The floor must not be slippery. Some finishes, for example ceramic floor tiles, are especially slippery, therefore dangerous, when wet. Bath mats must have a non-slip backing.
- Baths and showers for use by the elderly or children should have grips and a non-slip base, or a non-slip mat should be placed in the base. Showers are available with integral seats for the elderly.
- Never leave young children unattended in the bath – not even for a minute to answer the telephone or open the door. They can easily drown.
- Always test the water temperature before bathing a baby and run cold water first.
- Always supervise older children who are bathing.
- Water conducts electricity, therefore freestanding electrical appliances must not be used in the bathroom. There should not be a socket or switch in the bathroom; pull switches must be used for lights and fixed heating appliances. Special shaver sockets are the only type of power point for bathroom use.
- Never use an extension lead in a bathroom. Never bathe after drinking alcohol and do not have a very hot bath when very tired – you may doze off and slip under the water and possibly drown.
- The medicine cabinet must be out of reach of children.
- Razors and blades must be kept out of the reach of children.
- Heavy glass bottles or cosmetic jars and drinking glasses slip easily through wet hands, so keep them away from washbasin and bath.
- All areas must be kept clean.

KITCHEN SAFETY

- Water and electricity must be separated. Sockets should not be positioned near the sink and appliances should not be used when hands are wet.
- Flooring should be non-slip and broken flooring or loose matting which can slide around must not be used in the kitchen.
- If possible, the cooker should be away from the door to avoid any danger of the door being opened when someone is handling a large saucepan or container of hot food.
- Always leave enough space on the work surface to rest heavy or hot pots and pans.
- Knives and other sharp objects should be kept out of the reach of children.
- A stable, reasonably large area of work surface must be available when working in the kitchen. Preparing food in crowded conditions or on a rickety surface can be dangerous.
- All pan handles should be pushed backwards when in use on the cooker.
- Flexes must not trail from work-top appliances as they can easily be pulled down by children or caught by anyone walking by.
- Never leave food to grill or fry unattended.
- Plastic bags should be kept where children cannot reach them.
- Have a fire extinguisher and fire blanket in the kitchen.
- Keep strong, thick oven gloves close to the oven and use them.
- Practise high standards of personal and household hygiene in the kitchen, where food safety is important.

BEDROOM SAFETY

- Electric blankets should conform to the current national standard and should be used only according to the manufacturer's instructions. Electric blankets must be cleaned and serviced regularly when old.
- Babies and young children should not have pillows.
- Cots and bedding for young children must be safe and secure, with narrowly spaced railings on cots and cribs to prevent a child squeezing its head through the bars and becoming trapped.
- Items surrounding a cot must be secure and out of reach of the standing child.

- Windows should shut securely in a household with children, and lock if necessary, to avoid the danger of a child falling out.
- There should be some opening windows on upper floors to allow escape in the event of fire.

SAFETY AND CLOTHING

- Long dressing-gowns can be dangerous on stairs, particularly if you are carrying a tea tray.
- Long nightwear should be flame-resistant, particularly for children.
- Flapping sleeves can catch in door handles or on furniture.
- Long-sleeved items, dressing-gowns and loose clothing are not suitable garments to wear when you are doing jobs in the kitchen or, indeed, anywhere else; take extra care when making tea in a dressing-gown.
- Ill-fitting and worn slippers or house shoes are dangerous.
- Open shoes or slippers are not suitable for heavy work, such as home repairs or decorating, moving furniture, gardening or mowing the lawn.
- Eye or face masks, gloves and appropriate protective clothing should always be worn when sanding, using noxious substances or dangerous appliances, such as a chain saw.

FIRES AND HEATERS

- A fire guard should always be used with an unattended open fire.
- A child must not be left alone with any fire or infra-red heater without a large, closed, fixed guard in position.
- Open fires must be made safe last thing at night or before going out.

OUTDOOR SAFETY

- Pathways and steps should be well lit.
- Garages, sheds and other outhouses should be tidy and reasonably clean.
- Gardening and garage products and tools must be kept safely out of the reach of children.
- Great care must be taken when using sharp tools and with bean poles or sticks which can easily cause injuries – particularly to eyes.

- Garden pools and ponds, no matter how shallow, are potential death-traps for young children. Children should not be allowed to play unsupervised in a garden with a pool or pond as they can fall into the water and drown quickly before an adult has noticed the accident or has had time to rescue them.
- If children are allowed to play unsupervised in a garden, the fences and walls should be safe and secure. Gates should have a high catch to prevent young children wandering.

FIRE IN THE HOME

Here are some important points to remember.

- Get everyone out of the house as quickly as possible and dial 999 – in a neighbouring house if necessary.
- Take a towel to wrap around your face if you have to walk through smoke. If possible wet the towel, but do not waste time.
- If you are trapped on a first floor, with flames and thick smoke on the stairs, then jump out of a window and make children jump too.
- Crouch down or crawl if you are going through a smoke-filled area, as the smoke and hot air rises and it will be less dense near the floor.
- Do not attempt to put out a fire or to deal with smouldering furniture: the fumes are highly toxic and they kill in minutes.

CHIP PAN OR GRILL PAN ON FIRE

- Turn off the heat source if you can but do not lean across a flaming pan to do so.
- Do **not** pour water on the pan.
- Cover with a fire blanket or thick pad of fabric, a door mat is ideal, or put a large lid or sturdy plate straight down on top of the pan. Take care to avoid burning your hands and arms.
- Push the object down over the flames in a direction away from you.
- Turn off the heat source if you could not do so before.
- Leave the pan covered. If you could only lightly smother the flames, place another thick object on top of the pan. A baking tray, tin or other object will cut off the supply of air which keeps the fat burning.

FLOOD

Burst pipes caused by freezing and problems of malfunctioning valves or worn washers can result in flooding. Even minor 'floods' can be damaging and dangerous, so always adopt a 'better safe than sorry' attitude.

- Turn off the water at the main pipe – usually found in the kitchen.
- Turn off the electricity supply at the main switch; water conducts electricity and it can easily seep into sockets and connections.
- Turn on all the taps in sinks and bath, and flush the toilets to drain as much water out of the system as possible.
- If the flooding is severe or if it comes from the main outside your house, call the local water authority. Remember, too, that the Fire Brigade are used to dealing with flooding emergencies.

EMERGENCY SERVICES

In cases of emergency, dial 999 and an operator will ask which service you require; the functions of the various services are outlined below. State the service, the address or location, the problem and your name. Emergency calls are free – just dial.

Police For emergencies related to traffic accidents, offences such as burglary or violence and public disorder. Also remember that the Police can provide advice in an emergency if you do not know whom else to call for help.

Distinguish between an emergency call and a complaint or query and address the latter to the local Police station (number in telephone directory).

Ambulance In case of accidents causing injury, sudden or severe illness or other health or maternity problems requiring urgent hospital attention.

Fire Brigade In case of house fire, garden or country fires which are out of control, fire hazard in accident cases, severe flooding and any danger from chemical spillage or other serious problem with hazardous substances.

First-Aid

Read this chapter for future reference as the information it contains can save life. First-aid is the help given to a victim of injury or severe and sudden ill health. It is important to recognize life-threatening situations, when professional help is essential as fast as possible. This chapter deals first with such emergencies, then with other, equally important, aspects of first-aid which allow nominally more time for coping with the situation but still require prompt attention.

FIRST-AID KIT

Every home and car should have a first-aid kit; these can be purchased fully stocked, but it is just as easy to make up your own. Keep all the items together in a clearly-marked box, or neatly arranged in a cupboard. They should be easily accessible, but away from the reach of young children. Replace items as they are used or become out-of-date and discard opened packets of dressings which are no longer sterile.

The kit should contain medicines for dealing with everyday minor illnesses, creams and antiseptics for minor accidents and a variety of sterile dressings and bandages. Useful equipment includes such items as a small pair of scissors, safety pins, a pair of tweezers and some tissues; a concise, clear, illustrated first-aid handbook should be ready at hand. The exact selection of ointments and medicines is up to you; think about the likely reasons for needing minor first-aid – burns and scalds, bites, cuts, foreign bodies in the eye, stomach upsets, toothache, headache, sore throats, earache and so on – then select products to deal with these common problems.

SUGGESTED CONTENTS

- Antiseptic solution and cream
- Cream for stings and bites
- Surgical spirit
- Iodine
- Cream or lotion for skin irritations (for example, calamine lotion)
- Toothache tincture or oil of cloves
- Eye bath and eye-cleansing solution
- Aspirin for adults
- Similar product to above for children: take current advice from a chemist as opinions change and new products are often available.
- Product for easing upset stomachs
- Thermometer
- A good selection of plasters
- Sterile dressings and bandages
- Safety pins
- Cotton wool
- Tissues
- Sling

- Scissors
- Tweezers
- First-aid manual

The above is only a guide and there may be other items for your household situation.

LIFE-THREATENING EMERGENCIES

Dial 999 for an ambulance. In rural areas, where the nearest ambulance station is many miles away, the local doctor may be able to get to the patient more speedily. **In rural areas, keep the emergency number for the doctor near the telephone.**

EMERGENCY PROCEDURE

Check Airways Make sure that the person's mouth is not obstructed. Turn the head to one side and remove false teeth, if appropriate. Use fingers to clear out any food or vomit.

Check for Breathing Look for signs of movement in the chest and listen for the sound of breathing. If necessary, hold your ear to the person's chest to listen for breathing, or lean close to their face to feel any air movement.

Check Pulse for Circulation Checking the pulse tells you whether the heart has stopped beating. Practise this on yourself, a friend or relative. Hold your first two or three fingers to the neck, placing them in the hollow between the voice box and adjoining muscle; alternatively, turn the hand palm-up and feel the wrist on the thumb side. The neck is the more reliable area if you are familiar with the position. Do not use your thumb to feel the pulse as you may confuse your own pulse with that of the patient. If you cannot feel a pulse then the heart has stopped beating and heart compression must be applied immediately.

Coping with the Unconscious Patient Once you have checked the breathing and pulse, the patient should be put into the recovery position (see page 31) and treated for shock; then professional help should be sought immediately.

If there are any people within hearing distance, ask them to telephone for help while you deal with the patient.

THE KISS OF LIFE

If the patient has stopped breathing, give the kiss of life as follows:

1 Turn the person face upwards if possible. Turn the head backwards so that the chin is pointing up.
2 Clear the airways.
3 Tilt the head back again, pressing down on the forehead so that the chin points up – this ensures the tongue does not slip to the back of the throat to block the air passage.
4 Pinch the nose between thumb and forefinger of one hand.
5 Take a deep breath, then place your mouth over that of the patient to seal it completely; blow out steadily. The patient's chest should rise – this shows that the air you breathe in is reaching the lungs. If not, the air passage is blocked, possibly the head is in the wrong position or you are not sealing the patient's mouth with yours.
6 If the patient's mouth is inaccessible for the above, but you can keep it closed, then breathe in through the nose.
7 Give another breath, then remove your mouth for a moment before continuing to breathe into the patient.
8 Check for a pulse after applying breath four or five times. If the heart is beating, continue giving the kiss of life and do not give up until help arrives.
9 If there is no pulse, heart compression (see page 30) should be applied alternately with the kiss of life. If there is help available, apply both simultaneously.

Note Continue giving the kiss of life even if the patient does not immediately respond. It is sensible and not unusual to continue for period of twenty to thirty minutes.

BABIES

Since the face is very small, you should cover the nose and mouth of the infant completely.

ALTERNATIVE ARTIFICIAL RESPIRATION

If the kiss of life may not be applied due to facial injury, the following method should be adopted. It is less easy to apply and more exhausting but should be kept up as it can save life. This method is not suitable for patients with back, arm or neck injuries unless it is the only, vital method of respiration.

1 Lay the patient on the stomach, with arms above the head. Turn the head on one side, resting on the hands.
2 Hold the head and slide the chin up, neck back, to allow free access for air.
3 Adopt a semi-kneeling position above the patient's head, looking down his or her back. Lean on one knee by the patient's head and place the other foot near the patient's elbow.
4 Spread out your hands just below the shoulder blades, with thumbs towards the spine, then rock forward, keeping your elbows straight. Exert firm but not heavy pressure for about two seconds – this should make the patient breathe out.
5 Rock backwards, sliding your hands up the patient's upper arms to the elbows, then pull the arms straight backwards for about three seconds – this should make the patient breathe in.
6 Lower the arms, slide your hands back to their original position and continue the process. You may have to continue for some time, trying to ensure the patient breathes in and out about twelve times a minute.

HEART COMPRESSION

Also referred to as chest or heart massage, this must be applied if there is no pulse and the heart has stopped beating. It is essential to get the heart beating again so that blood is pumped to the brain.

The kiss of life should be given at the same time – if there are two of you, then take a task each and swop over occasionally. If you are alone, then alternate the treatment every few minutes to provide air and to try to stimulate the heart.

1 Lay the person face upwards, head back and chin up (as for the kiss of life). Kneel over the patient above the chest.

2 Find the breast bone, located down the middle of the chest. Move your hand along to the bottom of the breast bone, where you can feel the lower ribs meeting it, then move your hand back by 2.5 – 3 cm/ 1 – 1½ inches upwards from the end of the bone.
3 Place the heel of your hand on the bone. Cover with the heel of your other hand, interlocking your fingers to avoid digging them into the chest.
4 Keeping your elbows straight, lean down firmly on both hands to compress the chest by about 3 cm/1½ inches. Release the pressure at once.
5 Repeat this pumping process at a rate of eighty times a minute – that is more than one pump per second.
6 Check for breathing and give the kiss of life if necessary, applying two breaths between every fifteen heart compressions.
7 Check the pulse every three minutes and stop the heart compression once it returns. Keep giving the kiss of life and checking the pulse.

Note When the patient begins to breathe, move the body into the recovery position (see below): this prevents the air passage from being blocked by the tongue or other obstructions, such as vomit.

CHILD HEART MASSAGE

The process is lighter and faster – about one hundred compressions per minute. On a baby, the process is yet lighter and faster and two fingers should be used instead of the heel of the hand.

THE RECOVERY POSITION

An unconscious patient who is breathing and has a pulse should be placed in the recovery position. However, if there is any sign or likelihood of back or neck injury the patient must not be moved.

1 Kneel next to the patient.
2 Remove spectacles and any jewellery. Lay the patient on his back.
3 Tilt the head back and chin up. Cross the arm farthest away from you over the front of the body. Tuck the arm nearest you under the patient.
4 Roll the patient towards you so that the body moves on to its side. Use your knees to support the patient, and support the head as the body rolls.

5 The arms should support the body on its side. The arm which is facing towards the front should be bent and supporting the chest off the ground.
6 Bend the legs so that they support the patient on one side, with the chest slightly raised off the floor. The head should be to one side to allow easy breathing. Make sure that the chin is jutting out and that the neck is arched with the head up, not resting on the chest.

TREATING HEAVY BLEEDING

Heavy bleeding must be controlled promptly. Make the patient lie down, but do not move a patient who may have a back or neck injury. Press down firmly on the wound to ease the blood flow. Do not waste time trying to find a suitable cloth or dressing, just use your hand, even if it is dirty.

- If the wound is in an arm or leg, raise and support the limb to reduce the blood flow. Keep the pressure on the wound.
- Cover the wound with a sterile dressing or pad of clean cloth and wrap it firmly in place (use a tie, tights, sleeve of a jumper or whatever is to hand).
- If there is a gaping wound, try to bring the skin and flesh together to close it as far as possible.
- If there is something pucturing the wound or if there is debris in it, then apply pressure around the wound to ease the flow of blood.
- If blood is spurting from a wound, one of the arteries has been cut and immediate, direct pressure must be applied.
- When a wound is bandaged tightly, the flow of blood will be stopped or limited and it is vital to get immediate professional help as the blood supply should not be cut off for more than about fifteen minutes.
- Apply more pressure and dressings if the bleeding continues. Do not remove the first pad or dressing, simply add to it.
- If blood is spurting from the arm or leg, apply pressure to the main arteries to ease the blood flow.

Note If the blood is spurting from the body, one of the main arteries has been cut and prompt action is vital: immediate direct pressure must be applied by hand, with or without any cloth or dressing.

TREATING SHOCK

When a person is badly injured, the body goes into a state of shock; a weak condition which can result in collapse. As a general rule, in case of accident all patients should be treated for shock.

1 Put the patient in the recovery position or lay the person down, with feet up and head to one side.
2 Cover with a blanket, clothing or whatever is available to retain body heat.
3 Loosen tight clothing – tight belts or waistbands, neck ties or collars.
4 Call professional help.
5 Do not give anything to drink. If the patient is thirsty, you can moisten the lips with water.

CHOKING

In case of choking, or if there is some severe problem with breathing, give the person four firm thumps between the shoulder blades with the flat of the hand. If this does not release the blockage, get the patient to bend over so that the head is lower than the chest and apply a further four thumps.

CHOKING BABIES

Lay a baby or infant face-down on your lap, head and arms towards your feet, then slap between the shoulder blades four times.

PATIENTS NOT IN IMMEDIATE DANGER

If the patient is breathing, the heart is beating, they are conscious and not bleeding profusely, then you will probably have to cope with their state of fright and panic. Professional help should still be sought promptly but, if possible, ask someone else to telephone while you deal with the patient.

CONSCIOUS PATIENTS

1 Calm and reassure the patient. Treat bleeding at once.
2 If there is no risk of back or neck injury, then make them lie down, adopting the recovery position if there is likelihood of fainting or falling unconscious.
3 Treat for shock: keep warm and dry, loosen tight clothing and do not give anything to drink.

BROKEN LIMBS

If there is any chance of damage to the neck or back, do not move the patient. In the case of severe fracture, it is best not to attempt to move the limb but to deal with bleeding, treat for shock and call professional help as soon as possible.

COMMON ACCIDENTS AND SUDDEN ILLNESS

Even minor accidents should be dealt with promptly and efficiently to avoid any possible risk of infection. The following are all situations in which first-aid should be given.

ASTHMA ATTACK

This is indicated by difficulty in breathing and gasping for air. The person should sit down on an upright chair. If they are lying down, they should be helped into an upright position, leaning against pillows if in bed.

In a bad attack, face the person towards the back of the chair, legs astride the seat, and lift the arms to rest on the top of the chair back, so lifting as much body weight as possible off the chest.

Help the sufferer to find their inhaler or other medication and calm them. If the attack does not subside, call a doctor or ambulance. If the patient begins to turn blue from lack of breath, dial 999 and be prepared to give the kiss of life. If the heart stops, then heart massage should be applied.

BITES AND STINGS

Insect Bites The treatment depends on the severity but the majority of insect bites received in Britain are not dangerous. Cleaning the infected area with antiseptic, then drying it and applying a suitable cream is sufficient. The bite should not be scratched or the skin broken.

Wasp and Bee Stings These stings are not dangerous unless the person is known to be allergic to them or someone is attacked by a swarm. Use tweezers to remove the sting which is left in the skin, then clean the area with antiseptic. Place the area under cold water to reduce swelling or apply a cold compress of ice cubes in a clean dressing. If someone develops a severe reaction to a sting, call the doctor.

If the person has been stung by a swarm, call an ambulance and treat for shock.

Snake Bites The adder is the only poisonous snake in Britain, so any snake bites are unlikely to be highly dangerous. Do not try to suck the poison out of the wound, but make the person rest, loosen clothing and support a bitten limb. Wash the bite with antiseptic, keep the patient warm and either take them to hospital, call a doctor or call an ambulance.

Dog Bites Treatment depends on the severity of the attack. If the skin is not broken, the bite is unlikely to cause a problem and the person should simply be calmed. If the skin is broken, clean the wound and take the person to the doctor or hospital.

BURNS AND SCALDS

Burns may result from contact with fire or a heat source, boiling water or steam, electric shock or certain chemicals. Friction (for example by having a rope pulled through the hands) and contact with ice-cold metal can also burn the skin.

In cases of minor burns, give the following treatment:

- Loosen or remove tight clothing, shoes, jewellery or watch.
- Submerge the area in cold water or place under slow-running cold water. Do not place under fast-flowing cold water as this can further damage the skin and flesh.
- If you cannot get the burn under water, then douse the area well with cold water.

- Apply a sterile lint dressing and bandage it loosely in place. Do not cover with a fluffy dressing as this will stick to the wound.
- Do not burst any blisters. Do not rub creams, oils or ointment into the skin.
- Burns which cover an area larger than a medium-sized coin should be given medical attention.

Severe Burns In case of severe burns to large areas of the body, call an ambulance. Loosen tight clothing and treat for shock, keeping the patient warm and allowing sips of water.

Note If a small burn does not heal quickly, consult a doctor as the area can become infected.

CUTS AND ABRASIONS

Wash your hands and then wash the area under cool, slow-running water. Use antiseptic and cotton wool to clean the area gently, removing any dirt and debris. If there are any larger pieces of debris (such as gravel, splinters or glass) which can be easily removed with tweezers, do so. If the debris is embedded and your efforts are likely to push it further into the wound, then take the patient to the doctor or hospital. Otherwise, when the wound is thoroughly cleaned, apply a sterile dressing.

Change the dressing if it is obviously soiled or about twenty-four hours after it was applied. If the wound is not beginning to heal but shows signs of oozing pus, a doctor should be consulted as there is a risk of infection.

Larger cuts should be taken to the hospital or doctor immediately as stitches may be required to close the area and promote healing.

ELECTRIC SHOCK

Do not touch the person if he or she is still grasping the source of electricity.

- Turn off the power supply.
- If you cannot turn the supply off, use a dry, poor conductor to push the electric source away from the patient. If you touch the person, the electric current will pass on to you. A wooden broom handle, heavy plastic object, wooden chair leg or coffee table are all suitable – metal conducts electricity and should not be used.
- If the patient is conscious, deal with the burns and treat for shock, then call an ambulance.

- If the patient is unconscious, check breathing and pulse, giving the kiss of life and/or heart massage as necessary. Call an ambulance.

High-voltage Shock If the accident occurs with high-voltage outdoor cables, such as on a railway line, do not approach the person; call the emergency services at once. The power supply must be switched off before anyone can approach the patient. If there is no one in authority to see that the supply is switched off, call the Police as well as the ambulance; the fire service may also be called in to help.

EYE INJURY

Professional attention is vital to avoid any possibility of permanent damage. Take the person to hospital or the doctor, or call an ambulance, depending on the severity of the injury and the quickest solution.

If the person has something in the eye, this may be washed out with plenty of clean, cool water. Pour plenty of cold water over the affected eye, holding the head over the sink or wash basin.

If the object does not come out with washing, wash hands thoroughly before inspecting the eye; hold the top and lower part gently apart while the head is tilted back. Ask the person to look up, down and around so that you can see any foreign body. Most particles can be removed by gently touching them with the corner of a clean tissue or dressing.

The eye should be washed out with a suitable eye-cleansing solution and it should feel normal, if tired, within a few hours. If there is any prolonged discomfort, for example overnight, then visit the hospital or doctor.

FAINTING

People may faint due to tiredness or after very long periods of standing up. Hot and airless rooms can lead to faintness, as can distress or anxiety.

If a person indicates that they feel faint, dizzy and that everything is beginning to look slightly grey, they are about to faint. Make them sit down on a chair and lower the head between the knees. If a chair is not available, make the person lie down with the head on the floor and feet and legs raised on cushions, a low stool, a pile of books or any suitable object. Loosen tight clothing, belts and collar or tie. If the person has already fainted, then lower the head and raise the legs as above, loosening tight clothing.

Allow plenty of room around the person; ask onlookers to stand aside and increase the ventilation.

The person should come round quickly, but they should remain lying down or keep the head between the knees for a few minutes to recover. Then make the patient more comfortable, preferably lying down, and keep them warm. Once they are fully conscious again, provide a drink of water or a hot drink. The cause of fainting may be lack of food, in which case a sweetened drink can help.

Do not:

- try to lift or move a person who is fainting or about to faint
- pour any liquid into the person's mouth if they are about to faint or have fainted
- give any alcohol
- allow the person to walk away alone immediately they regain consciousness. Make sure they rest briefly and that they have company.

Note If the person does not regain consciousness within seconds, then hold their hand, speak to them clearly, encouraging them to come out of the faint. If this does not work rapidly, check the breathing and pulse: be prepared to apply the kiss of life and heart massage, if necessary. Call an ambulance or medical help.

FIT, EPILEPTIC

During an epileptic fit, the sufferer loses consciousness, becomes rigid, then the muscles will relax and contract causing the body and limbs to jerk and twitch. Following this the patient remains still for about ten minutes. The whole process takes about fifteen minutes in all. During the fit, the person may become temporarily incontinent.

Do not try to restrain the patient; however, do try to avoid injury by removing furniture and by preventing the person from falling. Loosen tight clothing and, once the limbs have stopped jerking, move the person into the recovery position (see page 31).

Towards the end of an epileptic fit, when the body begins to stop moving and starts to become rigid, there is a danger that the person may bite his or her tongue. It may be possible to place something between the teeth to prevent this (a handkerchief folded into a pad, for example); however, do not try to stuff something into the mouth which may consequently block air access.

There should be no cause for alarm if the person is a known sufferer and recovers quickly. If the person lapses into a second or series of fits, call an ambulance. If the person (adult or child) is suffering a first fit, then consult the doctor.

The patient may have medicine which should be taken and they may need help with this on recovering from the fit. Establish whether they have the necessary medicines or whether a doctor should be summoned for help before leaving the patient.

HEART ATTACK

A sudden heart attack without any warning and with dramatic symptoms is not common. If it does occur, the patient suffers severe pain down the left arm and up the chest, or towards the jaw. This is accompanied by dizziness or loss of consciousness and a grey pallor.

- Call an ambulance or doctor – whichever is quicker.
- Support the conscious patient in a sitting position to ease breathing and keep them calm. Keep them warm but loosen any tight clothing, belts and collars.
- If the patient is unconscious, check the breathing and pulse. Give the kiss of life, if necessary, and heart massage. However, do not apply heart massage if there is any sign of pulse.

NOSE BLEED

If this is associated with injury, for example in case of accident or fall, then call an ambulance. Keep the patient warm and treat for any other injury.

The majority of nose bleeds are harmless. The person should press the soft part at the side of the nostril to prevent the blood flowing and promote clotting. At the same time, they should breathe through the mouth and avoid coughing, sniffing or talking.

The bleeding should stop within ten minutes but the treatment may have to be continued for up to thirty minutes, with the patient resting, lying down if possible. If the bleeding continues for longer, then take the patient to the doctor or hospital.

Children often panic if they have a nose bleed, so it is important to calm them down and make them rest. Make sure they are breathing calmly through the mouth.

Do not blow the nose for several hours after a nose bleed. If nose bleeds are frequent, consult the doctor.

POISON

If a person has swallowed or eaten a poisonous or dangerous substance, either call an ambulance or take them to the hospital or doctor immediately, depending on which is quickest and most practical.

Do not try to make the patient sick, as this can increase the internal damage in some cases. If the person is vomitting, keep some of the vomit as it may be helpful in identifying the poison.

- Keep the person as calm and warm as possible, making sure tight clothing is loosened for easy breathing.
- If the person is unconscious, check breathing and pulse, applying the kiss of life or heart massage if necessary.
- Place in the recovery position (see page 31) once breathing has been established and the heart is beating.

Note If acid has been swallowed, make the patient drink milk but do not make them vomit.

FIRST-AID COURSES

These are available in most areas, run by local branches of national organizations and local authorities. They usually include practical instruction, which is invaluable in emergencies, and guidance on dealing with a broad range of situations as well as on current techniques. The benefits of attending such a course cannot be over-emphasized, especially to adults in a family household.

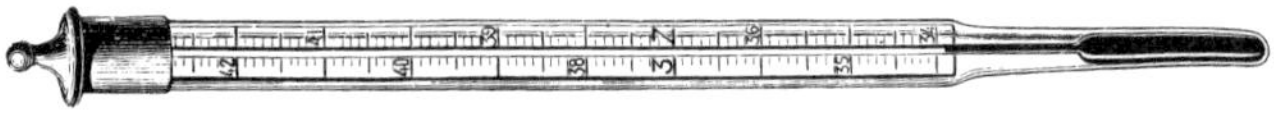

Microwave Cooking

Among the many twentieth-century changes in the kitchen, the microwave oven must offer the most revolutionary form of cooking. This chapter provides essential guidelines on making optimum use of this versatile appliance.

If you are completely new to microwave cooking take care to read and follow the manufacturer's instructions supplied with your appliance. This is most important probably more so than with any other appliance – as individual microwave ovens vary performance-wise even if they are based on the same power output.

All microwave information given in this book is based on an oven with an output of 650–700 watts. If your oven has a lower power rating, the food will take longer to cook; for a higher output, the cooking times should be shortened. The following terms have been used for the microwave settings: High, Medium, Defrost and Low. For each setting, the power input is as follows: High = 100% power, Medium = 50% power, Defrost=30% power and Low=20% power. Throughout the book, microwave notes and timings are for guidance only, and manufacturer's instructions should be consulted for basic cooking times as far as possible, or for the purpose of comparison.

BASICS OF MICROWAVE COOKING

Read the manufacturer's instructions for guidance on cooking utensils and techniques as well as for cooking times. Specific information on the use of metal depends on the particular appliance. Consult your handbook for more information.

GENERATING HEAT

Microwaves cook food by causing the molecules, or chemical particles, to vibrate to such an extent that the internal friction generates heat. This heat cooks the food. The amount of heat generated and the speed with which the food heats depends on the composition and quantity of the food.

VOLUME AND COMPOSITION

The greater the volume, the longer the food takes to get hot and cook. Foods which have a high water content take longer to cook than dry foods; for example, water takes a long time to boil in the microwave. So, adding boiling water to some dishes, such as soup, or adding the liquid in stages rather than all at once at the beginning of cooking, reduces the overall cooking time.

Foods with a low water content but high fat or sugar content heat very quickly and can therefore overcook speedily.

Dense foods take longer to cook or reheat than lighter foods. For example, potato takes longer to cook than egg. Mashed potato takes longer to reheat than cooked rice.

MICROWAVE PENETRATION

The microwaves penetrate food to a depth of up to 5 cm/2 inches, depending on the composition, shape and quantity of food. The remainder of the food, towards the centre, is cooked by conduction of the heat as during conventional cooking.

FOOD PREPARATION

Food that is evenly shaped cooks more evenly. Examples of such foods include boneless chicken breasts; similar-sized cubes of poultry or vegetables; similar-sized new or old potatoes; similar-sized cauliflower or broccoli florets; and fish steaks.

If pieces of food have thin or narrow areas, these should be arranged to receive less microwave energy than thicker or larger areas. For example, place the pointed ends of poultry breasts together towards the centre of the cooking dish and overlap thin ends of fish fillets or fold them under.

Areas that require little cooking should be treated as for thin areas, for example, broccoli florets should be placed in the dish so that the tender heads are towards the centre and the tougher stalks are around the outside.

Do not add salt to food before cooking unless there is a significant quantity of sauce. Never sprinkle salt over vegetables, meat or poultry as this results in dark, dehydrated patches. Sauces may be seasoned before cooking.

PRICKING FOODS

Any food that has a skin or membrane covering must be pricked before cooking, otherwise a build-up of heat within the food may cause it to burst during cooking. Whole potatoes, the skin on poultry and halved kidneys are typical examples. If you cook shelled eggs in the microwave, prick the yolks with a cocktail stick to prevent them bursting; eggs in shells must never be cooked in the microwave as they are liable to explode.

Chicken livers must be cut up, otherwise they pop and splatter as heat builds up within the membranes which cover them. The heat build-up can happen between cooked areas and the membrane, so large pieces of food are just as prone to splattering as whole food items.

STIRRING AND REARRANGING FOOD

During microwave cooking, food should be stirred or rearranged to promote even cooking, preventing some areas from being undercooked while others overcook.

As a general rule, the larger the quantity of food, the more often it has to be stirred or rearranged. However, the shape and size of container can influence the heating pattern. When heating liquid mixtures in small but deep vessels or in containers such as basins, bowls or wide casseroles, it is important to stir frequently to avoid having fierce hot spots which tend to froth over when the liquid is stirred at the end of cooking. If the heat is allowed to build up in the lower area of a container such as a coffee pot or similar container filled with liquid, the liquid can froth out through a spout or narrow opening. This also applies when heating a mug of liquid: if the liquid is not stirred a hot spot can froth over at the end of heating. Stirring prevents this problem from occurring.

COVERING

Many foods are covered during microwave cooking to retain moisture and heat, therefore promoting quick and even cooking. This applies to foods that are likely to dry out on the surface – fish or vegetables – as well as to items like rice, in which the moisture retained from the steam is necessary for successful cooking.

Lidded, microwave-proof dishes are ideal; however, suitable plates may be used instead of a lid.

When removing a cover, always take care to protect your hand and wrist, and, if possible, to lift the cover so that the escaping steam is directed away from you.

SHIELDING

Some areas which are prone to overcooking may be shielded with small pieces of smooth cooking foil. Typical examples include the wing tips on poultry and the tail end of a whole salmon. This technique should only be used where there is large portion of food exposed, so that the majority of the microwave energy is absorbed, and for part of the cooking time. Consult your manufacturer's handbook to make sure that this is recommended for your appliance.

STANDING TIME

During standing time, the heat generated by the microwaves is evenly conducted throughout the food. Standing time is important as it allows the food to cook evenly through to the centre. It ensures that heat is evenly distributed within the food, avoiding hot spots.

EQUIPMENT

METAL

Do not use metal utensils or containers with any metal trimming, including designs with metallic paint. The metal reflects the microwaves, causing them to arc and spark within the cooking cavity. Microwaves reflected back to the power source, the magnetron, may damage the appliance (with repeated misuse).

OVENPROOF GLASS

This is the most practical material for cooking containers. It is also suitable for use in the conventional oven and certain types are flameproof or suitable for use in the freezer. The thinner glass dishes absorb the least energy and give the best results; however all ovenproof glass is suitable and practical for use in the microwave.

Although inexpensive drinking glasses may be used for brief heating purposes (warming a glass of mulled wine or milk, for instance), drinking glasses are not suitable for cooking or boiling liquids. Do not use cut glass or lead crystal as this causes sparking.

CROCKERY

Crockery which will withstand the heat of the food is suitable for use in the microwave. Plates are useful for thawing or brief cooking as well as for covering dishes: mugs and jugs may be used with care (see Stirring and Rearranging Food, page 44). Some crockery absorbs microwave energy, slowing down the cooking process. Highly-glazed crockery can cause sparking. Delicate china is not suitable for use in the microwave.

PAPER

Absorbent kitchen paper, non-stick baking parchment and greaseproof paper are all useful for microwave cooking. Also, look for special browning paper, which has a coating to absorb microwave energy and brown food. Roasting bags and wrap are also suitable for microwave cooking. Boilable cooking bags may be used for moist dishes; however, they tend to melt under conditions of dry heat.

PLASTICS

Polystyrene is not suitable for microwave cooking. Boilable plastic basins may be used for short heating or thawing, as may some freezer containers; however, in general these plastics are not suitable as they melt when the food becomes hot. Some plastics also absorb sufficient microwave energy to cause softening, or even melting.

Cling film or plastic wrap should not be used as a covering directly on food. Special microwave covering may be used to cover bowls or basins containing a comparatively small amount of food but the wrap itself should never touch the food. Prick the wrap, or leave a small space for steam to escape.

MICROWAVE COOKWARE

There is a vast range of microwave utensils and containers on offer – many items are expensive and/or flimsy. These are not essential adjuncts to the microwave oven. Some are useful; many are gadgets which you may or may not find helpful depending on the type of food you cook. It is best to get to know your microwave oven and to decide on the use you intend to make of the appliance before investing in specialist equipment which may prove unnecessary; evaluate these items carefully before buying.

The quality of the basic material used in specialist utensils varies enormously and some of the flimsy, inexpensive containers do not withstand extensive use. Flimsy containers can be useful if you want a particular shape of dish to cook an occasional recipe; for example a ring-dish for making a pudding or chocolate cake.

The plastics used for microwave cookware are specifically manufactured to allow the maximum transfer of energy, so cooking times may be shorter when using these containers.

BROWNING DISHES AND WRAP

These have a coating which absorbs microwave energy and becomes hot. The hot surface browns the food as in traditional cooking methods. Wrap is usually designed for browning the base of items such as pizza or imparting some crispness to pastries when reheating them.

The use of a browning dish usually involves preheating it according to the instructions, for a given length of time at a certain setting. The food is then seared in the dish. In many cases, the heat of the browning surface is sufficient only to brown one side of food such as chicken joints lightly. The efficiency varies according to the particular container and the type of food, but for traditional browned results with foods such as meat, the browning dish may disappoint. Browning utensils include items such as burger makers. The range of browning gadgets is always changing – some give good results, others are less successful.

SUCCESSFUL MICROWAVE COOKING

The microwave may be used to cook a variety of foods successfully, with results as good as those achieved by traditional methods; other foods cooked by microwave energy may be less satisfactory, usually in terms of texture. In a combination microwave oven the failures are fewer than when using microwave energy alone, as the appliance includes a traditional heat source.

MICROWAVE COOKING: MOIST AND RAPID

Microwave cooking is a moist method, best compared to boiling or steaming. It is also rapid. Therefore foods which cook well by steaming or boiling often yield successful results in the microwave oven. However, tough foods which require long, slow cooking do not cook well in the microwave – braising or stewing meat does not have sufficient time to tenderize. A special microwave pressure cooker does give tender results with tough foods, when used according to the manufacturer's instructions.

TEXTURE AND BROWNING

Food cooked in the microwave does not become crisp and, on the whole, it does not brown. Some joints of meat brown slightly if large enough for the fat content to become hot enough and for long enough to cause some surface browning.

Foods that rely on a crisp crust for success are not suitable for microwave cooking. Choux pastry is a prime example: the paste rises and puffs dramatically while the microwave oven is operating; as soon as the power is cut off, the paste sinks. This is because the paste has to form a crisp outer shell to keep the shape of the baked item.

Other forms of pastry do not cook well in the microwave either – short crust dough is soft with a raw flavour and puffed or layered pastries do not form a crisp crust to set the light texture. With these types of pastry, the layers set only when the dough is so overcooked as to be dehydrated and unpalatable.

Traditional bread dough is too dense to cook well by microwaves; however, a yeasted batter will give reasonable results and can be useful for making small loaves or items. However, the results do not brown or have a crusted surface.

FLAVOUR

The microwave oven acts in the same way as a steamer to intensify, or bring out the best of some flavours. Vegetables usually have a good flavour when cooked by microwave and the natural flavour of fish is brought out to the full. As when steaming or boiling, herbs and spices and other strongly flavoured ingredients should be used in moderation, depending on the balance of the dish, as they can come through strongly to dominate. Onions and garlic should be cooked first with or without a little fat, otherwise they will have a raw flavour too strong for the majority of dishes. The same is true for traditional moist cooking methods.

Microwave-cooked meat does not develop the same flavour as grilled, baked or roast meat; instead it has a steamed or boiled flavour. Only the most succulent cuts are sufficiently tender for microwave cooking and the quality is not nearly as good as expected of traditional methods.

Minced meat is suitable for microwave cooking for meat loaves, burgers made with added breadcrumbs and seasonings and meat sauces. All give perfectly acceptable results, although a microwave-cooked meat sauce cannot be compared for richness with a long-braised one.

FOODS TO COOK BY MICROWAVE

Here is a checklist of some foods that cook well in the microwave.

Apples puréed or stewed
Artichokes both globe and Jerusalem
Asparagus when spears are small and tender; avoid woody spears
Aubergines for example in ratatouille
Bacon rashers rolls or chopped
Bananas for a quick pudding, cook with a knob of butter and a little orange juice
Battenburg cake as the mixture is cooked in two portions, then trimmed
Beetroot when young and tender
Broccoli with short, tender stalks
Brussels sprouts small whole, or halved
Cabbage for a result similar to stir-frying, particularly white or red
Carrots when young and finely cut but not when older or in large pieces
Celeriac cut up small
Chicken especially in sauce
Chicken livers must be chopped
Chocolate ring cake or cup cakes
Courgettes are better than by some traditional methods
Duck cook, then drain and brown well in a very hot oven or under the grill
Eggs scrambled only
Fish especially in sauce
Fruit most types poach well or cook perfectly for purées
Lentils particularly red
Liver cut small in sauces
Potatoes both small new and whole old but not for mashing or purées
Rice all types
Sauces savoury and sweet of all types
Steamed sponge puddings cook very quickly and taste wonderful
Turkey especially in small portions
Vegetables other types in addition to those listed

FOODS TO AVOID IN MICROWAVE COOKING

These are some of the foods that are either inferior or unsuccessful when cooked in the microwave.

Batters including Yorkshire pudding and pancakes
Bread dough is tough and unpleasant
Cakes (with a few exceptions, mainly chocolate or well-flavoured mixtures and cup cakes)
Choux pastry does not form a crust so will not set in shape
Eggs baked, fried or omelettes, the exception is scrambled eggs. Never attempt to cook eggs in shells in the microwave
Deep-fried foods are unsuitable. It is dangerous to heat large quantities of oil in the microwave
Fish fingers and other foods coated in egg and breadcrumbs
Fruit cake is too dense
Game the majority benefits from traditional roasting or long slow cooking, depending on type
Hamburgers traditional all-meat burgers are far better when grilled
Meat roasts can be partially cooked by microwaves to shorten the traditional roasting time
Omelettes are rubbery
Pancakes have to be fried
Pasta except very small amounts
Pastry except suet crust
Preserves except very small quantities
Sausages except frankfurters and other tender boiling types
Sponge cakes made by the whisked method
Stews of meat, game or less tender offal, except when cooked in a pressure cooker designed specifically for the microwave
Tougher cuts of meat offal and game

GENERAL GUIDELINES FOR THAWING FOOD

The microwave is undoubtedly an invaluable companion to the freezer as it makes possible speedy thawing without loss of quality. For good, safe results always remember the following points.

- Follow the microwave manufacturer's instructions regarding settings and timings.
- In the absence of a defrost setting or suggested alternative, use medium-low or low.
- Unwrap frozen food and place it in a suitable container. Most foods that benefit from retaining moisture should be covered during thawing; otherwise they may dry out on the surface.
- To make it easier to remove foods from their wrapping, it may be helpful to partially thaw them. Remove any metal tags or ties from the wrapping first, and do not put any wrappings with metal coating or foiled labels in the microwave. As soon as it is possible to do so, unwrap the food and return it to the microwave in a suitable container to complete thawing.
- Baked goods, such as bread, should be unwrapped and placed on double-thick absorbent kitchen paper. The paper absorbs excess moisture.
- Turn and rearrange food occasionally during thawing, breaking up blocks of food as soon as possible.
- Check on thawing progress and allow standing time halfway through and/or at the end of thawing. It is only necessary to allow standing time during the thawing process when handling large food items, such as joints or large birds.
- Thawed foods should be cold, not unevenly warm or cooked in parts.
- When reheating cooked food, such as a casserole, immediately after thawing, increase the setting when the food is just thawed to reheat it thoroughly and without delay.
- Small items or foods which thaw quickly may be speedily thawed by using a higher setting; however this is only useful when the food can be thoroughly thawed without any risk of cooking in parts.
- Pay particular attention to poultry, especially whole birds, ensuring it is thoroughly thawed before cooking to avoid any possibility of having undercooked areas when the poultry is served.
- Read and follow instructions on frozen convenience foods – most offer guidance on thawing and reheating or cooking by microwave when appropriate.
- Finally, always use or cook food promptly after thawing.

GUIDE TO COOKING TIMES

In the absence of the microwave manufacturer's cooking instructions and timings, the following information may be useful. All timings are for cooking on a High setting unless otherwise stated.

FISH

Fish can be cooked whole, in steaks or cutlets, in fillets or in chunks.

PREPARATION

Trim the fish, slitting the skin on whole fish to prevent it from bursting. Put into a suitable container and dot with butter or margarine or moisten with lemon juice, wine or water. Steaks, individual portions of fillet or chunks can be cooked in a sauce. Do not season with salt. Cover the dish.

COOKING NOTES

Thicker parts of the fillet, or the thick end of a steak, should be placed towards the outside of the dish. When cooking two or more large fish fillets, arrange them in a dish with head ends next to tail ends; tuck the thin tail pieces underneath to prevent overcooking. Chunks of fish should be placed as far apart as possible. Turn or rearrange halfway through cooking.

COOKING TIMES

Fillets, Cutlets or Steaks (White or Smoked Fish) The cooked fish should flake easily but it should still be very slightly translucent at the base of the flakes or towards the centre of the cutlet or steak. By the time the fish is removed from the microwave and served the residual heat will have completed the cooking process.

Fillets

100 g/4 oz	1½–2½ minutes
225 g/8 oz	4–6 minutes
450 g/1 lb	8–10 minutes

Cutlets or Steaks

1 medium	2–4 minutes
2 medium	4–6 minutes
3 medium	5–7 minutes
4 medium	8–10 minutes

Plaice

Fillets

2 fillets	1–2 minutes
4 fillets	3–5 minutes
6 fillets	4–6 minutes
8 fillets	7–9 minutes

Note For even results when cooking 6 or more fillets, roll the fillets and secure them in place with wooden cocktail sticks.

Mackerel

Whole Fish

1	2–4 minutes
2	4–6 minutes
3	5–7 minutes
4	7–9 minutes

Rolled Fillets (2 from each fish)

2	2–3 minutes
4	3–5 minutes
6	5–6 minutes
8	6–8 minutes

Mullet

1 grey mullet (about 1–1.5 kg/2–3 lb)	9–11 minutes
2 medium red mullet	8–10 minutes
4 medium red mullet	12–15 minutes

Note If the red mullet are very small, reduce the above times by 1–2 minutes in each case.

Herring

Whole Fish

2	2–3 minutes
4	4–6 minutes

Kippers

1 about 1 minute
2 1½–3 minutes
3 2½–4 minutes
4 4–6 minutes

Frozen Boil-in-the-bag Kippers

Pierce the bag and lay it on a plate or dish. Cook on High for 4–6 minutes. Leave for 1–2 minutes before snipping the bag. Look out for instructions on the packet – many brands of frozen foods provide microwave cooking instructions which relate to tests carried out on the product to give best results.

Whole Salmon

A whole fish weighing up to 2.25 kg/5 lb can be cooked successfully in the microwave. Prepare the fish as usual then slit the skin in several places. Curl the fish into a large flan dish. Cover the fish with special microwave film, wrapping two layers over the dish to keep the salmon firmly in place. Since the fish skin is discarded, it does not matter that the film lays directly on it.

Cook on High for 2–3 minutes per 450 g/1 lb. A 2.25 kg/5 lb fish will need 10–15 minutes. Leave the salmon to stand for 5 minutes before checking that it is cooked by piercing the flesh at the thickest point. The cooked salmon should be moist and the flesh should flake easily.

Salmon Steaks

Weigh the steaks. Secure the flaps of flesh neatly in the middle of the steaks with wooden cocktail sticks. Arrange as far apart as possible in a dish, with the thicker sides towards the edge of the dish. Dot with butter and sprinkle with 15 ml/l tbsp water. Cover and cook on High for 4–5 minutes per 450 g/1 lb. Turn the steaks halfway through cooking.

Trout

Prepare the trout, leaving heads on. Slit the skin in two or three places and sprinkle with 30 ml/2 tbsp water. Cover and cook on High for the following times:

1 trout 2–3 minutes
2 trout 4–6 minutes
3 trout 5–7 minutes
4 trout 8–10 minutes

Note It can be more practical depending on dish and microwave oven size, to cook four fish in pairs. When the first pair is cooked, wrap them in foil to keep hot while cooking the second pair.

POULTRY

Chicken and turkey both cook well in the microwave as they are tender meats, although turkey drumsticks are less successful. Duck cooks extremely well; for delicious results, drain off excess fat occasionally and at the end of microwave cooking, brown the whole bird or portions thoroughly in a very hot oven or under the grill before serving.

PREPARATION

For whole birds, complete the essential preparation and trimming as for conventional cooking then truss neatly, keeping the joints tied firmly as close to the body as possible. Prepare duck by pricking the skin all over to allow the fat to escape.

Boned birds cook particularly well, with or without stuffing.

COOKING NOTES

Cover the poultry during cooking. Whole birds may be placed in a roasting bag which should be partially closed with a microwave-proof tie. Stand the bird in its bag in a dish to catch juices.

When cooking portions, arrange thin parts or bone ends together towards the middle of the dish, with thicker areas around the perimeter. Rearrange the poultry during cooking, turning portions and whole birds over at least once.

Having prepared duck as described above, cook it in a fairly deep dish; drain off fat as necessary.

Place whole birds breast down for about two-thirds of the cooking time as this keeps the breast meat moist. When cooking large birds, such as turkey, shield the joint ends with small pieces of foil if they begin to overcook. Check in your manufacturer's handbook that this is permitted for your appliance.

STANDING TIMES AND CHECKING COOKING PROGRESS

Allow poultry portions to stand for 3–5 minutes at the end of cooking; whole birds should stand for 5–10 minutes, depending on size.

After standing times have been observed, test the poultry to make sure that it is cooked. The meat behind the thigh is thick and shielded, so always ensure it is done by piercing the meat with the point of a knife; look for any traces of blood in the cooking juices or pink flesh – both indicate that the poultry is undercooked. If this occurs, return the poultry to the microwave and continue cooking until the juices run clear and the flesh is firm.

COOKING TIMES

Whole chicken 7–9 minutes per 450 g/1 lb
Whole turkey 6–8 minutes per 450 g/1 lb

Chicken Quarters
1 5–7 minutes
2 10–12 minutes
3 15–18 minutes
4 21–25 minutes

Chicken Thighs or Drumsticks
1 2–3 minutes
2 4–6 minutes
3 5–7 minutes
4 7–10 minutes
6 14–16 minutes
8 18–22 minutes

Boneless Chicken Breasts or Turkey Fillets
1 2–4 minutes
2 5–8 minutes
3 9–11 minutes
4 12–15 minutes

Duck Quarters
1 4–6 minutes
2 7–9 minutes
3 12–15 minutes
4 17–20 minutes

Boneless Duck Breasts

1 4–6 minutes
2 8–10 minutes
3 12–15 minutes
4 16–18 minutes

MEAT

Some microwave ovens have automatic cooking programmes for meat, usually set according to the weight of the joint. Follow the manufacturer's instructions when using an automatic programme – the pre-programmed settings usually give best results as they are thoroughly tested by the manufacturer.

Avoid tougher cuts of meat that would require slow stewing or braising if cooked by conventional energy. If a joint is cooked completely in the microwave, the result will not be as good as if it were roasted conventionally. A better method is to partially cook the meat in the microwave, then complete the cooking in a conventional oven. Similarly, to speed up the cooking of small cuts, such as thick pork chops, cook them briefly in the microwave, then flash them under a hot grill to complete the cooking.

PREPARATION

Boneless cuts are a better shape for microwave cooking, particularly if the microwave is the main or only cooking appliance used.

Meat which is cut up for cooking – for example to make a stir-fry dish – is best cut across the grain into thin pieces. Slices or fine strips are more tender than cubes. Marinating the meat before cooking it imparts flavour and helps to tenderize it.

Joints should be tied into a neat shape – remember to avoid metal skewers. When cooking or partially cooking an unevenly shaped joint, shield any thin areas which begin to overcook by covering them with small pieces of smooth foil, provided this is permitted in your appliance.

Chops, cutlets and other small cuts should be arranged with any thin or small parts close together in the centre of the dish; failing this, keep thin areas together or overlapping as far as possible.

Do not sprinkle salt over meat and cover or partially cover the meat while cooking.

COOKING NOTES

The High setting may be used to partially cook a joint or for small joints or cuts and cut-up meat; however on larger joints, the outside tends to overcook before the middle is done. Medium is therefore the recommended setting. If you intend to start the meat off in the microwave before completing the cooking process in a conventional oven, use High.

Turn or rearrange the meat during cooking, stirring cubed or diced meat and breaking up mince.

Leave the meat to stand after cooking, allowing 5 minutes for small cuts, up to 15–25 minutes for joints.

MEAT THERMOMETER

A conventional meat thermometer may be used to check the internal temperature of the meat after it has been removed from the microwave. Heat the thermometer in readiness by standing it in hot water. Insert it into the centre of the joint, cover with foil and allow to stand, then check the temperature. If more cooking is necessary, remove the thermometer before returning the meat to the microwave.

Alternatively, if you often cook meat in the microwave, it may be worth buying a microwave thermometer. This is designed for use in the microwave oven and is free from metal. A skewer is used to make a hole in the meat and the thermometer is then inserted. Some cookers have a temperature probe which may be used for the same purpose.

COOKING TIMES

Times given are for complete cooking in the microwave.

Beef and Lamb

Joints: Cooking times per 450 g/1 lb on Medium

rare	10–12 minutes
medium	13–15 minutes
well-done	14–16 minutes

Joints: Cooking times per 450 g/1 lb on High

rare	5–6 minutes
medium	6–8 minutes
well-done	8–9 minutes

Minced Meat: Cooking time per 450 g/1 lb on High including pork or veal – 10–15 minutes

Note Timing for mince depends on other ingredients added.

Lamb Chops or Cutlets

Trim chops of excess fat before cooking and arrange them as far apart as possible on a shallow dish. Cover with absorbent kitchen paper. If the chops are cooked in a sauce, arrange the chops in a covered dish. Cook on High, rearranging the chops halfway through cooking.

1	2–4 minutes
2	5–7 minutes
3	6–8 minutes
4	8–10 minutes

Pork

Small cuts are best cooked in a sauce so that the lack of browning is less obvious. The following times are a guide to cooking on High.

Joints	7–10 minutes per 450 g/1 lb
Small cuts	6–8 minutes per 450 g/ 1 lb

Liver

Trim and slice the liver, then arrange the slices in a dish and dot with butter. Season with pepper. Cover the dish. Cook on High.

225 g/8 oz	2–3 minutes
450 g/1 lb	4–6 minutes

Bacon Rashers

Lay the rashers on a microwave cooking rack or large plate. Cover loosely with absorbent kitchen paper. Cook on High.

2 rashers	1½–2 minutes
4 rashers	2–3 minutes
6 rashers	3½–4½ minutes
8 rashers	5–6 minutes

Burgers

These times are for 100 g/4 oz burgers, cooked from frozen. Place the burgers as far apart as possible on a flat dish and cover loosely with absorbent kitchen paper. Cook on High.

1 2½–3½ minutes **2** 5–6 minutes **4** 8–10 minutes

VEGETABLES

PREPARATION

With the exception of frozen produce, the majority of vegetables should have a small amount of water added before cooking. Prepare the vegetables as usual then place them in a covered container with a little water. Do not add salt.

In some cases a knob of butter may be added instead of water: for example, with courgettes which are naturally moist, or wine or citrus juice may be used with or without a little butter.

When cooking large whole potatoes, arrange them as far apart as possible on a large plate, dish or double-thick absorbent kitchen paper. Remember to prick potatoes before cooking them so that they do not burst.

Arrange cauliflower and broccoli so that the tender heads are close together in the middle of the dish. The stalks, which are tougher and denser, should be spaced around the rim of the dish so that they receive the maximum microwave energy. This principle should be applied to all vegetables in which some parts are more tender than others. When cooking florets in a deep dish, arrange them with the stalks pointing outwards and upwards so that the tender heads are together in the middle.

QUANTITIES

Microwave cooking is excellent for small to medium quantities of vegetables; however large quantities are best split into two batches for cooking.

COOKING NOTES

Stir or rearrange vegetables once or twice during cooking, bringing small pieces from the outside towards the middle. The following times and notes are for cooking on High.

COOKING TIMES

Artichokes, Globe

1 6–8 minutes
2 9–11 minutes
3 12–14 minutes
4 15–18 minutes

Size and age affects cooking time. Leave the cooked vegetables to stand, still in their cooking container, for about 5 minutes, after cooking. To test that they are tender, pull off one of the outer leaves – it should come away easily.

Asparagus

Frozen asparagus does not take much longer than fresh but do not add water. Older spears which may be tough are best boiled or steamed.

225 g/8 oz – 4–6 minutes

BEANS:

Broad Beans

100 g/4 oz shelled fresh	3–4minutes
225 g/8 oz shelled fresh	6–7 minutes
450 g/1 lb shelled fresh	9–10 minutes
100 g/4 oz frozen	4–5 minutes
225 g/8 oz frozen	7–8 minutes
450 g/1 lb frozen	11–12 minutes

French Beans

100 g/4 oz fresh	3 –4 minutes
22 5 g/8 oz fresh	5–7 minutes
450 g/1 lb fresh	7 –10 minutes
100 g/4 oz frozen	4– 5 minutes
225 g/8 oz frozen	7–9 minutes
450 g/1 lb frozen	12–14 minutes

Runner Beans

450 g/1 lb fresh	6–7 minutes
225 g/8 oz fresh	4–5 minutes
100 g/4 oz fresh	2–3 minutes
100 g/4 oz frozen	3–6 minutes
225 g/8 oz frozen	6–8 minutes

Note Home-frozen runner beans that are in a block should be broken as they thaw. They take longer to thaw and cook than purchased frozen runner beans.

Broccoli

100 g/4 oz fresh	2–4 minutes
225 g/8 oz fresh	5–6 minutes
450 g/1 lb fresh	7–9 minutes

225 g/8 oz frozen	7–8 minutes
450 g/1 lb frozen	12–14 minutes

Leave for 2 minutes before draining and serving.

Brussels Sprouts

100 g/4 oz fresh	2–3 minutes
225 g/8 oz fresh	4–6 minutes
450 g/1 lb fresh	8–10 minutes
100 g/4 oz frozen	3–5 minutes
225 g/8 oz frozen	7–8 minutes
450 g/1 lb frozen	11–12 minutes

Cabbage Timing depends on personal taste. The following guide gives tender, crunchy results:

100 g/4 oz	3–5 minutes
225 g/8 oz	6–8 minutes
450 g/1 lb	9–11 minutes

Carrots

100 g/4 oz	2–3 minutes
225 g/8 oz	4–5 minutes
450 g/1 lb	6–8 minutes

Note Frozen carrots need very little cooking once they have thawed, so follow the above timings but do not add extra water.

Cauliflower

small whole cauliflower	10–12 minutes
large whole cauliflower	13 –16 minutes
100 g/4 oz florets	4–5 minutes
225 g/8 oz florets	6–8 minutes
450 g/1 lb florets	10–12 minutes

Note Frozen florets need very little cooking once they have thawed, so follow the above timings but do not add extra water. For best results, florets should be even in size and not too large.

Corn on the cob

1 fresh	3–5 minutes
2 fresh	6–8 minutes
3 fresh	8–10 minutes

4 fresh	11–13 minutes
1 frozen	5–7 minutes
2 frozen	8–10 minutes
3 frozen	12 –14 minutes
4 frozen	15–17 minutes

Note There is no need to add water to frozen corn.

Courgettes

225 g/8 oz	2–4 minutes
450 g/1 lb	4–6 minutes

Note Courgettes should be evenly sliced or cut in neat sticks. They cook well in a loosely-closed roasting bag.

Leeks

225 g/8 oz fresh sliced	4–6 minutes
450 g/1 lb fresh sliced	8–10 minutes
450 g/1 lb fresh whole	6–8 minutes
225 g/8 oz frozen sliced	5–7 minutes
450 g/1 lb frozen sliced	10–12 minutes

Note There is no need to add water to frozen leeks.

Marrow

The following times are for the prepared vegetable, cut into 2.5–5 cm/l–2 inch cubes.

225 g/8 oz	3–5 minutes
450 g/1 lb	7–10 minutes

Mushrooms

Whole Button Mix with olive oil or butter.

225 g/8 oz	2–4 minutes
450 g/l lb	4–6 minutes

Sliced Mushrooms Heat 25–50 g/1–2 oz butter in a dish on High for 30–60 seconds. Add the mushrooms and cook on High.

100 g/4 oz	1–2 minutes
225 g/8 oz	2–4 minutes
350 g/12 oz	3–5 minutes
450 g/1 lb	4–6 minutes

Parsnips The following times are for prepared vegetables cut into chunks. Cook with water in a covered dish on High.

450 g/1 lb	7–10 minutes
675 g/1½ lb	12–15 minutes

Leave to stand, still covered, for 3 minutes, then drain. Mash the parsnips or toss them in butter.

Peas Frozen peas do not require liquid; canned peas should be heated in the liquid from the can.

225 g/8 oz fresh	4–6 minutes
450 g/1 lb fresh	7–10 minutes
50 g/2 oz frozen	2–3 minutes
100 g/4 oz frozen	3–4 minutes
225 g/8 oz frozen	4–6 minutes
350 g/12 oz frozen	5–7 minutes
450 g/1 lb frozen	7–10 minutes
Small can (about 283 g/10½ oz)	2 minutes
Large can (about 425 g/15½ oz)	3–4 minutes

POTATOES:

Whole Potatoes The following times are for potatoes weighing about 350 g/ 12 oz each and cooking on High.

1	6–8 minutes
2	10–12 minutes
3	14–16 minutes
4	20–22 minutes

Old Potatoes Cut potatoes into large chunks, dice or slice; it is important to make sure the pieces of potato are fairly even in size. Place in a dish and add 45 ml/3 tbsp water. Do not add salt. Cover and cook on High, rearranging the potatoes once or twice during cooking.

450 g/1 lb	6–8 minutes
675 g/1½ lb	7–10 minutes
1 kg/2 lb	12–14 minutes

New Potatoes Select even-sized new potatoes. Scrub, then place in a dish with 45 ml/3 tbsp water. Do not add salt. Cover and cook on High, rearranging once or twice.

450 g/1 lb 5–7 minutes

675 g/1½ lb 6–9 minutes
1 kg/2 lb 8–11 minutes
Note Small new potatoes take slightly less time than evenly cut old potatoes.

Spinach
Place the trimmed, wet leaves in a bowl or large roasting bag. Cover or close the opening with a microwave-proof tie. Cook on High, rearranging halfway through cooking. Allow 5–7 minutes per 450g/1 lb on High. Drain well and use or serve as required.

Sweetcorn
100 g/4 oz frozen 2–4 minutes
225 g/8 oz frozen 4–6 minutes
350 g/12 oz frozen 6–7 minutes
450 g/1 lb frozen 7–10 minutes

Turnips
The following times are for prepared vegetables, cut into even-sized chunks. Very small whole turnips or halved small to medium vegetables may be cooked in the same way.
225 g/8 oz 5–7 minutes
450 g/1 lb 9–11 minutes
Leave, closely covered, for 5 minutes, then drain and toss in butter, adding a good grinding of black pepper.

COMBINATION MICROWAVE COOKING

A combination microwave oven combines microwaves with simultaneous conventional heat, so food cooks swiftly, at the same time browning and forming a crisp crust. The cooked flavour compares well with that achieved by traditional methods. Many foods which are not acceptable when cooked by microwave energy alone are excellent when cooked by this method. Read and follow your manufacturer's instructions and suggested cooking times. This section opens with an outline of what to expect from a combination microwave oven. Some foods which cook well by the combination method are listed overleaf. The chart on page 68 provides a guide to the temperature and microwave power setting to use, along with a likely cooking time for a selection of foods and recipes.

COOKING MODES

- Basic microwave facility
- Fan oven using conventional heat only
- Combination oven with the microwaves and conventional heat operating at the same time
- A grill may be included for use alone or with microwave energy

METAL

Unlike the majority of basic microwave ovens, combination ovens often come with specially designed metal racks. Always follow the manufacturer's instructions for using the accessories with the cooker.

To maximize the use of the microwave energy as well as the conventional heat it is best to use ovenproof glass and baking dishes.

COOKING INSTRUCTIONS AND RESULTS

Most combination microwave cooking employs a Medium microwave setting and conventional heat. The temperatures selected for the conventional heat are usually quite high by comparison with traditional methods: the microwave energy speeds up the cooking process, so a hotter oven is needed to brown and crisp the food in the shorter time. It is not always necessary to preheat the oven. Some combination microwave ovens have automatic cooking programmes based upon weight. Follow your handbook for instructions.

Meat Use Medium (some manufacturers recommend a Low setting) and a hot oven. Season after cooking. There is no need to cover the meat but joints should be turned to ensure even cooking. If roasting joints taking over 30 minutes, do not preheat the oven. The times in the chart (page 68) are a guide to minutes per 450 g / 1 lb, unless otherwise stated. Some ovens have preset combination cooking, and may not permit you to set the microwave control to Medium. In such cases, opt for the shorter cooking time.

Pastry Short crust, puff and flaky pastry all cook well to give crisp light results with good texture. Pastry flans, pasties and pies can be successfully cooked. Choux pastry does not cook well by this method. The times in the chart (page 68) are intended as a guide; exact timings will depend on the precise ingredients used.

Bread This cooks well, resulting in browned, crusty loaves with good flavour. The sides and underneath of the bread tend to be soft and pale when cooked but this is not a significant disadvantage. Preheat the oven.

Cakes Creamed mixtures cooked in combination ovens have brown tops and a good flavour. The sides and base are usually pale. Use baking dishes instead of tins, lining them with greased greaseproof paper first. Leave the cake in the dish for a few minutes before turning out. Use a standard mixture adding 30–60 ml/2–4 tbsp milk or extra liquid. Take care not to overcook as this results in a dry texture.

For example, a mixture of 175 g/6 oz each of fat, sugar and self-raising flour, 3 eggs and 30 ml/2 tbsp milk, baked in an 18 cm/7 inch deep dish, will require 12–15 minutes on 220°C/Medium. Preheat the oven.

Batters Yorkshire pudding or sweet batter puddings cook well. Make a batter from 100 g/4 oz plain flour, 2 eggs, 300 ml /½ pint milk and 30 ml/2 tbsp water. Heat a little fat in a flan dish, pour in batter and cook at 250°C/Medium for 10–15 minutes. Preheat the oven. For toad-in-the-hole, cook 450 g/1 lb sausages in a suitable dish at 250°C/Medium for 5 minutes. Add batter and continue to cook for 12–15 minutes.

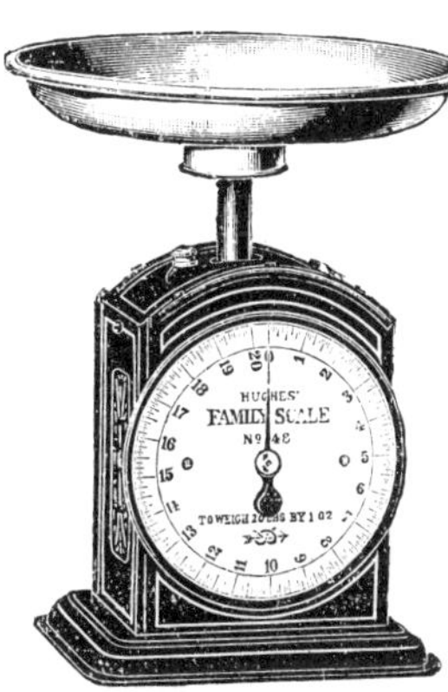

COMBINATION MICROWAVE COOKING: A GUIDE TO COOKING TIMES

Food	Setting	Cooking Time
Beef		
Joints: topside, sirloin, rolled rib (off the bone)	180°C/Medium	5–8 minutes
Steak: medium to well-done (not recommended for rare)	240°C/Medium	5–8 minutes
Note Times are a guide to minutes per 450 g/1 lb. Preheat the oven for steaks.		
Lamb		
Leg	190°C/Medium	9–11 minutes
Shoulder	200°C/Medium	10–12 minutes
Breast, boned and rolled	220°C/Medium	12–14 minutes
Note times are a guide to minutes per 450 g/1 lb		
Pork		
Loin, boned and rolled (reduce temperature after 10 minutes)	220–190°C/Medium	14–16 minutes
Loin, on bone (reduce temperature after 5 minutes)	220–190°C/Medium	14–16 minutes
Leg (reduce temperature after 5 minutes)	220–180°C/Medium	15–16 minutes
Chops	240°C/Medium	7–9 minutes
Note Times are a guide to minutes per 450 g/1 lb. Preheat the oven for chops.		
Short Crust Pastry Flan		
To partially bake a 23 cm/9 inch flan before filling, prick all over, then line with greaseproof paper and dried peas	250°C/Medium	5 minutes
Note Do not preheat the oven.		
Part-baked pastry with quiche Lorraine type of filling (3 eggs plus 300 ml/½ pint milk, cooked onion, cheese and ham or part-cooked bacon)	200°C/Medium	12–15 minutes
Note Preheat the oven.		
Short Crust Pastry Pie Crust		
Use pastry made with 175 g/6 oz plain flour, 75 g/3 oz fat		
With cooked steak and kidney filling	220°C/Medium	15 minutes
With half-cooked mince, onion and mushroom filling	200°C/Medium	20 minutes
Short Crust Pastry: Cornish Pasties		
4, with raw filling	220°C/Medium	18–20 minutes
Note Preheat the oven. Use rack for two-level cooking; swap dishes over halfway through time.		
Puff Pastry Pie Crust		
With cooked filling	220°C/Medium	10 minutes
Note Preheat the oven.		
Bread		
Dough made with 450 g/1 lb strong plain flour; risen in 23 cm/9 inch deep round dish	250°C/Medium	10–12 minutes
Half quantity of above, in 450 g/1 lb loaf dish	250°C/Medium	7–9 minutes

Freezing

The freezer and frozen foods have brought dramatic changes to our eating patterns. Fruit and vegetables are no longer seasonal specialities and, with the refrigerator, the freezer has done away with the need for frequent shopping. Follow the guidelines in this chapter for best results when freezing fresh food, and remember to use all food before the suggested storage time has elapsed.

BUYING A FREEZER

The choice of freezer depends on where you intend to site it and how you anticipate using it. Begin by considering the freezer space you require – think about family size, shopping and eating habits. Measure up, decide on the amount of space available, then thoroughly research all the models on offer before buying. Make a checklist before you shop around, adding features you like as you go.

Chest Freezer Top-opening with hinged lid. This is not suitable for a kitchen but is ideal for an unheated garage or utility room. Chest freezers should have a lockable lid to prevent children climbing in; also useful for keeping thieves out if the freezer is in an outhouse or garage. A large amount of food may be packed into a chest freezer but it is not always easy to reach all parts of the appliance, so the contents must be organized for easy access.

Upright Freezer More practical for a kitchen, this type is usually better designed to cope with a warm outside temperature. Also, access is easier. There are some large models of this type but the majority are smaller than chest freezers. Food is more easily organized and accessed in this type of appliance.

Fridge-freezer Generally smaller than an individual appliance (although some very large combination models are available), these are ideal for a kitchen site where the household is small. However, do not forfeit essential refrigerator room in order to gain freezer space.

PREPARING FOOD FOR FREEZING

All raw food should be prepared as for cooking. Produce should be trimmed, washed and dried. The majority of vegetables should be blanched.

Cooked items should be cooled as quickly as possible, then frozen promptly. Bought prepared foods or cooked items should be frozen as soon as possible after shopping.

Blanching Vegetables benefit from blanching. Enzymes, naturally present in the food, cause it to ripen, then eventually to become overripe and finally to rot. During freezing, enzyme activity is slowed down considerably but it is not fully halted; in some vegetables, therefore, the produce may deteriorate in quality if stored for long periods.

The enzymes are destroyed by exposure to temperatures equal to those of boiling water for a short period of time (this varies according to the food and enzyme). Blanching vegetables destroys the enzymes and improves the keeping quality during freezing.

However, if vegetables are to be frozen for short periods (2–4 weeks), there is no need to blanch them. Some vegetables keep well for far longer periods without blanching; others deteriorate rapidly, developing off flavours. This is particularly true of broad beans, which should always be blanched if storing for longer than 2 weeks.

Blanching Method To prevent food from being cooked during blanching it is important that it is placed in rapidly boiling water, which is brought back to the boil as quickly as possible, then drained immediately. To facilitate speedy cooling, the drained food should be immersed in iced water. This prevents continued cooking by residual heat.

Blanch manageable quantities at a time – if large batches are processed the water takes longer to come back to the boil and the vegetables tend to cook.

Have ready a large saucepan, a wire basket and a large bowl (or thoroughly clean sink) of iced water. Place the prepared vegetables in the basket and plunge them into the boiling water. Bring the water back to the boil, then time the blanching exactly. Remove the vegetables and plunge them straight into iced water as soon as the required time is reached. Drain well, pat dry on absorbent kitchen paper, then pack the vegetables and freeze.

PACKING FOR FREEZING

To avoid the development of cross-flavours between foods in the freezer and to prevent deterioration in quality, it is essential that all food is adequately packed.

Packing Materials These must be waterproof; they should form an airtight seal when closed. Plastics, whether containers or bags, are ideal. Although foil keeps moisture in, it tends to be too fragile and tears easily.

Sheets of plastic tissue may be used for interleaving stacked items, such as chops or burgers.

Bags should be heavy gauge; thin ones do not keep in moisture, nor do they prevent exposure to the air from causing the food to dry out.

Freezer Burn This results from poor packing: the surface of the food dries out, looks pale, and on meat or fish the flesh is slightly shrunken and heavily grained. It is caused by dehydration and is not remedied on thawing and cooking.

Open Freezing This is a useful technique for fish cakes, sausages, strawberries, raspberries and other individual items which are best frozen separately. The food should be prepared, then spread out on trays lined with freezer film or foil. The trays are placed in the freezer until the food is hard, then the items should be packed in airtight bags. This allows large quantities to be packed in one bag, and because the items are free-flowing, small amounts may be removed as required.

Removing Air It is important to remove air from freezer packs as it is a factor in the formation of freezer burn and can cause some fatty foods, such as bacon, to become rancid.

To displace the air, the pack of food may be immersed in a bowl of water. Once all air has been removed, the opening should be sealed with a wire tie. The exterior of the pack should be dried before freezing.

Labelling Always label packs of food with details of the food or dish, the date and any notes about potential use. For example, note any quantity of sugar added to a fruit purée.

USING FROZEN FOOD

Vegetables should be cooked from frozen. Fruit may also be prepared straight from frozen but the majority of other items should be thawed before use.

Thawing Food The safest way to thaw food is to unwrap it and place it in a covered container in the refrigerator overnight.

The important point to remember is that as the food thaws, the bacteria and enzymes contained in it slowly become active as the temperature rises. While the food remains very cold there is no risk of it being open to contamination by bacterial growth; however if the food is left in a warm room for a long period, parts, if not all, of it will become sufficiently warm for bacteria to grow. Foods left in this manner for long periods may develop high levels of bacteria with the possible consequence of food poisoning.

It is therefore vital that food thawed at room temperature should be frequently monitored. It should be used as soon as it is thawed, while still very cold.

Cooking from Frozen Fish fillets and steaks thaw quickly and may be cooked from frozen; however their texture and flavour is improved if they are thawed first.

Poultry and meat should be thawed before cooking, the only exception being very small or thin items, such as fine strips of meat or poultry, burgers or similar products and thin escalopes. Meat joints may be cooked from frozen but results are not as good as when the meat is thawed. If you must cook from frozen, reduce the cooking temperature to very low and increase timing to ensure that the centre of the joint is adequately cooked. The drawback with this method is that the outside of the joint may be overcooked or dried out.

Never cook poultry portions or whole poultry from frozen. Poultry may contain bacteria which cause food poisoning and unless the meat is thoroughly cooked these bacteria, or their spores, may survive. Thick areas of poultry should be pierced to check that they are thoroughly cooked; if there is any sign of blood, the poultry should be returned to the oven at once.

Microwave Thawing The microwave is useful for thawing food. Always read and follow the manufacturer's instructions. As a general guide, use a Low or Defrost setting. Unpack the frozen food and ensure it is free of metal (for example, clips used to keep poultry limbs in place), then place it in a suitable covered dish. Turn or rearrange items during thawing and observe recommended standing times with larger items to ensure even thawing.

FISH

Only freshly caught or bought fish which has not previously been frozen, then thawed, should be frozen. Clean and prepare fish completely and pack in polythene. Separate steaks or fillets with interleaving film.

MEAT, POULTRY, AND GAME

Ask the butcher to freeze large quantities of meat, because this would take 3 or 4 days in a home freezer which is not acceptable and would result in poor-quality frozen meat. Smaller quantities of meat, poultry, and game can be frozen successfully at home. Meat must be frozen quickly and the fast-freeze switch should be turned on well ahead of freezing time, following the instructions in your handbook.

Most game must be hung for the required time, then plucked or skinned, and drawn. Surplus fat should be removed, and the meat will take up less space if boned and rolled. Any bones should be padded with a twist of foil or paper before the meat is packed in polythene. Pack chops, steaks, and sausages in small quantities or open-freeze them first. Remember that salted meats have a limited storage life since they quickly become rancid.

VEGETABLES

All vegetables should be young, fresh and clean, and frozen as soon as possible after picking. Open-freeze blanched vegetables, then pack them in free-flow packs so that small quantities can be removed as required. Vegetables should be cooked from frozen. Since they are blanched, they cook quickly; however the time taken to thaw them means that the overall cooking time is about the same, or slightly less, than for fresh produce. Add the frozen vegetables to boiling water, steam them or toss them in hot butter, according to type.

COOKED AND OTHER PREPARED DISHES

Add rice, pasta or potatoes to liquid dishes after thawing. For long freezer storage, use onions, garlic, herbs and spices with care, as flavours can deteriorate or mature during freezing.

Pack cooked foods in freezer containers, or in ordinary dishes which will withstand freezing and heating. Label carefully if additional ingredients have to be included during reheating. Use cooked foods within 2 months to retain high-quality. Thaw all dishes and make sure they are thoroughly reheated to the original cooking temperature.

CAKES, PASTRY, AND BREADS

Icings and fillings made from fat and sugar are best frozen separately. Fruit or jam fillings in cakes become soggy after thawing, and are better added just before serving. Decorations are also better added then, since they absorb moisture during thawing and may stain the cake. Sweetened whipped cream can be frozen like a cake filling. Pack cakes carefully to avoid crushing during storage. It is better to open-freeze decorated cakes before packing.

FRUIT

Freeze only fresh, top-quality fruit. Fruit can be frozen dry and unsweetened, with sugar, in syrup, or as purée, and in cooked dishes. Although the use of sugar or syrup was considered to be important at one time, good results are obtained by freezing fruit without sweetening. Open freezing prevents crushing. Apples discolour; therefore they should be blanched before freezing if not cooked.

Fruit Purée Prepare purée from raw raspberries or strawberries, but cook other fruit in a little water first. Sweeten to taste before freezing and when packing, leave a little headspace to allow for expansion.

Fruit Juices Prepare fruit juice and freeze in ice-cube trays. Wrap frozen cubes individually in foil and store in polythene bags. For long storage it is best to bring juice to the boil and boil it rapidly for a minute, then cool it quickly by standing the pan in iced water.

DAIRY PRODUCE

Most cheeses can be frozen but tend to crumble. They should be frozen in small pieces, and cut when still slightly hard. Cream and cottage cheese tend to separate and should not be frozen, although cream cheese can be used for cooking if well-beaten after thawing. Only homogenized milk in waxed cartons should be frozen, and then only in small quantities which can be used quickly. Whipped double or whipping cream may be frozen but single cream does not freeze well. Eggs should be very fresh. They should be washed and then broken into a dish to check for quality. They should be frozen already beaten or separated, in rigid containers, with sugar or salt added in the proportions shown in the chart (page 78) to prevent coagulation.

FREEZER REMINDERS

- Keep a record of the contents of your freezer and update it regularly even if you do not do so whenever you remove food from the freezer.
- Move items to be used promptly to the top or front of the freezer.
- Freeze food which is in good condition and produce in its prime.
- Always consider how you intend using food before you freeze it.
- Pack all food in sealed containers or bags.
- Exclude as much air as possible from packs except when freezing liquid items which require headspace to allow for expansion.
- Always label packs – even though the contents may be evident when fresh, they are far more difficult to identify when frozen.

FRUIT FREEZING CHART

Type of fruit	Preparation for freezing	High-quality storage life
Apples	Peel, core, and slice. Blanch in boiling water with lemon juice added for 1 minute.	12 months
Apricots	Skin and cut in halves or slices. Add lemon juice to pack.	12 months
Blackberries and raspberries	Clean and hull.	12 months
Blueberries	Wash and drain. Crush slightly to soften skins.	12 months
Cherries	Chill in water for 1 hour and stone.	12 months
Cranberries	Wash and drain.	12 months
Currants (red, white, and black)	Strip fruit from stems.	12 months
Damsons	Wash, drain, and stone.	12 months
Gooseberries	Clean, top, and tail.	12 months
Greengages and plums	Cut in half and stone.	12 months
Lemons and limes	Peel and slice, or without peeling and pack for drinks.	12 months
Peaches and nectarines	Skin, cut in halves or slices, and brush with lemon juice. Alternatively, make a raw purée with 15ml/1 tbsp lemon juice to 450g/1lb fruit.	12 months
Pineapple	Peel and cut in slices or chunks.	12 months
Rhubarb	Wash in cold water and trim sticks.	12 months
Strawberries	Clean and grade for size.	12 months

COOKED DISHED FREEZING CHART

Type of dish	Preparation for freezing	High-quality storage life
Casseroles and stews	Slightly undercook vegetables. Do not add rice, pasta or potatoes. Remove surplus fat.	2 months
Flans (sweet and savoury)	Prepare and bake. Open-freeze, then wrap.	2 months
Ices – fresh fruit purée	Fully prepare.	3 months
– ice-cream	Fully prepare.	3 months
– sorbets and water ices	Fully prepare.	3 months
– bombes and other moulded desserts	Fully prepare.	3 months
– ice cream gâteaux	Fully prepare.	3 months
Meat	Do not freeze cooked joints or grilled meats they can become tough, rancid and dry. Sliced cooked meat thinly and pack in sauce or gravy.	2 months
Meat pies	1) Bake and cool. Wrap. Cook meat filling. Cool and cover with pastry. Wrap.	1) 2 months 2) 2 months
Mousses	Prepare in freezer-tested serving dishes.	1 month
Pancakes	Cool and pack in layers with interleaving film.	2 months
Pasta dishes	Pack pasta and sauce in foil dish with lid.	1 month
Pate	Cool completely and wrap.	1 month
Pizza	Bake. Cool and wrap. Alternatively, par-bake base, then add topping and freeze.	1 month
Rice	Slightly undercook, drain well, cool, and pack.	1 month
Sauces (savoury)	Prepare completely, but season sparingly. Pack in rigid containers, leaving headspace. *Do not freeze sauces thickened with eggs or cream.*	1 month
Sauces (sweet)	1) Fresh or cooked fruit sauces should be packed in rigid containers, leaving headspace. 2) Thickened pudding sauces with cornflour and pack in rigid containers, leaving headspace. *Do not freeze custard sauces.*	1) 12 months 2) 1 month
Soup	Do not include rice, pasta, barley, potatoes, milk, cream or eggs. Pack in rigid containers, leaving headspace.	2 months
Steamed and baked puddings	Steam or bake puddings in foil containers. Cool and cover.	2 months

DAIRY PRODUCE FREEZING CHART

Dairy produce	Preparation for freezing	High-quality storage life	Thawing instructions
Butter or margarine	Overwrap in foil or polythene.	6 months (unsalted) 3 months (salted)	Thaw enough for 1 week's use in refrigerator.
Cheese – hard	Cut in 200 g/7 oz pieces and wrap in foil or polythene. Pack grated cheese in polythene bags. Double wrap blue cheese.	3 months	Thaw in open wrappings at room temperature for 3 hours. Cut while slightly frozen to avoid crumbling.
– cream	Blend with double cream.	3 months	Thaw in container in refrigerator overnight. Blend with fork to restore smoothness.
Cream	Freeze double and whipping creams in cartons. Do not freeze single, soured or half-cream.	6 months	Thaw in carton at room temperature and stir with a fork to restore smoothness.
– whipped	Sweeten with 30 ml/2 tbsp sugar to 600 ml/1 pint cream. Freeze in containers, or open freeze piped rosettes.	6 months	Thaw in container at room temperature. Rosettes thaw in 15 minutes at room temperature.
Eggs	Do not freeze in shell. 1) Mix yolks and white, adding 5 ml/1 tsp salt or 10 ml/2 tsp sugar to 5 eggs. 2) Mix yolks, adding 5 ml/1 tsp salt or 10 ml/2 tsp sugar to 5 yolks. 3) Put whites in containers with no addition.	12 months	Thaw in refrigerator but bring to room temperature before use.
Milk	Only homogenized milk can be frozen. Leave 2 cm/¾ inch headspace.	1 month	Thaw at room temperature and use quickly.

FISH/SEAFOOD FREEZING CHART

Type of Fish	Preparation for freezing	High-quality Storage life	Thawing instruction
Crab, Crayfish and lobster	Cook and cool. Remove flesh before packing. Live crustaceans may be packed in clean polythene carrier bags, then frozen. This is an acceptable method of killing them and they should be cooked from frozen.	1 month (cooked) 3 months (raw)	Thaw in container in refrigerator and serve cold, or add to cooked dishes.
Mussels	Scrub and clean thoroughly. Put in a large pan over medium heat for 3 minutes to open. Cool, remove from shells, and pack in rigid containers with juices or in sauce.	2 months	Cook raw crustaceans as usual, allowing an extra 5–10 minutes cooking, depending on size. Thaw in container in refrigerator before adding to dishes.
Oily fish (herring, mackerel, salmon)	Clean well, fillet, cut in steaks or leave whole. Exclude as much air as possible from packs.	2 months	Thaw large fish in refrigerator but cook small fish from frozen
Oysters	Open and reserve liquid. Wash in brine (5 ml/1 tsp salt to 500 ml/ 17 fl oz water). Pack in own liquid.	1 month	Thaw in container in refrigerator and use promptly for cooked dishes.
Prawns and shrimps	Freeze raw or cook and cool in cooking liquid. Remove shells and pack. Shrimps may be covered in melted spiced butter.	1 month	Thaw in container in refrigerator and serve cold, or add to cooked dishes.
Smoked fish	Double pack in polythene bags.	2 months	Thaw in refrigerator to eat cold, or cook haddock and kippers from frozen.
White fish (cod, sole)	Clean, fillet or cut in steaks, or leave whole. Separate pieces of fish with interleaving film. Wrap, excluding air carefully.	3 months	Thaw large fish in refrigerator, but cook small fish from frozen.

- Separate different types of food in the freezer for easy access. Large, colour-coded polythene sacks are available for the purpose or clean supermarket carrier bags are equally practical.
- Keep the freezer plug taped into its socket if there is any chance that it may be removed by mistake and not replaced.
- If you have children in the household be aware of the safety aspects of freezer ownership. Keep a chest freezer locked so that young children cannot climb into it. Pay particular attention to safety when buying a secondhand chest freezer – look for one which has a lid which opens from inside or one which locks securely.

MEAT, POULTRY AND GAME FREEZING CHART

Type of meat, poultry, & game	Preparation for freezing	High-quality storage life	Thawing instructions
Cubed meat	Pack in small quantities, pressing together tightly.	2–4 months	Thaw in refrigerator for 3–8 hours.
Ham and bacon	Commercial vacuum packs are best. Otherwise, exclude as much air as possible.	2–6 weeks (sliced) 3 months (joints)	Thaw in refrigerator.
Offal	Wash and dry well, remove blood vessels and cores.	1 month	Thaw in refrigerator for 3 hours.
Joints	Trim, bone, and roll, if possible.	9–12 months (beef) 9 months (lamb and veal)	Thaw in refrigerator allowing about 4 hours per 450g/1lb.
Minced meat	Use lean mince and pack in small quantities.	1 month	Thaw in refrigerator for 3–8 hours.
Sausages and sausagemeat	Pack in small quantities or open-freeze.	1 month	Thaw in refrigerator for 3–8 hours.
Steaks, chops or sliced meat	Pack in small quantities or open-freeze.	6–12 months (depending on meat)	Thaw in refrigerator.
Chicken, guineafowl or turkey	Hang, pluck, and draw, if necessary. Truss or cut in joints. Chill for 12 hours. Pack without giblets. Do not stuff.	6 months	Thaw in refrigerator. Must be completely thawed before cooking.
Giblets	Clean, wash, dry, and chill.	2–4 weeks	Thaw in refrigerator for 2 hours.
Duck and goose	Hang, pluck, and draw, if necessary. Chill for 12 hours. Pack without giblets.	6 months	Thaw in refrigerator. Must be completely thawed before cooking.
Grouse, partridge, pheasant, pigeon	Hang as liked after removing shot and cleaning wounds. Pluck, draw and truss, and pad bones.	6 months	Thaw in refrigerator.
Plover, quail, snipe, woodcock	Prepare as other game.	6 months	Thaw in refrigerator.
Hare	Clean shot wounds and hang, bleeding the animal and collecting the blood if required. Paunch, skin, clean, and cut into joints. Pack blood separately.	6 months	Thaw in refrigerator.
Rabbit	Paunch, skin, clean and prepare: as for hare.	6 months	Thaw in refrigerator.
Venison	Pack convenient-sized joints. Open-freeze steaks, cubes or minced venison.	12 months	Thaw in refrigerator.

BAKED ITEMS FREEZING CHART

Type of cake, pastry or bread	Preparation for freezing	High-quality storage life	Thawing/baking instructions
Biscuits	Form dough into 2 cm/¾ inch diameter roll. Wrap. **Note** Baked biscuits are best stored in tins without freezing.	2 months	Thaw in refrigerator for 45 minutes. Cut in slices and bake at 190°C/375°F/gas 5, for 10 minutes.
Bread	Pack in polythene bags. Crusty bread quickly loses its crispness in the freezer.	1 month	Thaw at room temperature for 4 hours.
Breadcrumbs (plain)	Pack in polythene bags.	3 months	Use from frozen.
Brioches and croissants	Pack in rigid containers to prevent crushing, immediately after baking and cooling.	1 month	Thaw at room temperature for 30 minutes and heat in oven or under grill.
Cakes (un-iced)	Cool completely and wrap.	4 months	Thaw at room temperature for 2–3 hours.
Cheesecakes	Make baked or refrigerated variety in cake tin with removable base. Open-freeze and pack in rigid container. Types relying on gelatine for texture and shape are best avoided as they become very soft on thawing.	1 month	Thaw for 8 hours in refrigerator
Choux pastries	Bake but do not fill or ice. Pack in polythene bags or boxes.	1 month	Thaw at room temperature for 2 hours. Crisp for 1 minute in the oven.
Crumpets and muffins	Pack in polythene bags.	1 month	Thaw in wrappings at room temperature for 30 minutes before toasting.
Danish pastries	Bake but do not ice. Pack in foil trays with lids, or rigid containers.	2 months	Thaw at room temperature for 1 hour. Heat if liked.
Fruit pies	Brush bottom crust with egg white to prevent sogginess: 1) Bake, cool, and pack. 2) Use uncooked fruit and pastry, open-freeze, and pack.	1) 4 months 2) 2 months	Thaw to serve cold, or reheat. Bake from frozen at 200°C/400°F/gas 6 for 1 hour.

Type of cake, pastry or bread	Preparation for freezing	High-quality storage life	Thawing/baking instructions
Pastry cases	Freeze baked or unbaked, using foil containers	4 months	Bake frozen cases at recommended temperatures for type of pastry. Re-heat baked cases, or fill with hot filling.
Sandwiches	Do not remove crust. Spread with butter or margarine. Do not use salad fillings, mayonnaise or hard-boiled eggs. Separate sandwiches with interleaving film and pack in foil or polythene. Cheese, diced chicken with soft cheese, diced ham and grated cheese or mashed sardines are examples of suitable fillings.	1 month	Thaw at room temperature and remove crusts, or toast under grill while still frozen.
Scones	Pack in small quantities	2 months	Thaw at room temperature for 1 hour. Bake frozen scones at 180°C/350°F/gas 4 for 10 minutes.

VEGETABLE FREEZING CHART

Type of vegetable	Preparation for freezing	Blanched time	High-quality storage life
Artichokes (globe)	Remove outer leaves, stalks, and chokes. Add lemon juice to blanching water.	7 minutes	12 months
Artichokes (Jerusalem)	Peel and slice. Cook and purée.		3 months
Asparagus	Trim and cut in lengths.	2 minutes (thin) 3 minutes (medium) 4 minutes (large)	9 months
Avocados	Mash pulp with lemon juice (15ml/1tbsp juice to each avocado).		1 month
Beans (broad)	Shell small young beans.	1½ minutes	12 months
Beans (French)	Top and tail young beans. Leave whole or cut into 2 cm/¾ inch chunks.	3 minutes (whole) 2 minutes (cut)	12 months
Beans (runner)	Cut as preferred.	2 minutes	12 months

Type of vegetable	Preparation for freezing	Blanched time	High-quality storage life
Beetroot	Cook very young beet, under 2.5 cm/1 inch in diameter. Peel and leave whole.		12 months
Broccoli	Trim stalks and soak in brine for 30 minutes. Wash before blanching.	3 minutes (thin) 4 minutes (medium) 5 minutes (thick)	12 months
Brussels sprouts	Trim and prepare for cooking.	3 minutes (small) 4 minutes (medium)	12 months
Carrots	Use very young carrots. Wash and scrape. Leave whole, dice or slice.	3 minutes	12 months
Cauliflower	Wash and break into florets. Add lemon juice to blanching water.	3 minutes	6 months
Corn on the cob	Use fresh tender corn. Remove husks and silks.	4 minutes (small) 6 minutes (medium) 8 minutes (large)	12 months
Courgettes	Cut courgettes into 1 cm/½ inch slices without peeling.	3 minutes	2 months
Herbs	Wash and pack whole sprigs or chop.		6 months
Leeks	Clean and cut into rings.	2 minutes	12 months
Mushrooms	Wipe but do not peel. Pack or open-freeze without blanching.		3 months
Onions	Skin and chop or slice. Double wrap.	2 minutes	2 months
Parsnips, turnips, and swedes	Peel and dice.	2 minutes	12 months
Peas	Shell young sweet peas.	1 minute	12 months
Peppers	Remove seeds and membranes.	3 minutes (halved) 2 minutes (slices)	12 months
Potatoes	Cook and mash, or make into croquettes. Jacket, baked and roast potatoes can be frozen. Fry chips for 4 minutes but do not brown.		3 months
Spinach	Remove any stalks and wash leaves very well. Press out moisture after blanching.	2 minutes	12 months
Tomatoes	Purée and pack in rigid containers.		12 months

Menu Planning

The success of any snack or meal, both in aesthetic and dietary terms, hinges upon the combination of food or dishes which comprise it. A few important guidelines summarize the approach to planning menus for every day as well as for special occasions.

The key points to consider when planning a menu, apart from the likes and dislikes or dietary restrictions of the diners, are the flavours, textures, colour and weight of the meal. A well-planned menu balances all these elements. Additional, practical, aspects to consider are your ability and confidence as a cook; the budget for one meal or for a weekly – or monthly – run of meals; and the cooking facilities available.

FLAVOURS AND TEXTURES

As well as considering the accompaniments for the main dish, remember that a strongly-flavoured starter will put a lightly seasoned main course in the shade, just as a very spicy main course will ruin the palate for a delicate dessert. Balance strong flavours and aim to accentuate more subtle dishes.

Texture is a less obvious but equally important characteristic of food. A meal that consists solely of soft food is dull, and three courses of dry or crunchy dishes can be a disaster, leaving everyone gasping for water. Balance soft and smooth mixtures with crunchy textures; combine moist dishes with dry ones. Offer crisp salads with zesty dressings to counteract rich fried foods; serve plain, crunchy, lightly cooked vegetables to balance heavily-sauced casseroles and stews.

COLOUR AND WEIGHT

The importance of colour in a dish and on a menu does not simply refer to the piece of parsley dropped on to a grey sauce. The ingredients used in individual dishes, the quality of cooking juices and sauces and the choice of accompaniments are all factors in achieving a menu that looks appealing. Some cooked foods inevitably look uninteresting; this is when the choice of accompaniments is vital. Remember that flavour and texture must also be considered.

The overall weight of the meal is important. Light dishes should balance richer foods. A filling dish should always be flanked by delicate courses.

FOOD VALUE

The chapter on Nutrition and Diet outlines the importance of eating a balanced diet. Dinner parties and special meals are occasions for breaking or bending the rules and indulging in favourite foods. When planning everyday meals or snacks, however, it is very important to consider food value alongside the flavour, texture and appearance of the dishes. Applying rigid guidelines to every meal is not practical but considering the overall food value of the day's diet is prudent. Taking a sensible, overall view of food eaten over a period of a few days, or within a week, is also a reasonable way of ensuring that snacks and meals provide a balanced diet. From breakfast through to supper, whether considering the main meal of the day or an in-between meal snack, variety is one of the keys to success, both in the range of foods eaten and the cooking or serving methods used.

CATERING FOR SPECIAL DIETS

Be aware of any dietary restrictions for social or medical reasons, planning them into the menu for all diners as far as possible. In some cases, for example when catering for vegartarians as well as meat eaters, it is quite possible to provide one menu to suit everyone. Contemporary vegetarian dishes are acceptable to all, not simply to those who avoid animal products; it is far trickier to plan a vegan menu to suit all tastes. Limitations imposed for health reasons may be more difficult to accommodate; if in doubt, check details with the prospective guest or consult an official source of information for guidance.

If the whole menu cannot be adapted to suit everyone, plan the meal around one or two of the key dishes. It is usually quite easy to serve a first course to suit all diets. Either the main dish or vegetable accompaniments should be selected for their versatility: if the main dish is unsuitable for certain diners, then the vegetable accompaniments should make equally interesting main dishes on their own. For example, ratatouille, a mixed vegetable gratin or stir-fried vegetables with noodles are all suitable for serving with plain meat dishes but they are equally good vegetarian dishes when served with appropriate accompaniments.

Adopt this approach whenever you plan meals and snacks but pay special attention to the food value of restricted diets if you cater for them on a regular basis. Make up for nutrients lost in banned foods by including compensatory alternatives.

PARTIES

The choice of party food depends on the number of guests and the budget – these factors influence the style of food, choice of ingredients, balance of hot and cold dishes and the number of courses. Whether you are planning a formal meal or cocktail-style buffet with snacks and nibbles, remember the following points as they are crucial to the success – or failure – of the menu.

- Time available for food preparation.
- Refrigerator space for storing ingredients and/or dishes which require chilling.
- Kitchen facilities, particularly oven and hob space.
- Freezer space and suitability of dishes for preparing in advance.
- Availability of crockery and cutlery for serving.
- The time available for last-minute work, finishing dishes, garnishing and so on.
- Your own ability as cook – opt for a menu which you will tackle with confidence.
- Ease of serving and eating the food: the only thing worse than a host or hostess who is overstretched by last-minute cooking between courses at a formal dinner party is the poor guest who is struggling with a knife and fork while standing and balancing a plate, glass and napkin, at the same time as chatting politely to other guests.

COOKING IN QUANTITY

Forward planning is all-important when cooking for a crowd, from considering the likes and dislikes of guests, planning the menu, checking the serving arrangements and crockery through to clearing up afterwards. It is vital to select a menu which is manageable kitchenwise and to batch cook ahead, if possible, to avoid running out of oven space, cooking utensils or equipment for one massive cooking session.

The following are all practical choices for buffets for large numbers up to fifty (or more), for informal parties or occasions such as weddings. The dishes selected may either be cooked ahead and frozen but they are also a sensible choice for same-day cooking. Remember that you can hire large cooking pans for potatoes or rice that require last-minute cooking. When batch baking these recipes, double the quantities; this is practical and speedy.

Chicken Mayonnaise Allow 1 small boneless chicken breast per person, skinned. Roast, covered, cool and chill the day before. The chicken may be diced before chilling. Coat with mayonnaise thinned with a little cream or yogurt and dress with chopped parsley, chives and tarragon. For a well-dressed dish, allow 600 ml/1 pint mayonnaise and 300 ml/½ pint plain yogurt or cream for 25 chicken breasts. Browned flaked almonds or grated lemon rind may be sprinkled over instead of the herbs.

Baked Ham Order a whole cooked ham, preferably on the bone, from a good butcher, delicatessen or large supermarket. The rind may be removed and the fat coated with brown sugar, then browned in a hot oven before serving the ham.

Carbonnade of Beef Cook in double quantity batches, with slightly less liquid; each batch to serve 12. Cool and freeze well ahead, packing in small quantities that thaw quickly. Thoroughly reheat in the oven just before serving the carbonnade.

New Potatoes Scrub and boil small new potatoes, then drain and toss in butter with chives or mint. They should be scrubbed the day before, boiled early on the day of the party until only just cooked, then drained and tossed in butter. Cool quickly and reheat well in their butter before serving. Allow 1.8–2.25 kg/4–5 lb for 16–20 portions; 5.5–6.75 kg/12–15 lb for 50 portions.

For a delicious salad, cook the potatoes completely, then toss them in an oil and vinegar dressing, adding lots of snipped chives and chopped parsley, cover and cool.

Cooked Rice Allow 50 g/2 oz per person as a side dish, 75 g/3 oz per person as part of a main dish (for example, risotto) on a buffet. Cook with twice the volume of water. If serving hot, cook ahead, cool and chill promptly. Reheat thoroughly to a high temperature in covered serving dishes and serve promptly: do not reheat more than once and do not allow to stand, lukewarm, on the buffet for long periods. Rice salads should be kept chilled until served.

Quiche Make, chill and freeze quiches in advance, allowing 10–12 portions from a 20–23 cm/8–9 inch round quiche, depending on other buffet food. Thaw and reheat just before serving.

Salad Green salad is practical and a refreshing accompaniment to most buffet food; however, it is seldom eaten in any quantity. Select a crisp lettuce and shred or cut all ingredients finely. A salad of 1 large lettuce, with cucumber, spring onions and green pepper will yield up to 30 portions as part of a buffet. Serve dressing separately.

Meringues Make ahead – when thoroughly dried, meringues keep well in airtight containers in a cool place for at least a couple of weeks. Pile them high in a dish and serve with a bowl each of whipped cream and strawberries for a do-it-yourself dessert. Allow 600 ml/1 pint cream, whipped to serve 15–20 and 75 g/3 oz strawberries per portion.

Brownies These make a good dessert for freezing ahead. Thaw on the day of serving, stack them up and serve with a bowl of whipped cream.

Sacher Torte Make ahead and freeze, assemble and coat the day before. Serve with whipped cream.

ADAPTING RECIPES

There are a number of important factors to bear in mind when catering in quantity. If you are planning to scale up a favourite recipe, you must first look at it carefully to see if it contains any strong flavourings. These do not need to be scaled up in the same proportions as the meat or vegetable content of the recipe, as a small amount of flavouring will penetrate quite large quantities of food. Spices, garlic, strong herbs, and proprietary sauces all need to be handled with care.

The liquid content of the dish also needs to be looked at carefully. A fish dish with sauce, for example, will not need as much sauce when produced in quantity. Stews and casseroles, too, may not need the same proportion of liquid.

Apart from the logical reasons for these differences when increasing quantities, there is also a psychological factor. When dishes are prepared for four or six people, the cook wishes the food not only to be sufficient but to look sufficient, and very often enough food is made for five or seven. Unless this factor is taken into account when scaling up, the resultant recipe for fifty would actually feed sixty or more.

APPROXIMATE QUANTITIES OF BASIC FOODS PER PERSON

Bread

French bread 2 slices (with dinner; more may be eaten with salad); 3–4 slices (served with just wine and cheese)
Rolls 2

Butter 25 g/1 oz

Cheese 100 g/4 oz (served at wine and cheese party); 50 g/2 oz (served as last course of dinner)

Pate 50 g/2 oz (as first-course dish)

Soup 150 ml/¼ pint

Meat
On the bone 150– 225 g/ 5–8 oz (main course: depending on whether used in casserole with vegetables or on its own)
Off the bone 100–150 g/4–5 oz (main course: depending on whether used in casserole with vegetables or on its own)

Chicken
On the bone 150–225 g/5–8 oz (main course: depending on whether used in casserole with vegetables or on its own)
Off the bone 100–150 g/4–5 oz (main course: depending on whether used in casserole with vegetables or on its own)

Fish Fillet or steak 100–150 g/4–5 oz (depending on whether main or subsidiary course)

Vegetables 100 g/4 oz (served with one other vegetable and potatoes as accompaniment to main course)

Rice 25–50 g/1–2 oz (uncooked)

Pasta 50–100 g/2–4 oz (depending on whether main course or subsidiary)

Gravy/sauces 75–100 ml/3–3½ fl oz (served with main dish)

Salad dressings 15–20 ml/3–4 tsp (smaller quantity for French dressing, larger for mayonnaise)

Desserts
Ice-cream 50–75 ml/2–3 fl oz (depending on richness, whether an accompaniment, etc)
Fruit 150 g/5 oz (for fruit salad)
Pouring cream 75 ml/3 fl oz

Tea 5 ml/1 tsp tea leaves per person
125 ml/4 fl oz milk for 4 people

Coffee 125 ml/4 fl oz per person; 125 ml/ 4 fl oz cream for 4 people

For finger buffets and cocktail canapes, check by making a mental picture of one of each of all the items you are planning to serve set out together on a plate. This will give you an idea of the quantity allowed for each person.

OUTDOOR EATING AND PACKED LUNCHES

The days of the Great British Picnic, when teams of servants set up groaning tables in field and forest, may have passed, but eating out of doors can still be a significant social occasion, with several families or friends gathering for an outdoor party or a sophisticated meal at a sporting event or an alfresco theatrical performance.

Food which can be cooked ahead and eaten cold, salads that travel well without becoming limp and crusty bread are all ideal. Make sure the food arrives in prime condition by using chiller bags for perishable foods. Sturdy plastic containers which seal well are ideal for salads and desserts as well as savouries such as stuffed vine leaves or an array of cooked cold meats.

When ease of preparation takes priority over economy, shop for salami, cooked ham, pork pie, cooked continental sausages, smoked chicken or turkey and smoked mackerel, trout or salmon. Opt for thinly sliced rye breads and a variety of rolls, then make a good mixed salad and take a jar of dressing to toss into it at the last minute.

Finger foods, selected for their portability, are always acceptable. Tiny pizzas, individual filo pastries, quiches or pasties, spiced chicken drumsticks, crudites with a selection of dips, pinwheel sandwiches, filled bridge rolls or prawns will all prove popular.

PACKED LUNCHES

These are far more down-to-earth than picnics. They may be a regular meal, in which case special attention should be paid to food value.

Sandwiches are practical and easy, and do not have to be boring. Keep the fat content low, particularly in an adult's daily lunch-box, by doing away with lashings of butter: it is not essential and once you are accustomed to sandwiches without butter or margarine. Low-fat spreads and soft cheeses are worth considering but they are not necessary.

Combine salad ingredients such as cucumber, lettuce, tomatoes and spring onions with cold cooked poultry, meat or cheese. Peanut butter provides food value as well as flavour; it goes well with lettuce and cucumber.

Easy-to-eat pasties and pies can be included from time to time, but pastry products contribute a significant amount of fat, so should be used sparingly. Mixed salads are excellent and easy to eat – with a chunk of bread or a roll they can be satisfying and nutritious.

Small vacuum flasks are ideal for soup or hot drinks and can equally well be used for cold drinks in summer. Milk drinks, hot or cold, are nutritious for young children who may be less eager to eat all the packed lunch provided. Fresh fruit is the simplest and most nutritious sweet. Bananas, apples and pears are the most practical choices; oranges, peaches and other refreshing fruit are suitable but can be messy to eat. Dried fruit, boxed in individual portions, is another option, and it is also possible to buy individual cans of fruit with ring-pull tops, as occasional treats. Yogurt may also be offered. Small insulated containers are available, which will keep yogurt cartons cool. Don't forget to pack a teaspoon.

It is best to avoid crisps, sweet biscuits or chunks of sweet cake as regular lunch-box features. Semi-sweet biscuits, scones and teabreads are all easy to pack and are not too sugar-rich.

Remember that food which is packed early in the morning should be kept as cool as possible until it is eaten. Insulated lunch-boxes and small chiller bags are ideal for this purpose.

BARBECUES

Make sure that you have sufficient charcoal and enough grilling space for the food to be cooked. Light the barbecue at least 30 minutes before you plan to cook: depending on the size barbecue, you may need to light it up to 1 hour ahead. The barbecue is ready for cooking when the coals have stopped flaming. When cooking for a crowd, part-cook chicken in the oven and finish it on the barbecue.

Plan your menu around the barbecuing: have nibbles and drinks for guests while the food is cooking. Dips and crudités are ideal starters. Serve salads, baked potatoes or crusty bread as accompaniments. Have relishes and chutneys with plain grilled foods. Desserts should be simple and fruit may be grilled on the barbecue.

Pay special attention to safety at all times, from lighting up to over-imbibing and risking an accident. Always ensure children are supervised and pets restrained.

VEGETARIAN ALTERNATIVES

Combining a part-vegetarian menu with fish, poultry or meat dishes requires planning. Include a side dish which is ideal as a vegetarian main course, then plan the meat main dish. For example, vegetables or ratatouille with a gratin topping, a vegetable curry or chilli may be served on their own or as accompaniments for grilled fish, poultry or meat. Remember to cook a slightly larger quantity to allow for main dish servings as well as asides. Baked potatoes, rice or pasta are also versatile and a salad offers a palate-refreshing accompaniment for both options.

Everyday packed lunches seldom cause problems but the person who is entertaining may be concerned about providing suitable, interesting vegetarian picnic and barbecue food. Apart from salads, tempting vegetable or bean pasties, pastes and spreads, made from beans and pulses, and quiches with vegetable and dairy fillings are ideal. Vegetables can be delicious grilled on the barbecue, either threaded on skewers to make kebabs or marinated and grilled whole. Aubergines, peppers, courgettes, small whole onions and tomatoes are typical examples. Vegetable or lentil burgers and Haloumi cheese also grill well. Remember to set aside a distinct area or separate grill to avoid any contact between poultry or meat and vegetarian food.

The most important point when entertaining vegetarians is to avoid offering miserable plain vegetables or a completely separate dish which is not served to other diners.

MENUS AND PREPARATION PLANS

Having a complete meal perfectly cooked and served with the minimum of fuss requires either experience or careful planning, or in some cases both. Here are a few examples of typical menus, with a guide to the order in which to prepare the food. The aim of this section is not to provide a detailed schedule which must be slavishly followed, but rather to provide a blueprint to help you plan – and cook – with confidence.

Preparing or cooking vegetables in advance and keeping them fresh in iced water, or covered for reheating, is useful for special occasions but not recommended for everyday cooking when it is important to conserve the nutrients.

SUNDAY ROAST

Roast Beef
Yorkshire Pudding
Roast Potatoes
Boiled Fresh Vegetables
Gravy

~

Apple Tart
Custard

The day before

- Make the pastry for the tart, wrap it in polythene and chill it.
- Note the weight of the beef and determine the cooking time. Make a note of what time it will need to go into the oven.

Sunday morning

- Prepare the meat for the oven and set it to roast on time.
- Lay the table.
- Prepare the potatoes and other vegetables. Unless they are very large leave the peeled potatoes for roasting whole. Add them to the roast about 30 minutes after it has started cooking; baste them with a little fat.
- Finish making the apple tart.
- About 1 hour before the meat is cooked, make the batter for the Yorkshire pudding. Transfer a little fat from the beef to the cooking tin for the pudding

and place it in the oven to heat 35 minutes before the meat is cooked. Pour the batter into the tin after 5 minutes heating time, when the fat should be very hot.

- Place the tart in the oven at the same time as the Yorkshire pudding.
- Warm serving plates and vegetable dishes. Make sure carving knife is sharp.
- Prepare the saucepans and water for vegetables, adding each according to its cooking time: green vegetables which are best cooked very briefly should be added to boiling water just before the gravy is being prepared.
- Set plates and serving dishes to heat. Get out the ingredients for the custard. The custard can be made at this stage, covered with dampened greaseproof paper and stood in a bain-marie to keep hot.
- When the meat and roast potatoes are cooked remove them from the oven as quickly as possible. Transfer them to serving dishes, leave to rest or keep hot. Tent meat under foil if leaving to rest. Do not cover roast potatoes.
- Use the meat juices to make gravy, straining the cooking water from the vegetables to use as well as, or in place of stock.
- By the time the gravy has simmered, the Yorkshire pudding should be cooked. Quickly reheat the vegetables and serve the main course, or carve the meat first, then serve.
- The apple tart should be cooked about the same time as the Yorkshire pudding but it may be left in the oven, with heat turned off.
- If you have not already done so, make the custard after the main course is finished.

NO-FUSS INFORMAL SUPPER

Tzatziki or Hummus
Crudités
Pitta Bread

~

Quiche Lorraine
Baked Jacket Potatoes
Green Salad

~

Cheese and Biscuits and/or Bananas in Rum

The day before or early in the day

- Prepare the hummus, if serving, or buy good quality alternative, place in a serving dish, cover and chill.
- Prepare the pastry case and bake blind. Prepare all other filling ingredients ready to go into the quiche; cover and chill. The quiche may be cooked in advance and reheated just before serving, but it is best freshly cooked.

2 hours before serving

- Lay the table.
- Scrub the potatoes, prepare the salad ingredients and wash, peel or scrub the vegetables for the crudités.
- Make the tzatziki, if serving. Place in a serving dish, cover and chill.

1½ hours before serving

- Set the potatoes to cook, setting the oven at the temperature for cooking the quiche.
- Cut the crudités and arrange them on a dish, cover and keep cool.
- Make a dressing for the salad.
- Mix the salad ingredients in a bowl. Do not add the dressing. Cover and set aside in a cool place.
- Have the ingredients ready for the bananas and prepare a pan for cooking them.
- Prepare the cheese and biscuits, keeping both covered at room temperature.

45 minutes before serving

- Sprinkle the prepared ingredients into the pastry case for the quiche. Beat the eggs and milk and pour in, then set the quiche to cook.
- Warm serving plates and have a napkin lined basket ready for the potatoes.
- Set the pitta bread to heat in the oven for 5 minutes.
- Serve the pitta, tzatziki or hummus and crudités.

Serving the quiche

- Transfer the potatoes to the basket and the quiche to a serving platter or place on a table mat on the table.
- Toss the salad with dressing.

After the main course

- Serve cheese and biscuits before the dessert if preferred.
- Put dessert plates to warm for the bananas.
- Cook the bananas just before they are served.

FORMAL DINNER PARTY

Vichysoisse or Asparagus Soup
Hot Bread Rolls

~

Coquilles St Jacques Mornay

~

Coq au Vin
New Potatoes
Glazed Carrots
French Beans

~

Port Wine Jelly
Red Fruit Salad
or
Gâteau de Pithiviers
Whipped Cream

~

Cheese and Biscuits

The day before

- Make and chill the chosen soup.
- Prepare the ingredients for the coq au vin, setting the chicken to marinate.
- Make the port wine jelly, if serving.
- Prepare the gâteau de Pithiviers, if serving. Chill it uncooked – it will benefit from being cooked on the same day as serving.

Early on the day

- Prepare the red fruit salad, if serving, cover and chill.
- Bake the gâteau de Pithiviers, if serving.
- Prepare the coquilles St Jacques mornay up to the final stage of baking.
- Prepare the vegetables: scrub the potatoes, peel or scrub and slice the carrots, then leave covered with iced water. Trim and wash the beans.
- Lay the table; set out all crockery.

2½ hours before serving

- Complete the preparation on the coq au vin, ready to go into the oven.
- Prepare the beurre manié for thickening, cover and set aside.
- Whip the cream for dessert, cover and chill in a serving dish.

- Ladle the vichysoisse into serving bowls and chill. Alternatively, place the asparagus soup into a pan ready to heat.
- Drain the carrots and place them in the cooking pan with the glazing ingredients; cover and set aside ready to cook at the last minute.

1½ hours before serving.
- Place the coq au vin in the oven.
- Prepare the croûtes of bread for garnishing the coq au vin.
- Place the bread rolls on a baking tray ready to heat.
- Cook the potatoes until only just tender, drain and set in a pan with butter, cover.
- Prepare a pan with water for cooking the beans.
- Turn out the jelly if serving, then chill.
- Prepare the cheese board and biscuits, cover and set aside at room temperature.

20 minutes before serving
- Warm serving plates and dishes.
- Finish the coq au vin, replacing the chicken in the thickened sauce in the ovenproof dish. Cover tightly and replace in the oven: this saves having to thicken the sauce between courses.
- If serving the asparagus soup, heat it gently.
- Put the coquilles St Jacques to bake at the same temperature as the coq au vin – remembering they have to reheat completely and noting that they are being cooked at a lower temperature than when prepared according to the recipe.
- Heat the bread rolls and serve the soup course.

After the soup
- Set the buttered potatoes over low to medium heat.
- Set the carrots to cook and the water to boil for the beans.
- Serve the coquilles St Jacques.

After the fish course
- Add the beans to the cooking water and boil rapidly.
- Transfer the potatoes to a serving dish.
- Increase the heat under the carrots, if necessary, to glaze them, then transfer to a serving dish.
- Drain and serve the beans.
- Garnish the coq au vin with the croûtes and serve.

After the main course

- Serve the fruit salad, port wine jelly or gâteau.
- Take the cheese and biscuits to the table.
- Set the water to boil for coffee, or prepare the coffee machine.

SUMMER BARBECUE

Crudités

~

Chicken Wings with Ginger
Lamb Shish Kebabs
Sausages
Potato Salad
French Bean and Tomato Salad
Fennel and Cucumber Salad
Hot Garlic Bread or French Bread

~

Oranges in Caramel Sauce
Bananas on the Barbecue
Cream or Yogurt

The day before

- Prepare the lamb and chill overnight.
- Prepare the oranges in caramel sauce.
- Cook the potatoes for the salad in their skins. Drain and rinse under cold running water. Drain and cover. Cool, then chill overnight.
- Prepare the garlic bread, wrap tightly in foil and chill.

Early on the day

- Prepare the chicken wings and place them in a roasting tin, ready to half bake them before putting them on the barbecue. Cover the tin and chill.
- Prepare the kebabs, placing them in a dish; cover and chill until ready to cook.
- Make the potato and French bean and tomato salads; cover and chill.
- Prepare the crudités. Place in polythene bags and chill ready to put out in dishes just before serving.

1½ hours before serving

- Light the barbecue.

- Make the fennel and cucumber salad, cover and keep cool.
- Preheat the oven, ready to par-cook the chicken.

1 hour before serving

- Put the chicken wings in the oven.

30 minutes before serving

- Transfer the chicken to the barbecue to finish cooking.
- Heat the bread in the oven.
- Serve the crudités.
- Add the kebabs to the barbecue about 10 minutes before the chicken is cooked, then add sausages as required.
- Stagger the serving, offering the chicken wings first while the kebabs and sausages are cooking.
- Serve the kebabs and sausages with the salads and bread.
- Cook the bananas in their skins individually on the barbecue, as required, until the skins are blackened outside. To serve, make two lengthways slits along the top of each banana. Remove a section of skin, so that the cooked banana flesh may be scooped out using a teaspoon. Offer the cream or yogurt separately. Serve the oranges.

Table Laying

Following dining trends, there are many options for table laying, from formal settings to casual, yet attractive, presentations.

PLACE SETTINGS

If soup is to be served, round soup spoons or dessertspoons should be provided. Special fish knives and forks can be laid for the fish course; the knives are blunt with a slightly pointed end which enables the bones to be eased out of the fish without cutting the flesh. Large knives and forks are laid for the main meat course, with a small knife for bread and butter and cheese. Steak knives with a serrated cutting edge are often used for grilled steak or chops. A dessertspoon and fork are provided for the sweet course, or a teaspoon if the dessert is to be served in small dishes or glasses. If fresh fruit is being served, the appropriate knives and forks should be provided.

TABLE DECORATIONS

Flower arrangements should be low and flowers must not be overpoweringly scented. Candles should match table linen and/or room decor. Wine should be placed ready on the sideboard or side table together with a jug of iced water and soft drinks. Sauceboats should have a stand or saucer to avoid drips on the tablecloth.

THE BUFFET TABLE

The art of laying a buffet table is to show off the food to its best advantage while making serving easy.

For buffets to serve 50 people or more, place plates and cutlery at either end of the buffet table so that there at least two serving points. This means that there must be two platters (at least) of each dish so that guests may help themselves from either end of the table. Drinks, and later coffee, should be served from a side table. Depending on the space available, the dessert can be displayed ready on a side table, or served from the main table when the main course is finished. Use cake stands for gâteau-type desserts to vary the height of the display. The most convenient way to lay cutlery is to wrap a set for each person in a table napkin. Distribute cruets along the table, and accompaniments (salad dressing or sauce) near the appropriate dishes. Place bread or rolls with butter at each end of the table. Cheese boards should be brought in with the dessert and placed at each end of the buffet with celery, biscuits and butter, and, of course, small plates and knives. For small buffets, it is usually possible to lay everything on one table with cutlery and plates at one end only.

TRADITIONAL FORMAL SETTINGS

Lay the knives, blades pointing inwards, on the right of the dinner plate and the forks on the left in the order in which they will be used (first to be used on the extreme right or left and the last next to the plate). The dessertspoon and fork can either be laid in neat alignment across the top of the setting, with the spoon handle to the right and the fork handle to the left, or at the sides of the plate, spoon on the right, fork on the left; either arrangement is correct. Fruit knives and forks can be laid across the top of the setting with the dessertspoon and fork, or at the side. Alternatively, they can be handed round with the dessert plates. The small knife for bread may go next to the dinner plate, on the right-hand side or vertically across the side plate, which should be on the left of the place setting. The soup spoon is placed on the extreme right-hand side as this is the first implement to be used. Line up the cutlery neatly and as closely together as is practical, with the handles about 1 cm/½ inch from the edge of the table.

Glasses should be arranged in a straight line across the top of the right-hand cutlery, in the order of use; for example, a glass for white wine on the right, then one for red, and a port or liqueur glass on the left of the row. If you include a tumbler or stemmed glass for water, place this before the liqueur glass. The last glass should be placed just above the meat knife. If you are laying a single wine glass, put it anywhere above the right-hand cutlery.

Finger-bowls, if used, are placed to the left just above the line of forks. Table napkins can be put in the centre of the place setting, on the side plate or in one of the glasses.

ALTERNATIVE SETTINGS

A completely different approach to table laying is sometimes suitable for casual or everyday entertaining. Place mats are widely used instead of tablecloths, on both formal and casual occasions. The table setting may be changed completely to reflect the food as when Chinese bowls, chopsticks, spoons and forks replace the traditional cutlery. For an informal, one-course meal, the cutlery (usually a knife and fork) may be placed neatly together on a napkin on the side plate in the centre of the setting. Match bright china with colourful napkins, flowers or ribbons to emphasize the lighthearted approach.

CUTLERY AND CONDIMENTS

Whatever the type of meal, always have the necessary serving utensils on the table.

Traditionally, serving spoons and forks are paired at both ends of the table, according to the number of dishes, arranged as for the dessert cutlery. Have all the implements for serving the main course on the table; those for the dessert may be brought in later.

Salt and pepper, or just a pepper mill, and any other condiments or accompaniments, should be positioned centrally but to one side of the table. For a large dinner party, it is customary to have more than one set of condiments and two plates of butter. Place a butter knife near the butter.

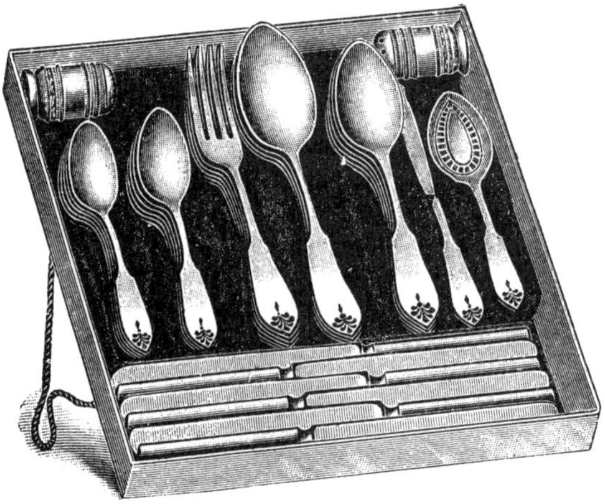

Nutrition and Diet

A basic understanding of nutrition leads to an awareness of the food we eat in relation to its use by the body and, consequently, to an appreciation of the importance of eating a balanced diet.

Food is the essential fuel for life, maintaining the body as well as building and repairing it. Foods are made up of a combination of different nutrients and, as the body digests the food, these nutrients are released and utilized. General guidelines are provided regarding the nutritional needs of the population; however, individual requirements vary. Factors that influence anyone person's dietary needs include gender, age, build, lifestyle and health.

BALANCED DIET

A balanced diet provides all the essential nutrients and sufficient energy to meet an individual's needs and to maintain a healthy body weight without causing obesity. In young people, the diet must also include sufficient nutrients to sustain growth. Nutritional requirements relating to pregnancy, lactation, illness and special conditions should be provided by a doctor and/or dietician. A balanced diet should include a wide selection of different types of foods, prepared and cooked in a variety of ways. Fresh foods and 'whole' foods are important in providing a balanced variety of nutrients. Raw and lightly cooked fruit and vegetables are also essential.

In general terms, the carbohydrate and vegetable content of the diet should dominate the protein and fat. A diet that lacks carbohydrate, fruit and vegetables is likely to have too high a fat content and to be lacking in fibre. Fibre, from vegetable and cereal sources, is also a vital ingredient for a balanced diet.

BASIC GUIDE TO NUTRIENTS

PROTEIN

Used by the body for growth and repair, protein foods are composed of amino acids, in various amounts and combinations according to the food. There are eight specific amino acids which are an essential part of an adult's diet as they cannot be manufactured by the body from other foods; an additional one is necessary for young children, to sustain their rapid growth. In addition, nine other amino acids are widely available in protein foods, although a high intake of these is not vital as the human body can manufacture them if they are not adequately supplied by the diet.

The quality of any one protein food is determined by the number and proportion of amino acids it contains. Animal foods have a higher biological value than vegetable foods because they provide all the essential amino acids. Generally, no single vegetable food provides all the essential amino acids and they are not present in the proportions best suited to the human body. There are, however, important exceptions to this rule; certain non-animal foods are excellent sources of protein; notably soya beans, some types of nut and mycoprotein (quorn). Other beans and pulses, nuts and cereals are also excellent sources of good quality protein. Since the amino acid content of vegetable foods varies, by mixing different foods and eating them in sufficient amounts, the necessary types and quantities of amino acids may be obtained.

As amino acids are not stored in a digestible form in the body, a regular supply is essential.

This is most easily obtained from a mixture of animal and vegetable sources; if fish, poultry and meat are not eaten, then it is vital that a broad selection of vegetable sources and dairy foods are included to provide sufficient quantities of amino acids.

CARBOHYDRATES

These are the energy-giving foods and may be divided into two main categories: starches and sugars. Starch is obtained from vegetables, cereals, some nuts and under-ripe bananas; sugar is found in fruit (including ripe bananas), honey, molasses and cane sugar.

Carbohydrates in the form of starch, known as complex carbohydrates, should form a significant proportion of the diet. For example, they should be eaten in larger quantities than protein foods, such as meat, poultry and fish. The sugar content of the diet should be limited.

If the diet is deficient in carbohydrates, the body will break down other foods to supply energy, eventually including proteins which have a more valuable role to play.

FIBRE

At one time referred to as roughage, fibre is a complex carbohydrate which is not totally digested and absorbed by the body; however, it is vital as a carrier of moisture and waste products through the digestive system.

Fibre is obtained from cereals and vegetables. Good sources are whole grain rice, oats, wholemeal flour and its products. Sources of vegetable fibre include beans and pulses, some types of fruit, as well as vegetables.

Raw and lightly cooked foods (where appropriate) generally provide more fibre than well-cooked foods; similarly more refined foods offer less fibre than wholefoods and unrefined ingredients.

FATS

Fat and oils provide energy as well as being important sources of certain vitamins and fatty acids. They may be loosely divided into saturated fats and unsaturated fats. Unsaturated fats may be further grouped into polyunsaturated and monounsaturated, depending on their chemical compositions. Although the majority of fatty foods contain both saturated and unsaturated fats, as a general rule animal sources have a higher proportion of saturated fats and vegetable sources are richer in unsaturates.

The recommended fat intake is calculated as a percentage of the total energy value of the diet. The energy value (in calories or joules) of fat eaten should be no more than 35% of the total energy intake with the major proportion of fat in the diet being the unsaturated type.

It is important to remember that young children (under five years of age) should not follow low-fat diets. Although their meals should not contain high proportions of fatty foods (fried foods, chips, high-fat snacks), their fat intake should not be limited by the use of skimmed milk, low-fat cheese and low-fat spreads.

VITAMINS

Although each of the vitamins has specific functions within the body, they also play vital roles in regulating metabolism, helping to repair tissues and assisting in the conversion of carbohydrates and fats into energy. Vitamin deficiency results in general poor health as well as certain specific illnesses.

Vitamins fall into two groups; fat-soluble and water-soluble. Fat-soluble vitamins include A, D, E and K; water-soluble vitamins include C and B-group vitamins. Fat-soluble vitamins can be stored by the body, whereas any excess of the water-soluble type is passed out. This means that a regular supply of water-soluble vitamins is essential and that an excess is unlikely to be harmful. Conversely, the fat-soluble vitamins which are stored in the body should not be consumed to excess as this can result in a condition known as hypervitaminosis. It is important to remember that an excess can be dangerous when taking vitamin supplements, or when eating a very high proportion of foods which are particularly rich in anyone (or more) of the fat-soluble vitamins.

Vitamin A Found in fish liver oils, liver, kidney, dairy produce and eggs, vitamin A is important to prevent night blindness. It also contributes to the general health of the eyes and to the condition of the skin. Carotene, found in carrots and yellow or dark green vegetables such as peppers and spinach, can be converted into vitamin A in the body.

If the diet is excessively rich in vitamin A, or supplements are taken for a prolonged period, it is possible for stores to build up to toxic levels in the human liver.

B-group Vitamins This is a large group of water-soluble vitamins, linked because of their importance and use in the body. They play vital roles in promoting chemical reactions, in the release of energy from food and in the efficient functioning of the nervous system. They are essential for general good health and deficiency diseases occur comparatively quickly if these vitamins are missing from the diet.

Thiamin (vitamin B1), riboflavin (vitamin B2), vitamin B12, vitamin B6 (pyridoxine), nicotinic acid, folate, pantothenic acid and biotin are all included in this group (or complex) and each has its own particular characteristics.

In general, meat, offal, dairy produce, and cereals are good sources of B-group vitamins. Some of these vitamins are destroyed by prolonged cooking, notably thiamin, and long exposure to sunlight destroys riboflavin which is found in milk. Refined flour and bread are fortified with thiamin to meet natural levels in comparable wholemeal products. Breakfast cereals are also emiched with, or naturally rich in, B-group vitamins.

Vitamin C or Ascorbic Acid A water-soluble vitamin, this cannot be stored in the body, therefore a regular supply is essential. The main function of this vitamin is to maintain healthy connective tissue (the cell structure within the body) and healthy blood. It also plays an important role in the healing of wounds. A deficiency can lead to susceptibility to infections.

Vitamin C is found in fresh and frozen vegetables, notably peppers and green vegetables, and in fruit, particularly blackcurrants and citrus fruit. Many fruit juices and drinks are fortified with vitamin C. Potatoes are also a valuable supply; although they are not a rich source, when eaten regularly and in quantity they make an important contribution to a healthy diet.

Vitamin C is the most easily destroyed of all vitamins and may be affected by light, heat, staleness, exposure to air and overcooking. The vitamin is also destroyed by alkaline substances, such as bicarbonate of soda.

Note Raw, fresh fruit and vegetables and lightly-cooked vegetables are an important source of vitamins, particularly C. Vegetables should be freshly prepared and cut up as little as possible before cooking. They should not be soaked in water. Cook them lightly and quickly in the minimum of liquid and use the cooking liquid, whenever suitable, in sauces and soups to benefit from any vitamins lost.

Vitamin D Essential in promoting calcium absorption, a deficiency will result in an inadequate supply of calcium being made available for building and repairing bones and teeth. A diet which is too rich in vitamin D can result in excessive calcium absorption and storage which can be damaging, so supplements should only be taken on medical advice.

Vitamin D is manufactured by the body from the action of sunlight on the skin – this is the primary source for most adults. The vitamin is naturally present in cod liver oil and oily fish such as herrings, mackerel, salmon and sardines. Eggs contain vitamin D, and it can also be manufactured from vegetable sources. Some foods, such as margarine, are fortified with vitamin D.

Vitamin E This vitamin is found in small amounts in most foods and the better sources include vegetable oils, eggs and cereals (especially wheatgerm).

Its role in the body is not clearly established, although unsubstantiated claims are made about its contribution to fertility, healthy skin and its role in improved circulation.

Vitamin K Widely found in vegetables and cereals, this vitamin can be manufactured in the body. Vitamin K contributes towards normal blood-clotting. Deficiency is rare, due to a ready supply being available in a mixed diet.

MINERALS

Minerals and trace elements are essential for a healthy body as they play important roles in metabolic processes relating to to the nervous system, glands, muscle control and the supply of water. They are only required in minute quantities and a well-balanced diet containing plenty of fresh and whole foods should provide an adequate supply. Mineral supplements should only be taken on medical advice as overdoses can be dangerous.

Iron An essential constituent of red blood cells and important in muscles, iron can be stored in the body. The diet must maintain the store as, if it becomes depleted, anaemia can result. An adequate supply of iron is especially important during menstruation and pregnancy, as both use up the iron supply.

Found in meat, offal and green vegetables, such as spinach, and eggs, the iron in meat and offal is the most readily absorbed; it is less easily utilized from vegetable sources. The availability of vitamin C is important to promote iron absorption; other factors, such as the presence of tannin, can impair absorption.

Calcium Important in building and maintaining healthy teeth and bones, as well as for normal blood clotting, muscle function and a healthy nervous system, calcium is obtained from milk, cheese, bread, fortified flour and vegetables. The calcium found in milk and dairy produce is likely to be more easily absorbed than that in green vegetables or whole grains (although the system can adjust to utilizing the mineral from less ready sources) and an adequate supply of vitamin D is necessary for efficient calcium absorption.

Phosphorus Along with calcium, this is valuable for bones and teeth. It is widely distributed in food and deficiency is unknown in man.

Potassium, Chlorine and Sodium These play an important role in the balance of body fluids and they are essential for muscle and nerve function. Sodium and chlorine are added to food in the form of salt; sodium is found naturally in meat and milk, and it is added to bread, cereal products and manufactured foods. Potassium is found naturally in meat, vegetables and milk.

Trace Elements These are required by the body in very small amounts and include iodine, fluorine, magnesium, zinc, manganese, cobalt, selenium, molybdenum and chromium. An adequate supply of trace elements is almost always found in the diet and deficiency is extremely rare. Unprescribed supplements should be avoided as they can be detrimental to health.

SPECIFIC NEEDS

Most people have particular dietary needs at some time during their life, if only as babies or young children.

BABIES

Breast milk is the ideal food for young babies as it provides all the nutrients they require for the first few months of life. Even if this method of feeding is not continued in the long term, it is a very good idea to breast-feed a baby for the first few days, as valuable antibodies are passed from the mother to help the baby fight infection in the early months.

Bottle-fed babies should be given a manufactured milk formula. These should be prepared exactly according to the manufacturer's instructions or according to the health visitor's or doctor's advice.

Regular checks on the baby's progress are important and any problems should be brought to professional attention immediately.

The weaning process varies from infant to infant; however, between the ages of four to six months a baby should be ready to try a little solid food. By eighteen months, the infant should be able to cope with a mixed diet based on adult foods, following general guidelines for balanced eating. Milk is still an important supplement during this time of rapid growth.

TODDLERS AND YOUNG CHILDREN

Fads and eating difficulties are common in young children, who are too busy discovering the world around them to concentrate for the length of time necessary to learn about meals. Since toddlers and young children are quickly satisfied, it is important that they are introduced to good eating habits and that their meals are nutritious; sweet or fatty snacks are to be avoided and bread, milk, vegetables, fruit, cheese and other valuable foods should be introduced. New foods should be presented in small amounts, along with familiar ingredients. Milk is still an important source of nutrients, particularly for difficult eaters.

Providing a meal-time routine and making the process of eating a pleasure is all important. Children should not be encouraged to play with food, but they should look foward to eating it. Small, frequent yet regular meals, are ideal: in theory, these occasions should be relaxed, free of distractions from the business of eating, and traumatic scenes relating to food rejection should be avoided.

SCHOOL CHILDREN

Fast-growing and active children need a highly nutritious diet, so the substitution of sweets, fatty snacks, sweet drinks and sticky cakes for meals should be avoided. These types of foods should be rare treats.

Breakfasts and packed lunches need special attention. The first meal of the day should be nutritious and provide sufficient energy to keep the child on the move until lunchtime: bread, cereals and milk, eggs and fruit are all practical and useful foods. Raw vegetables, semi-sweet biscuits and crackers are practical mid-morning snack foods but they should not spoil the appetite for lunch. Packed lunches, if eaten, should contain a variety of foods – bread, salad vegetables, some form of protein and a piece of fruit. If a packed lunch is the norm, tea and an early supper are important meals.

As a general guide, every meal should provide growing children with a good balance of valuable nutrients, and additional milk drinks (whole or semi-skimmed) are excellent sources of the calcium which is so important for strong teeth and bones, as well as other nutrients. Sweet foods and confectionery should be avoided as they cause tooth decay and can lead to obesity; similarly, fatty cooking methods and high-fat foods should not be a regular feature in the diet. The importance of fibre, raw fruit and vegetables must be stressed.

ADOLESCENTS AND TEENAGERS

This group also requires a highly nutritious, energy-packed diet, but unfortunately, young people are particularly prone to food fads and fashions and it can be difficult to get a teenager to eat a balanced diet. While it is essential to provide all the necessary nutrients, it is important to avoid obesity in this group. Reduced-calorie diets are not recommended, but overeating must be controlled and the types of food eaten should be carefully monitored.

During this period of rapid growth and development, adopting an active lifestyle and participating in regular exercise is of equal importance as eating well. Young people in this age group should be encouraged to take an interest in nutrition, food and the relationship between a balanced diet, health and fitness.

Parents should try to pass on an understanding of food shopping, meal planning and food preparation, together with an appreciation of the positive benefits of a good diet. This is particularly important for young people who are about to embark on their first experience of living alone and catering for themselves.

PREGNANCY AND LACTATION

A woman should pay special attention to diet during pregnancy as she will need to provide sufficient nutrients and energy for her own needs as well as those of the growing baby. The nutritional requirements continue after birth and during lactation, when the mother is feeding the new baby. The doctor or clinic should provide dietary advice, recommending supplements as necessary.

The mother's responsibility is to ensure that her diet is varied, with emphasis on foods rich in minerals, vitamins and energy. Sweets, chocolates and foods which satisfy without offering nutritional benefit should be avoided in favour of fruit, vegetables, dairy produce, bread and protein foods.

ELDERLY PEOPLE

Problems relating to nutrition and the elderly are often linked to social factors. The cost and effort of eating well can deter some elderly people from shopping for a variety of foods and therefore from cooking fresh ingredients. Although many elderly people are extremely active, others may have physical difficulty in shopping or spending long periods standing to prepare meals; in this case help should be sought with planning a practical diet. Equally, dental problems restrict some elderly people from eating well and these can, and should, be overcome by visiting a dentist.

Hot, solid meals are important, particularly in winter. Some elderly people get through the day by eating lots of snacks and this can be detrimental to health; cakes, biscuits and favourite puddings may be pleasant and comforting but they do not constitute a balanced diet. The appetite is often reduced, particularly as the person becomes less active, so meals that are small must contain a high proportion of valuable nutrients. Wholemeal bread, dairy products and cereals with milk are all practical snacks.

The pleasure often disappears from eating when meals are lonely occasions and the palate is not as efficient as it once was. Special centres and meal services exist and these should be used, not only by those who are prevented from cooking for themselves by physical limitations, but also by all who need the company and contact that such services offer.

SPECIAL DIETS

Individuals and whole sections of the population follow special diets for different reasons: religion, medical and health-related conditions, cultural and personal factors can all influence the choice of food. Many diets are self-imposed, others are dictated by society and some are prescribed by a dietician or doctor. The following brief notes indicate some typical dietary restrictons. Remember that some diets are influenced by food fashions while others have genuine social or medical backgrounds.

DAIRY-FREE

Young children under three years old are sometimes unable to digest the protein found in cows' milk; however, they tend to grow out of this. Adults may react adversely to lactose, the carbohydrate found in milk. This means that all milk products have to be avoided, including butter, cheese, cream, yogurt, dishes containing milk and milk drinks.

Soya milk is a useful altemative as it is a non-dairy product. It may be used for cooking as well as for adding to drinks.

DIABETIC

Insulin, a hormone produced by the pancreas, plays a vital role in sugar absorption. If the pancreas fails to produce insulin, or slows down production to inadequate levels, the condition known as diabetes results.

The control of the condition varies according to the individual case; however, attention to diet is always an important factor. Sugar, in all its forms, is avoided or used in small, carefully controlled amounts. In some cases the overall carbohydrate intake may be controlled, as starch is also converted into sugar during digestion.

As well as direct carbohydrate control, other factors affecting carbohydrate metabolism must be taken into account and, for general good health, a balanced diet is essential.

GLUTEN-FREE

People suffering from coeliac disease react adversely to gluten, a protein found in wheat. This means that all wheat products such as flour, bread, traditional pastry, biscuits, sauces thickened with wheat flour and so on, have to be avoided.

The gluten in wheat flour is the substance which gives it its strength and makes it ideal for yeast-risen bread doughs. For those on a gluten-free diet, alternatives are available for most wheat-based products: cornflour and rice flour are typical thickening agents which may be used in place of wheat flour. Rice crackers and cakes may be used instead of savoury wheat crackers and specially manufactured breads, biscuits and cakes can also be found.

LOW-FAT

Under normal circumstances the value of a rational approach to fat in the diet must be emphasized. In the right proportions, fat is important in the diet and extremely low-fat or fat-free diets are not generally recommended. If, for medical reasons, a low-fat diet is imposed or suggested, then the doctor's or dietician's advice should be followed. Full-fat dairy produce, fatty meat, margarine, butter and high-fat convenience foods are typical examples of food to avoid; frying, particularly deep-frying, and other cooking methods which employ fat should also be avoided.

LOW-SALT

This is another example of a diet which should not be taken to extremes as a certain amount of salt is essential in a normal diet. By eating a balanced diet, with plenty of fresh foods or a watchful choice of ready-prepared items, and by avoiding the use of large amounts of salt either in cooking or at the table, a sensible salt intake can be maintained. Careful, light seasoning should provide a good flavour without being harmful; sprinkling extra salt over cooked, seasoned food, with a few rare exceptions, should be avoided. Remember, many convenience foods and snacks have a high salt content, so eating them frequently in large quantities is not advisable.

REDUCED-CALORIE

In order to lose excess weight, a person's calorie intake must be reduced, ideally in combination with a sensible exercise programme. A very low calorie diet should be avoided as this can result in the breakdown of muscle for energy as well as nutrient deficiency.

Often, unless the problem is simply one of eating far too much food for the body's requirements, the cause of obesity is a diet too rich in sugary and/or fatty foods. The first steps should be to cut out sweetened foods and to significantly reduce the amount of fat consumed, substituting plenty of vegetables and sufficient carbohydrate, along with fibre. Foods should be baked, steamed or grilled; frying, especially deep-frying, shold be avoided.

The doctor should be consulted before embarking on a major weight-loss programme or prolonged diet. As well as dietary guidelines, he/she will provide a general health check and advice on increasing the exercise level to improve the body's energy consumption and reduce excess fat stores.

SEMI-VEGETARIAN

This dietary option involves avoiding meat. Fish, and sometimes poultry, are eaten, as are dairy products.

VEGETARIAN

Fish, poultry and all types of meat are avoided in any form; however, dairy products may be eaten. By ensuring that the diet is mixed, including a variety of vegetables and pulses as well as dairy produce, the vegetarian diet can provide all the essential nutrients. There are two factors of which to be aware: firstly, by eating large amounts of dairy produce to replace meat, fish and poultry the fat content can be high; secondly, nutrient deficiency can result if dairy foods are avoided to reduce the fat content without substituting high-value vegetable foods. The importance of variety and balance must be stressed.

VEGAN

The vegan diet excludes all animal products, including dairy foods, and it is often related to other food restrictions. Following a diet which limits nutrient intake to this extent is not recommended. Ensuring that the body receives essential vitamins and minerals in sufficient quantities and in a form which is available is difficult, resulting in the necessity for consuming a large bulk of vegetable foods. This type of diet should never be imposed on children or young people.

The Home

Regardless of changing fashion and individual taste, your living accommodation – whether a bedsit or a palace – should be a home; that is, a place in which you feel secure and relaxed.

The qualities and virtues considered necessary for the proper management of a modern household are nothing like as daunting as they were a century ago. However, we have the same responsibility as any mistress of that day to create a household which is equally secure, pleasing and relaxing for all residing therein.

With few exceptions, today's household is a place for the family without a team of staff, yet running even the smallest home successfully is no mean task – and not necessarily one for which we are adequately prepared. This chapter takes an overview of accommodation and the way in which it grows into a home.

RENTING OR BUYING

Individual circumstances have to be taken into account when deciding whether to rent or buy accommodation, such as employment and job security, the length of time you expect to be living in an area, your financial situation and personal responsibilities. The current economic situation in the country and prevailing social trends will also play a role.

Young people who leave school may well choose to live in their parents' home while they continue their education or first start work. When they have settled in their new working life, they may opt for rented accommodation, then to go on and buy. Often the decision to purchase is made due to improved financial status or, in many cases, young people decide to pool resources when they marry, making house purchase possible. An unmarried couple who live together may buy instead of renting or two friends, without any personal relationship, may decide on a joint purchase.

TAKING ADVICE

Before renting or buying a property, it is wise to find out about your current rights as a tenant or owner. Check the telephone directory or local library for the address of the Citizens' Advice Bureau or Consumer Advice Centre. There you will find relevant leaflets, particularly on renting. The majority of tenants or home purchasers will not need to fight for their rights, but being aware of the laws relating to your situation is sensible.

HOUSE-HUNTING

Even Mrs Beeton referred to the 'horrors of house-hunting'. Looking for your first home is exciting, but the novelty can quickly pall. Before embarking on a home-hunt, make lists of points to remember, special requirements and things to do. Divide your lists into three main sections:

- Maximum price
- Area
- Accommodation type

Maximum Price Before deciding to buy, find out about borrowing money. Borrow only from reputable sources, such as major banks and building societies. Find out about 'hidden costs', which may include fees to agents, solicitors, surveyors and so on – these can come as a nasty shock if you are not prepared. Budget for all these items before deciding on the price you can afford to pay for the property or in rent.

Consider all other financial commitments such as fuel bills, local authority charges, any other outstanding long-term loans and travelling expenses. Also, remember to budget for food, clothes and other basic living costs in addition to the price of the accommodation.

Area Get to know a new area – buy a street map and local paper for information. Investigate public transport, local shops and other necessary facilities. Visit the library for information on the area.

Accommodation Type By looking at what's available over a period of time and comparing prices to your budget, you will soon have some idea of what you can afford. Working within sensible limits, draw up a list of requirements.

Think in terms of the number of rooms, or bedrooms you need, parking or garage facilities, other key features (such as separate lounge and dining room or a kitchen large enough to serve as a dining room for family meals), and whether or not you want a garden, patio or balcony – remember, a large garden can be a burden if you loathe gardening.

Whether renting or buying, watch out for any signs of damp, such as peeling wallpaper or mould and rotting woodwork around windows or windowsills. Pay attention to the standard of plumbing and heating in use and check that essential facilities such as kitchen and bathroom are in good working order. If you are intending to buy, it is always advisable to have an independent survey carried out before signing a contract.

When owners are showing you around property, it is obviously important to be polite, but avoid giving a false impression by being overenthusiastic if you are not genuinely interested in the property.

Although taking young children around every property you view is not always practical, when you find somewhere suitable do take the children to see the house.

PROGRESSING THE BUYING PROCEDURE

Taking shortcuts can lead to problems, so always follow the normal channels, seeking the necessary surveys and raising any problems or queries with your solicitor as soon as they arise.

RENTING PROPERTY

You may be renting through an agent, from a local authority or through a housing association. If you are dealing with an agency, you should not pay a fee unless you rent accommodation which they have presented.

The relationship between landlord and tenant is, in terms of the law, a complex one. For this reason, check up-to-date information before embarking on any agreement. Do not sign any document until you have read it carefully and considered the implications. Before renting, make sure you have a clear agreement over what is covered by the rent, for example, fuel costs, maintenance, cleaning of the common parts and so on. Information on the use of coin-operated meters in rented property is available from Citizens' Advice Bureaux or Consumer Advice Centres. Also, an inventory of fixtures and fittings, or furnishings in furnished accommodation, should be made as much for the protection of the tenant as for the landlord.

Once you are renting, you should keep a written record of all outgoings and receipts for all deposits, bills and rent paid.

MOVING HOUSE

Obviously, the extent of the operation depends on the size of your family and the quantity of your possessions. Moving into a first bedsit with a few boxes of belongings is rarely a major problem; moving from one family home to another is quite a different proposition.

MAJOR MOVES

The moves which require most forethought and planning are those involving large pieces of furniture, significant quantities of possessions and complicated family arrangements.

IN ADVANCE

Schools and Family Matters Settling a young family into a new home, particularly in a new area, requires advance planning. Finding out about schools and facilities for children is a key priority in the search for a home. Remember to make the necessary arrangements and confirm details as soon as the decision to move is finalized.

Similarly, find out about doctors and dentists before moving – your existing surgery will provide details on how to transfer. The local health authority or general practitioners' association provides a list of practices. Plan ahead and it is one thing less to sort out once you are in the new home.

Removal Companies If you intend using a removal firm, investigate suitable companies as soon as you have decided on the move. Do not wait until dates are fixed and details confirmed before assessing different companies.

Look for companies that are members of a professional association of removal firms. Before inviting companies to visit and give a quotation, note any particular points you wish to make. For example, list any valuable items of furniture which require special attention, note any items which may be unusual (porcelain collections, quantities of glassware, pictures and so on), any garden furniture or garden items to be moved, contents of attic, garden shed or garage. It is easy to forget to point out these things to someone who is estimating the work and it avoids any confusion at a later date – or on the day of the move.

Compare quotes and raise any queries with companies before making a decision. It is usual, if you are planning significantly far ahead, to make a provisional booking for the removal date, then to confirm it within an agreed period.

Do-it-yourself Removal Moving yourself is an option when vacating a small property. This involves hiring a van (check details of the minimum age for drivers) and organizing friends who are able and willing to help with lifting and carrying.

Services Remember to inform suppliers of services in advance of your move – gas, electricity, telephone, water, newspapers, milk and so on. Similarly, they should be informed of your arrival at your new home, or new suppliers selected.

Pets It is wise to book cats into a boarding cattery for the period of the move, usually from the day before (when the home is being packed) until everything has been moved into the new property. Cats should be kept indoors until they are accustomed to the new home, otherwise they may stray. It is not a good idea to keep a cat shut in one room while the contents of the home are being packed; someone is quite likely to open the door and the frightened animal will run off and hide.

Dogs may have to be boarded for the day of the move – this depends on the animal. Make sure you have some plan for looking after your dog, ensuring it does not take fright and run off, especially when introduced to the new home. Similarly, do not neglect small caged pets and make arrangements in advance for them to be looked after by a friend on the day of the move.

SORTING AND PACKING

It is best to begin sorting out cupboards, attic and other storage areas as soon as the move has been confirmed. Moving home is a great opportunity for a really good clear-out.

If you are using a removal company, they will probably include packing and unpacking in the quote. Generally, most companies insist on doing the packing for insurance purposes: if you pack, their insurance does not cover any breakages.

If you are packing yourself, think ahead and acquire sturdy boxes for unbreakable goods, such as books. Tough plastic sacks are ideal for clothes, linen and soft furnishings. Sturdy tea chests are most suitable for china and delicate items. Save newspapers for packing delicate goods. Old blankets or sheets should be used to protect furniture surfaces in the van. When you move yourself, remember to pack boxes that can be carried easily. Tie boxes securely with string and label them.

Food storage areas need special attention; run down stocks over the months and weeks before the move, particularly in the freezer. If you do have to move frozen food, it should be kept in the freezer. The freezer should be switched off at the last minute, packed last and then unpacked first. However, follow the manufacturer's instructions when moving freezers as they can be permanently damaged if handled incorrectly.

HEATING AND FURNISHING THE HOME

HEATING

The new home may have satisfactory arrangements but you may have to alter or install a heating system. Installing a new system is likely to be a fairly expensive operation unless it is a very small property, so always take professional advice from a reputable source. Make sure the system complies with the current safety standards and is installed by a member of the relevant professional association.

The choice of system depends on your budget, your lifestyle (factors such as whether you are at home during the day or spend long periods of time away from home, and so on) and the availability of services in the area. Compare running costs before deciding on which of the systems outlined below would suit you best.

Central Heating A central heating system operates by heating water and distributing it to radiators throughout the property. It may be fuelled by gas, electricity, oil or solid fuel and the hot water supply is run off the same system. In some cases, cooking facilities may also be provided (for example, when using an Aga or Rayburn) .

Heating by Electricity There are a number of options, including night-storage systems, convector heaters and warm-air systems. One or more of these facilities can be combined to provide a system which can be pre-programmed and controlled to suit your requirements.

Solar Heating This is a comparatively new method of heating which utilizes sunlight to heat water by means of solar panels, usually installed on the roof. The installation process does not involve major structural work, but it is important to note that the resulting system is unlikely to provide sufficient hot water and heating on its own. Although the economic and environmental aspects of using solar energy for hot water and heating are extremely attractive, the success of the system relies on the number of hours of sunlight and on the cloud cover. Developments of this type of system include links with alternative fuel supplies and its main potential lies in the prospect of building new purpose-planned property, rather than in converting old systems.

Heating Individual Rooms Heating the whole house is the preferred method but, when the cost is too great, it is important to ensure that rooms can be heated individually as needed. A fixed heat source is best in the main living area and portable convector heaters or similar appliances may be used in rooms which are not in constant use.

Special arrangements are necessary for bathrooms, where fixed heaters must be used and the use of electric appliances is limited according to type.

Open Fires These are appealing but they involve a lot of work, so are not practical as the only source of heat in living areas. Also, different types of fireplace produce varying amounts of heat and smokeless fuel must be used in some areas. Open fires are ideal as an optional extra to a central heating or other system which produces background heat throughout the house.

Other Heating Options Various alternative systems can be found, usually based on a dry heating system and generally powered by electricity. Hot-air heating distributes the air through a series of ducts to the various rooms. Other alternative systems that may be used include underfloor or overhead heating, with these tending to feature in new property.

FIXTURES AND FITTINGS

If these are unsuitable, they should be replaced before decorating. The first criteria for replacement must be safety; any very old appliances, such as water heaters or gas fires, should be checked and replaced if necessary. Normally, the standard of wiring and, possibly, plumbing is checked as part of a pre-purchase survey.

On an aesthetic level, remember that accessories can be a great help in disguising fittings which are not to your taste. Pots, bottles, jars, plants, rugs, curtains or blinds, or towels in toning colours may all be used to distract from bathroom fixtures which are a disagreeable colour or unattractive style.

Instead of replacing kitchen units, you may find that you can purchase alternative cupboard doors at less cost and without delay. Similarly, new work surfaces and flooring can create a completely different impression.

DECORATION

The urgency for decorating a new home depends on the standard of the existing decor and obviously any structural work should be completed first. If the paintwork is in bad condition throughout, it is just as well to decorate, finances allowing, before completely unpacking. If the decor is in good condition and not unsuitable, then any re-decorating can be done gradually, room by room.

If the existing colour schemes are unacceptable to your taste but time and cost prohibit thorough re-decoration, refreshing the walls by applying several coats of white paint can be a practical, short-term measure.

Decide on colour schemes to match existing furnishings if you have not budgeted for replacing these. Blend colours which do not quite match by introducing linking tones in cushions, curtain tie-backs and other trimmings.

FLOORING

The choice of flooring depends on the decor of a room, what it is used for and your budget. Kitchens, hallways and living rooms are typical heavy-use areas, particularly in a home with a large number of occupants, and will need sturdy, hard-wearing flooring. Floors in kitchens, utility rooms, bathrooms, shower rooms and cloakrooms should withstand dampness as well as the occasional soaking.

Wood Flooring Floor boards, wooden tiles or wooden sheeting may be stained, varnished or painted.

Floor boards should be in good condition if they are to be left uncovered. Even, unsawn floor boards without too many nail holes can be sanded until smooth and then stained or painted, if required, before being sealed with several coats of a suitable floor varnish, clear in the case of paint or stain.

Wooden tiles are available treated or untreated and may be ready-stained. Wooden sheeting or chipboard are inexpensive options that can be very successful. It is important that the finish which is applied is used in sufficient quantities, sanded and dried according to the manufacturer's instructions to withstand hard wear.

Floor Paint Ordinary paint can be suitable for some wooden floors when finished with a sealant. Special paint is also available for use on concrete floors; this can be practical for cellars or other ancillary areas.

Ceramic Tiles These are suitable for solid floors and work well in the kitchen, utility room, cloakroom and conservatory. Ceramic tiles are expensive, but wear well. They do, however, feel rather cold.

Marble Tiles These are expensive but attractive for conservatory or cloakroom and they are ideal for solid floors. Although they are washable, marble tiles do scratch and mark easily.

Quarry Tiles Expensive but hardwearing, these are cold underfoot but easy to keep clean and ideal for solid floors.

Vinyl Flooring Available as tiles or by the roll, vinyl is washable and feels quite warm underfoot. There is an excellent choice of colours and designs, but it is worth remembering that the quality varies according to the price. This type of flooring is practical for kitchen, utility room, conservatory, cloakroom and bathroom.

Cork Tiles The quality varies enormously, but these can be an excellent, inexpensive option and, if properly sealed, last well for a number of years. Cork tiles are suitable for solid floors and are warm underfoot.

Carpet Carpet is available in a wide range of types, quality, backing, weaves, finishes, patterns, colours and, of course, prices. It may be fitted wall-to-wall, it may be fitted within a fixed wooden carpet edging border in the middle of a room or along a hall, or it may be a set size, leaving a border of bare, polished floor boards around the edge of the room.

Before buying, always check that the particular carpet is suitable for the type of floor and for the use of the room or area. Also, check underlay requirements recommended by the manufacturer.

As a general guide, carpet for a bathroom, cloakroom or shower room should contain a high percentage of man-made fibre, as this is not absorbent; wool-rich carpets which absorb moisture tend to rot if they remain damp. Also, carpet with special backing is sold specifically for bathroom use.

Carpet tiles can be a good alternative for heavy-use areas, as worn tiles can be individually replaced. However, these do vary in quality and appearance. Carpet or carpet tiles made specifically for the kitchen are particularly tough and moisture-resistant.

Rugs and Matting These can look attractive on polished floors or on a plain base of fitted carpet and can be useful to cover worn parts of existing carpets or flooring. However, they can be dangerous when placed on slippery floors; in particular, loose rugs are not suitable for hallways and kitchens where they can cause accidents.

FURNITURE

The choice is entirely dependent on individual taste. Without attempting to comment on styles, there are various options to consider when looking for furniture. With a little effort and ingenuity, you can furnish a home most attractively on a fairly low budget.

Second-hand furniture can be an excellent buy. Look for junk shops as well as secondhand furniture stores and antique shops. Bargains can also be found in auctions and through the local paper.

Before buying second-hand furniture, check it for breakages or damage and for small holes, particularly fresh-looking ones, which indicate that the furniture has had woodworm and may be infested. This is easily cured by using an appropriate product (see page 141), but the furniture should never be left untreated as the worm will spread to other furniture or woodwork in the house.

When buying new furniture, think practically, considering aspects of durability, ease of cleaning (especially upholstery) and so on, in relation to the use they will be put to in your household. When buying sofas and chairs, look for those manufactured to current recommended standards, particularly with reference to flammability. A mixture of second-hand and new furniture can be combined most successfully. For example, although it is worth buying a new bed of the best quality you can afford as poor sleeping conditions result in long-term discomfort, a good-quality new mattress can be used with a second-hand base, or even a home-made, wooden base.

Remember that furniture is not necessarily a once-only purchase and it is practical to think in terms of up-grading particular pieces, circumstances permitting.

SOFT FURNISHINGS

Curtains, chair covers and cushions can bring a room together; they can enliven dull colour schemes, add pattern to plain furnishings and give a completely new look to a room. Curtains are also a valuable form of heat insulation when they are drawn, particularly those made from heavy fabric and hung over large windows. Insulated curtain lining can be a good choice for French windows, patio doors or large windows.

Curtains, cushions, tie-backs and trimmings may be purchased ready-made, you can make them yourself or have them made. As well as ordering through major stores or manufacturers, look through the local paper for individuals offering a soft furnishing service. Remember to add the cost of linings, tapes and trimmings when comparing the price of making curtains to buying them ready-made.

On a practical basis, the choice of colours and fabrics should reflect the wear they are likely to have. Dramatic, plain, pale chair covers can be stunning in an elegant adult environment, but they are not as successful in a house full of growing children. Check for flammability, finish, cleaning or washing instructions. If the furnishing is for a bright, sunlit room, check that it is not likely to fade.

As well as practical aspects, choice of colour and style, consider the position of the furnishings and their impact in their setting. For example, a stunning, vibrant, flowered fabric may look wonderful in the shop, but will it be too overpowering for curtaining patio doors opposite the sofa in a lounge? Consider what kind of environment you want to create – lively or restful, cosy or sophisticated?

As alternatives to curtains, look at the various types of blinds, net curtaining and decorative drapes.

LIGHTING

The correct choice of lighting is important for safety as well as comfort. Bright lighting in the kitchen and bathroom is essential for practical tasks such as food preparation and shaving. Stairs and hallways must also be well lit to avoid accidents; the front and back doors or porch should be well illuminated, as should outside steps or pathways that are used at night.

There are areas which benefit from soft lighting; the lounge, bedroom and dining room are places to relax. However, these places should include several lighting options, to provide adequate light for acitivities such as reading, sewing, dressing and clearing away after a meal.

Achieving good lighting means including different sources throughout the room. Well-directed light is invaluable over work surfaces or mirrors. Central ceiling lighting is practical for some work and, by using a dimmer switch, this can be adjusted to suit the mood. Wall lights tend to be softer and cast interesting shadows, while standard lamps can be used to create soft areas of light as well as for providing bright light by which to read.

Type of Light The common incandescent filament lamp, with bayonet or screw fitting, is widely used, more often with pearl glass or tints which provide a softer effect than clear bulbs. The higher the wattage, the brighter the light: 60-watt bulbs are commonly used in living areas, with 100-watt bulbs to provide bright lighting for areas such as halls. Filament light bulbs come in a variety of shapes and long-life or low-fuel types are available at an initial extra cost, but with long-term savings.

Reflector lamps for spotlights or down-lighting throw out powerful beams of light which are ideal for areas in need of high illumination. Special bulbs for downward-facing wall lights or similar fittings have silvered caps to spread the area of illumination for a broader, less harsh effect.

Tungsten halogen sources provide more light for an intense, bright, white effect. These are used for up-lighting standard lamps, desk lamps or alternatives to spotlights on track systems. The replacement lamps are expensive but they have a long life.

Fluorescent lights provide more light than an incandescent bulb for the same electricity consumption and, therefore, fluorescent tubes are suitable for working areas. They may also be concealed behind pelmets or cupboards to provide up-light against ceilings or down-light for working areas. In the latter case, they are far more economical than spotlights. Small fluorescent tubes are also available for bed-head lights, mirror lights and so on.

Emergency Lighting Every home should have an emergency light. A powerful torch, either battery-powered or rechargeable and kept topped up, is most practical. Candles, gas or oil lamps are other options. Keep a torch near the fuse box along with fuse wire, so that you can see to mend a fuse. So that you know where to go in case of a power cut, designate a home for the torch – somewhere practical where it is easy to find in the dark.

HOME SECURITY

This section concentrates on fire and theft or burglary, two key dangers which should be safeguarded against as a matter of course.

BURGLARY

Any goods that fetch a reasonable second-hand price are valuable to the casual burglar, and the majority of homes have something to offer: television, computer, camera, microwave cooker, silver, jewellery and so on. If you own items of significant value, then it is sensible to take professional advice on security systems and to consider appropriate insurance cover. Security systems are many and varied, complex and expensive, and a separate specialist subject. The following notes apply to basic security standards and practice which should be adopted in every home, no matter how humble.

Away From Home Most burglaries take place when the occupier is out, usually during the day. A 15-minute trip to the corner shop can provide ample opportunity for the casual burglar. A house that is empty every day is an ideal target and the fact that you are away on holiday can be all too obvious if home security is poor.

- Deliveries should not advertise your absence; milk, mail, papers and leaflets left on the doorstep or visibly piled inside a porch should be avoided. Make sure the letter box is flexible enough for items to be pushed through easily. If you do not find unsolicited papers of interest, then put a notice near your gate or door to stop people delivering them. Ask a friend or neighbour to remove deliveries if you are away (even for a couple of days). Cancel milk and papers before holidays. The Post Office offers a mailholding service for a fee.
- Unattended, closed curtains are a sign of absence, particularly if left on a daily basis before going to work or during holidays.
- Leaving only the hall light or outside light on when you are out in the evening is a sure sign that you are out; leave various lights on throughout the house.
- An open, empty garage is both an indication of your absence and an invitation to the thief to take his pick. Make sure you close the door, even if you are only going out for a short trip.
- Do not put your full address in the telephone directory; your name and street are sufficient, without the necessity for house name or number.
- Telephone answering-machine messages can be a sign of absence. A message which indicates that you use the machine when you are at home as well as when you are out is a good idea – the 'too busy to take your call' type of message is better than 'out at the moment'.
- Never leave a note on the door to let welcome callers know you have popped out.
- Do not let strangers or casual acquaintances know of holiday plans. If possible, ask a friend or neighbour to take you to the station instead of ordering a taxi. If you do take a taxi, do not tell the driver where you are going on holiday or for how long. Do not put your name, address and destination on luggage until you reach the airport or coach station.

Everyday Security When you move to new property, contact the local Police for information on home security. They often provide free advice and a home visit as well as information on crime prevention schemes in the district.

- Windows and doors should be secured whenever you are out. Also, if you are in the garden or out of hearing distance of the door, then keep it shut tight (locked, if necessary).
- High-quality locks should be fitted to all doors and to windows, particularly older windows which tend to be less secure than newer, sealed units. The local Constabulary offer advice on types of locks for windows and doors and they provide information on reputable companies or individuals to do the work.
- Garages, sheds and outhouses should be locked. Ladders and tools should be locked away.
- Lights are useful deterrents. Leave a living room or kitchen light on if you are out for the evening, use a time-switch to activate discreet living room or bedroom lights if you are away for a few days or longer and make sure the entrances to the house are well lit.
- Noise can lead the casual burglar to believe the home is occupied. Leaving a radio on when you are out for a short while is a good idea and a time-switch to activate the radio can be useful for longer periods.
- Callers who are not familiar should not be admitted without first presenting formal identification. Have a door chain or lock which restricts entry, then check identification before opening the door to strangers.

Neighbours and Friends Aside from social reasons, it is sensible to make contact with your neighbours; if they are familiar with you, your family and your comings and goings, they will be able to notice any strange activities while you are out. If you are going away, ask a friend to check the property and leave a key so that they can remove deliveries from sight. Remember to offer to do the same for your neighbours and friends.

FIRE

Take sensible precautions against fire at all times. Here are some basic points to remember.

- Have electric wiring checked in an older property and never overload electric circuits or sockets.
- Do not try to repair or use old or unsafe electrical appliances. Frayed wires and loose plugs must be replaced.

- Electrical fuses blow for a reason; if a fuse repeatedly blows it means there is a fault or that the circuit is overloaded. When a main fuse or trip switch blows frequently, call in a professional electrician. Never substitute larger fuses or fuse wire.
- If you smoke, always ensure you use an ash tray and never leave lit cigarettes to burn unattended. Do not smoke in bed.
- Keep matches and any other potential fire risks out of reach of children.
- Pay particular attention to paraffin heaters, keeping them clean and safe according to the manufacturer's instructions. They must stand on a stable surface in a ventilated area. Never try to fill a lit heater.
- Never leave gas or electric fires burning unattended and always place a guard in front of an open fire. Never leave a child in the room with a fire, without a fixed guard.
- Always let an open fire burn down before going to bed or going out and tidy it up: rake ashes and burning coals, ensuring they will not fall out of the grate, brush up ash and dirt from the fireplace, remove any nearby flammable items and place a fine mesh guard in front of the fire.
- Have chimneys swept regularly.
- Always observe kitchen safety. Grilling or frying must be supervised at all times.
- Fit at least one smoke alarm: contact the local fire brigade who advise on fire prevention.
- Keep a fire blanket and/or extinguisher in the kitchen.
- Shut interior doors at night as, in the event of fire, they will hold back smoke and fumes for sufficient time to allow you to escape.
- Pay particular attention to fire exits, provisions and precautions in flats and bedsits.

HOUSING PROBLEMS

In the case of problems with housing, whether related to renting or buying, seek authoritative advice immediately. Do not let a situation drag on in the hope that it might resolve itself; find help promptly.

Typical problems include disagreements with landlords or neighbours, difficulties relating to rent or mortgage payments, problems caused by accidents or damage in the home, problems arising from poor health and various problems resulting from changed family circumstances. Remember that other people have incurred similar troubles and that help is always available – never be ashamed or frightened about asking for advice, as it is the most sensible course of action.

As always, the library is a useful source of information for the addresses of consumer centres, Citizens' Advice Bureaux and professional associations. The local council offices will also provide information, if not direct advice or help. Do not dismiss the value of a brief interview with a trusted, family acquaintance, typically the doctor, religious leader or solicitor. Anyone of these people may be able to suggest organizations which offer guidance and support.

In dealing with purchasing problems, always speak directly to someone in authority at the mortgage company. Do not simply pour out all your problems to the clerk or receptionist; make an appointment to discuss the matter with the manager or someone who is in a position to advise about your account.

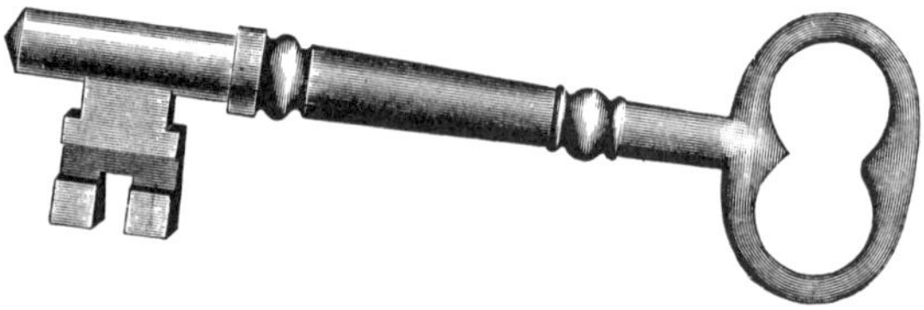

Pests and Fungi

Maintaining a high standard of cleanliness and hygiene is vital to discourage some household pests; other infestations require specialist attention. This chapter deals with most common pests and fungi, and offers advice on dealing with them.

Dealing promptly with a minor pest problem is important to avoid major infestation. If simple methods do not appear to work, seek professional advice. The local council deals with requests for advice or eradication of pests, helping with anything from wasps' nests to problems with vermin such as rats. They are also in a position to tackle problems covering a larger area than your property. Private companies specializing in pest control can be found in your local telephone directory.

ANTS

Paraffin or boiling water can be used to destroy ants' nests outside the house, around the base of a wall or under pathways. Special insecticides are also available and can be obtained from hardware shops and garden centres. These should be applied around exterior walls, across entrances and around windows.

BED BUGS

Found in warm, dirty rooms and old, dirty bedding, bed bugs have an unpleasant smell and bite humans. Contact the local authority as these should be removed by fumigation.

CARPET BEETLES

The beetles may originate from birds' nests in the eaves or attic, so these should be cleared.

Moth crystals may be used to clear the beetles and carpets and curtains should be sprayed with insecticide available from hardware stores.

COCKROACHES

Living in cracks and the fabric of the house, cockroaches come out at night. They are attracted to kitchens by the food and warmth, therefore scrupulous cleanliness is vital.

Once established, cockroaches can be difficult to remove, especially in flats or adjoining houses. Contact the local council or a private pest control company immediately you are aware of cockroaches to eliminate the pests before they can establish a large colony. Continue to maintain a high standard of household cleanliness, paying particular attention to cupboards. crevices and areas behind appliances in the kitchen.

DRY ROT

This condition affects damp wood and is more destructive than wet rot as it spreads far and fast. It will even spread through masonry boundaries – which can be a severe problem in older, terraced houses.

Signs of dry rot include crumbling or soft wood. warping or cracks, reddish dust, fungus and a distinctive mushroom-like smell. White 'wool' strands are a typical symptom and plasterwork on the walls tends to bulge.

The problem of damp must be solved and all affected wood must be cut out, along with adjacent materials, to a radius of about 1.5 metres/5 feet. Fungicide has to be applied to surrounding wood and masonry to prevent re-infection.

Serious cases of dry rot will involve major work and corresponding expense and should be carried out by a reputable company and be covered by a guarantee. The work may include the complete replacement of floor joists, the insertion of a reliable damp-proofing system into the masonry, a review of ventilation in outside walls, re-plastering and so on.

FLEAS

These tiny creatures have flattened bodies and may be light brown or almost black in colour. The most common are those living on animal hosts – cats or dogs. Fleas which actually live on humans are rarely found, but animal fleas will bite humans.

The pet should be treated with a flea wash or spray, preferably obtained from the vet. It is also important to treat all areas in the house where the pet wanders, particularly the pet's bed. All carpets should be thoroughly vacuum-cleaned or brushed, corners and floor edges should be cleaned and then all areas should be sprayed with a suitable product. Most sprays for animals can also be used to spray the house.

Treating the animal at the first sign of a problem (frequent scratching) and treating the house at the same time prevents the problem from becoming severe. Treating a pet (even if they do not have fleas) before they are sent to kennels or a cattery often prevents infestation.

If you have a very serious problem with fleas, the local council will fumigate the property.

FLIES

The common house fly is an unpleasant insect which carries germs and disease. Flies feed on animal excrement, then they enter a kitchen to land on food, or on surfaces which come in contact with food. They vomit on potential food in order to reduce it to a form which can be ingested by their bodies.

Areas around rubbish bins are prime targets for flies, therefore they should be kept clear of open bags and as clean as possible. Bins should be washed frequently, and rubbish should be placed in plastic sacks which can be securely sealed.

Never leave food uncovered in the kitchen. Use a suitable fly deterrent in warm weather and keep kitchen windows closed when preparing food to prevent flies entering.

MILDEW

This condition is caused by condensation and the only way to prevent growth is to sort out your condensation problem.

Condensation is caused by warm, moist air striking a cold surface. It is familiar on bathroom windows on a cold day, when the warm, moist air from hot bath-water hits the cold window pane. Reducing condensation is not easy, particularly in winter. Good ventilation is important, so an extractor fan in kitchen or bathroom is a useful alternative to opening the window.

Even warmth is more effective than alternate cold and hot periods. Condensation can be a problem in houses that do not have continuous heating, where a heater is used to raise the temperature rapidly for times when the various rooms are in use. Oil heaters give off a lot of moisture, therefore they are best avoided.

Fine polystyrene lining paper may be used on walls to increase the surface temperature and therefore reduce the condensation. A combination of good insulation (for example, in the attic or loft) and ventilation in humid rooms tends to help by evening out the extremes of temperature and reducing the moisture in the air.

In the short term, cleaning off the mildew with bleach or fungicide helps, as does painting with fungicidal paints; however, these are not permanent solutions.

MITES AND WEEVILS

Found in flour, cereals, dried fruit and other storecupboard ingredients, these creatures break out of closed packets and rapidly develop into a major infestation. They thrive in a warm environment, so cupboards near a heater, boiler or cooker are not suitable for storing ingredients.

Mites and weevils may originate from a packet of grain and multiply profusely in warm conditions, spreading rapidly. Once you have discovered mites, throw away all food from the cupboard; careful checking will inevitably reveal the minute creatures somewhere, even in unopened packets. Thoroughly scrub all cupboards, inside, outside and in all cracks and crevices, using plenty of bleach. Apply an insecticide to surrounding walls and clean out all surrounding cupboards.

RODENTS

Rats and mice will be attracted by food refuse around dustbins. However, the occasional visit by mice normally living outside may simply be due to the combination of a warm environment and a ready supply of crumbs or food in the kitchen.

To avoid visits from rodents, stop up holes in the brickwork in external walls, such as those found beside pipes running out behind a kitchen sink. Thorough cleanliness is vital; avoid leaving crumbs of food on the floor, behind cupboards or appliances and around work surface edges. It is also important to clean out ovens and grill pans and to empty and clean toasters regularly.

Tiny black droppings are a sign of mice and if you suspect that you have even one mouse, then you must take the precaution of storing all food in sealed containers, if not in the refrigerator.

To get rid of mice you can use traditional mousetraps or one of the various brands of poison available, some of which are incorporated in plastic traps. However, if the problem is more than an occasional visit, then this should be dealt with professionally. Rats are a more dangerous proposition and should be reported to the local council immediately.

SILVERFISH

These are unpleasant but not particularly harmful. They are found in damp places under flooring or in damp cupboards. Thorough and frequent cleaning is important and cupboards should be aired and kept dry, particularly under the sink or in similar areas which are prone to damp. Once again, an appropriate insecticide can be obtained from hardware stores.

SPIDERS AND OTHER SMALL INSECTS

Unless these are present in large numbers, they are unlikely to be a severe problem. Good general standards of cleanliness throughout the house should keep them at bay, with frequent brushing and vacuum-cleaning of hidden areas behind furniture and so on.

WASPS

Wasps sometimes nest in the attic or under the eaves of a house but they do not return to the same nest on successive years. Local councils are accustomed to ridding nests of wasps and specialist companies offer a similar service. The specialist may have to gain access from inside the attic as well as approaching the nest from outside the house.

WET ROT

Tiny organisms grow in wood which is continually saturated. The organisms eat away the wood which becomes dark, soft and splits. Paintwork flakes and strands of fungus may appear, fanning out from the wood.

The source of the dampness has to be eliminated, the wood replaced and the new wood treated with a suitable preservative.

WOODLICE

These oval grey insects have an armour-like exterior and come into the house through doors, windows and cracks or cavities in walls. Woodlice tend to live in damp, cool and shaded outdoor areas and, although they are not hazardous, they are unpleasant. Insect powder or suitable disinfectant may be used across doorways and around the outside of exterior walls. Keep interior floors clean, particularly corners. An interior insecticide can be sprayed around skirting boards and into cracks and crevices to prevent woodlice from entering and to kill any which live in the walls.

WOODWORM

Wood which is peppered with tiny holes has been infested with woodworm; however, holes that look old, with the wood well dried around their edges are unlikely to be a problem. The holes are made by tiny grubs boring through the wood and fresh or active holes will be accompanied by a residue of very fine dust.

STRUCTURAL TREATMENT

If there are signs of wood worm in the structural timbers of the house, or as a precaution against possible infection in older houses, a professional pest control company should be called in to spray all joists and floor boards. The treatment which is applied usually also prevents the onset of other likely wood disease and pests.

Make sure that the company you choose is a member of a professional association, or take a recommendation from the local authority or other reliable source. The work usually involves completely clearing each floor of the house, one at a time, including the attic. To prevent damp in older houses and protect against the pest infestation that occurs in damp wood, a damp-proofing treatment may also be inserted around relevant areas of the ground floor at the same time. Make sure that you receive a guarantee once the treatment is completed.

FURNITURE TREATMENT

Treating woodworm in furniture is far simpler and there are various brands of fluid and aerosols available to do the job. The furniture should be brushed with fluid, inside and out, or sprayed according to manufacturer's instructions. If there are clear signs that the worm is active, a syringe should be used to inject the fluid into the wood, via the holes. The fluid should be injected at 10 cm/ 4 inch intervals.

Once the treatment has dried, the holes may be filled with a suitable wood filler and the wood polished, varnished or painted.

Health Care

An appreciation of everyday factors which contribute to good health and a common-sense approach to medical conditions or illness, as well as to the medical profession, are important aspects of household general knowledge.

Thankfully, today, professional support is likely to arrive in minutes rather than hours in the case of accident or serious illness, and broader access to comprehensive professional health care has eliminated the need for crude or dangerous home treatment. However, thoughts on hygiene, diet and the life-saving importance of understanding first-aid are just as relevant to the contemporary reader as to those of the last century.

This chapter covers basic information on professional medical care, with useful background notes on various common ailments and conditions. In addition, there are a few reminders on caring for a patient at home, such as an elderly relative, a child or someone convalescing after illness or an operation.

THE DOCTOR

Medical Card This must be kept safe as it shows your National Health Service number and proves that you are entitled to NHS treatment. It shows the address of your local family practitioner committee as well as the name of your existing doctor. This card should be shown when registering with a new doctor or changing doctors.

Family Practitioner Committee This is your link with the local health authority. The address is shown on your health card, or it may be obtained from the local library or through the telephone directory. Contact the FPC if you lose your medical card.

The FPC can provide a list of doctors, dentists, opticians and pharmacists in your area, and provide information on health services which are available, including family planning and maternity clinics. If you have special needs or a problem finding a doctor or other health care, then contact the FPC for help.

CHOOSING A DOCTOR

It is essential to register with a local general practitioner when you move to an area – do not wait until you are ill. If you live in a larger town with a choice of health centres or surgeries, make some enquiries about the various options before making your choice. The district family practitioner committee provides lists of local doctors – as usual, the local library or internet is the first stop for information.

Before registering with a doctor, find out about the way in which the practice is run. For example, are patients seen by an appointment system or does the practice operate an open surgery where the patients simply queue?

The location of the surgery is important. You should be able to visit the doctor easily from home and the doctor should be able to get to you in time to cope with an emergency.

The best approach is to visit the surgeries of local doctors and ask the receptionist for information. Many practices provide leaflets detailing the way in which they are run and listing the doctors.

When you have made a decision, take your medical card to the surgery and explain that you would like to register. Remember the doctor is not obliged to accept you.

Once you have been accepted, your medical records will be transferred from your previous doctor through the family practitioner committee system. This may take some time.

Many surgeries like to do a health check for new patients and continue to do so at regular intervals.

VISITING THE DOCTOR

The following pointers will help towards a successful relationship with your doctor.

- If the doctor is likely to want to examine you, wear clothing that is easy to remove and put back on again. This saves valuable time.
- Explain your problem simply and clearly, giving the doctor as much relevant detail as possible. It's a good idea to write a few brief notes beforehand so that you remember exactly what you wanted to say.
- If you do not understand any of the doctor's questions or comments, then ask for an explanation so that you can give accurate information or follow the advice properly.
- Take note of the doctor's advice and follow it. Do take any course of treatment which is suggested. Do not leave the surgery and dismiss the medical or social care which has been given.

HOME VISITS

These are intended for emergencies which occur outside surgery hours – that is, when the problem cannot wait until the following surgery time – or for those who are too ill to attend surgery or unable to do so for some other reason. Home visits are not intended for your convenience, they should only be requested when they are essential.

If you need a home visit, then ring the surgery as early as possible in the morning, certainly before 10 am.

In an emergency, if you do have to call the doctor out of surgery hours, explain the problem as clearly as you can over the telephone as this will help the doctor decide whether a visit is necessary.

THE DOCTOR'S PARTNERS IN PROVIDING CARE

The doctor has a back-up team of professionals who fulfil specific roles. The district nurse visits patients at home to perform routine medical tasks, such as changing dressings, giving injections and so on. Many practices employ nurses who are available in the surgery to attend to visiting patients and the practice nurse will perform the same duties as the district nurse for those who are able to visit the surgery. In addition, the nurse is able to ease the load on the doctor by checking blood pressure, giving some routine health checks and injections.

The midwife provides ante- and post-natal care to a doctor's patients as well as, occasionally, delivering babies in the home. The latter depends on the attitude and professional judgement of the doctor.

Health visitors provide important back-up before and after childbirth and with any other social aspects related to medical care.

Home helps are also linked to the back-up provided by a doctor. For example, they work with elderly people providing the support needed for independence. Their contribution is also of value in maintaining the comfort and good health of many people.

THE DENTIST

It is important to find a local dentist in whom you have confidence and to visit the surgery for regular check-ups. Children should be introduced to the dentist at an early age by the example of their parents. If you make regular visits to your dentist, you will find that today's treatments are quick and relatively painless.

A list of dentists who offer NHS treatment is available from the family practitioner committee. A dentist is not obliged to accept you as a patient and some dentists provide only private care. The FPA or the dentist's receptionist will be able to provide details of concessions and other aspects of treatment relating to the NHS.

GENERAL DENTAL CARE

Most dentists offer leaflets and advice on how to take care of your teeth. Your diet and dental hygiene are both important.

- Avoid eating large or regular amounts of sugary foods.
- Avoid frequent and large quantities of acidic drinks.
- Clean your teeth at least twice a day, brushing between and behind the teeth and around the gum area.
- Use a toothbrush as recommended by your dentist – this should not be too harsh.
- A balanced diet is vital to the development and continued maintenance of teeth.

THE CHIROPODIST

The chiropodist specializes in foot care. The doctor may refer patients to the chiropodist, for example elderly or diabetic patients, and treatment may be available on the National Health Service. However, you do not have to be referred to the chiropodist by a doctor and many people have regular, private, appointments.

If you do have a problem with your feet and are not registered with a chiropodist, then it is sensible to consult your doctor first for advice.

GENERAL FOOT CARE

The choice of footwear and hygiene are two main aspects of foot care.

Children and young people with growing or developing feet should wear shoes which provide support as well as room for growth and do not restrict or bend the feet or toes. Children should have their feet measured at a reputable shoe shop before buying shoes. Tight shoes and restrictive styles cause permanent damage to the feet.

Although most women have some frivolous shoes for special occasions, daily footwear for adults should be comfortable and suitable for their lifestyle. Similarly, footwear for sport must be suitable for the activity, providing support and cushioning as appropriate.

Slippers or equivalent shoes for use in the home should be warm and, preferably, washable if worn without socks or stockings.

Feet should be thoroughly washed and dried every day. Using a proprietary foot cream helps to keep the skin and nails in good condition; many also promote good circulation. Regularly massaging cream into the feet is also good for the circulation – equally important for men as as women.

Nails should be cut or filed straight across, not down at the sides. Rough skin should be removed using a pumice-stone or suitable cream. Foot powders, antiperspirants and other products are all helpful in the prevention of foot odour and for comfort; however, these should complement a rigid hygiene routine, not replace it.

THE OPTICIAN

An ophthalmic optician is someone who is qualified to give sight-tests as well as to provide spectacles; a dispensing optician is not qualified to test the eyes but is able to supply and fit 'optical appliances' (the official term for spectacles).You should visit an optician regularly even if you do not wear spectacles as sight does change with age and health. When you have had an eye-test you will be given a prescription for spectacles if you need them. You are free to take this prescription to any dispensing optician to buy new spectacles. The optician will provide details about NHS treatment and concessions it is a good idea to ask when you make a first appointment or before you begin to select frames for spectacles, as there is a range available for a fixed charge through the NHS.

You may decide to investigate the possibility of wearing contact lenses instead of glasses. You should be examined specifically for this purpose and your eyes should be examined following fitting to ensure that you are adapting to wearing lenses.

SUPPORT GROUPS AND OTHER ORGANIZATIONS

As well as standard health and welfare care, your doctor will be aware of local groups and national organizations dealing with your problem, condition, long-term or terminal illness or disability, offering moral support and technical assistance as appropriate.

PRIVATE HEALTH CARE

There is a large network of professionals offering private health care; some working for the NHS as well. Your NHS doctor can refer you to a private practitioner if you wish, for example for consultation on a problem or for specific treatment. You may also opt for the private medical system for your choice of general practitioner.

The most popular form of private medical care is through a personal insurance policy. There are a number of large organizations specializing in this field and many large companies offer free membership to a private health scheme as an employment bonus.

In addition to on-going health care, there is the option for occasional use of private facilities for a particular purpose, such as birth control or dental treatment.

HOSPITALS

You may have to visit a hospital as an outpatient on a one-off occasion for tests or a consultation, or for a series of visits while undergoing treatment. Alternatively, you may have to be admitted for a period of time.

No-one enjoys going to hospital but there are ways of easing the process. You are going to be dealing with an organization of considerable size, so fitting in makes for smoother progress through the system.

Find out as much detail as possible about your visit and the treatment you will be having in advance. If you are going to stay in hospital, pack sensible nightwear that is fairly cool and comfortable – most hospitals are well-heated. Pack a practical dressing gown and slippers, a toilet bag and towel, a small bedside clock (but not one with a loud tick) and something to read or do while lying in bed. On the formal side, make sure you take any regular medication with you and any letters of introduction from your doctor.

Do not take valuable jewellery, watches, clothes or lots of money. Ask a relative or friend to come in with you and take your clothes away when you are admitted. Keep a small amount of change for using the payphone (mobile phones interfere with some medical equipment), buying a newspaper and so on.

While you are in hospital, try to maintain a positive outlook and friendly approach to fellow patients and to staff. Being miserable, negative and grumpy will not help your condition and will make life unpleasant for everyone else. On the other hand, being the life and soul of the party when other people are trying to rest is equally undesirable, so try to strike a happy medium.

Make sure friends and relatives are aware of visiting arrangements and adhere to them.

When the time comes to go home, make arrangements for someone to bring your clothes and organize your journey home, remembering that you may not feel fit enough to cope with public transport. Make sure that there is someone at home to welcome you, with some essential food supplies in store, the heating turned on and so on. Before leaving, make sure you are clear about any after-care, such as how to cope with a wound while it is healing.

CARING FOR A PATIENT AT HOME

If you have to take care of a sick member of your family, put the patient in a single bed (if possible) with a firm mattress. Place the bed so that you can walk all round it. Ideally the bed should be by a window, so that the patient can look out. Make sure that the light is good enough to read by. The less furniture there is in a sick-room the better: a minimum of two chairs to put the bedclothes and pillows on when you make the bed, and a bedside table for books, drinks, a lamp, etc. It takes two people to make a bed easily; the aim is to leave the bed flat, clean, and unwrinkled. A sick person usually needs four pillows behind him to be able to sit up enough to eat and drink, and where there is difficulty in breathing he will need a back rest so that he can sit upright, or a bed-table on which he can lean forwards. A foot-rest will keep him from sliding down the bed.

The areas of skin that need attention in the bedridden are over the heels, elbows, shoulders and hips, knees, buttocks, and the lower part of the back. The position of the patient must be changed at least every two hours to prevent the pressure falling on the same area of skin all the time; the skin must be kept dry and clean and must never be irritated by wrinkles in the lower sheet. If redness develops in the places mentioned above, skilled attention is necessary. In some cases bedclothes must be kept away from the legs and feet; if you cannot get a bed cradle, use a pillow at each side of the legs to raise the bedclothes.

Do not use an electric blanket or pad in a sick-bed. Never fill a hot-water-bottle with boiling water, and always use a cover on it.

Wash the patient's face and hands two or three times a day, as it is refreshing, and make sure that toe nails as well as finger nails are properly cut. Attend to the hair regularly; this is good for morale.

The doctor will tell you whether a special diet is needed. Always make sure that the sick person has enough to drink within easy reach, for in most short, acute illnesses solid food is not nearly as important as water. The patient must never become dehydrated, especially when the bowels are upset. One can often get children to drink by making up flavoured drinks with soda water; in very difficult cases try giving plain or flavoured ice to suck. When patients improve they become hungry, and common sense suggests nourishing soups, boiled or grilled fish, scrambled eggs, chicken, bread and butter – no fried food.

Old people and children easily become bored and lonely, and need to be kept occupied. People get better much more quickly if they are contented.

PRIVATE NURSING HOMES

Rest homes are establishments providing a caring environment and assistance for people who are convalescing, but they do not necessarily offer professional nursing or medical support except through local doctors. Private nursing homes provide in-house nursing facilities and medical back-up. However, the standards vary enormously. Selecting a nursing home is difficult, particularly if the stay is expected to be long term. Your doctor will be able to provide a list oflocal nursing homes and may well be able to provide guidance on current information available from charitable, private and health authority sources. Find out as much as you can about the options available before making a decision and visit a few homes (if there are that many available) to assess the differences. The following points will be helpful in choosing a suitable nursing home:

- Nursing homes must be registered with the local authorities – check this first.
- Find out about fees: what the fee covers, any extras, the source of payment should the stay be extended beyond the period originally planned, and so on.
- Find out about the staffing in the home, the facilities offered and any links it has with other organizations.
- Take a thorough look around the home; ask to see typical residents' rooms and public rooms, dining facilities, gardens, etc.
- When you are visiting take note of the general standards of cleanliness and neatness – look at floors, walls, curtains and furnishings.
- Be aware of the occupants – are they bright and cheerful or asleep and bored? Are they suitably occupied and aware of you as a visitor when you

walk through public areas?

- Be aware of needs for privacy and safety factors such as alarm buttons near beds.
- If shared rooms are the norm, then find out who the person sharing will be.
- Check arrangements for medical as well as social care – can the occupants remain registered with their existing doctors or do they have to re-register with the home's doctor?
- Can the occupants take some items of their own furniture, have private televisions, radios or pets?
- What about the staff? Are there plenty of them around, neat and clean in appearance, cheerful and friendly in their attitude to the residents?
- Think about the general atmosphere. The home should be clean and fresh, pleasant and homely, active and alive.

It is difficult to assess all these things in one go but it becomes easier once you can compare several different places. However, miserable surroundings, general poor standards of housekeeping and unpleasant smells, such as a prevailing odour of boiled cabbage or stale urine, are fairly obvious to the visitor.

HOSPICES

The hospice movement is growing rapidly in more than forty countries, but there are still many people who have only a hazy notion of what a hospice is. Primarily, hospices exist to offer specialized care to patients with severe and progressive diseases such as advanced cancer or AIDS. They also provide respite care for patients who are not yet in the final stages of their disease, but who would benefit from a short stay in such a caring environment – or whose relatives would benefit from a break from the often exhausting task of caring for someone who is seriously ill.

The aim of all hospices is to improve the quality of life. The control of pain and other symptoms is a priority, as is the provision of a calm, supportive and dignified environment for both patients and their families. Many hospices have day centres, which provide an opportunity for patients being cared for at home to receive clinical assessment, nursing care and support through creative and leisure activities.

Admission is normally arranged by the patient's own doctor or hospital, and care is usually free of charge. Charitable hospice organizations share with the

NHS the principle of free access, based only on the criteria of medical, social and emotional need.

ALTERNATIVE MEDICINE

The various health-care practices which do not fit directly into the current medical system of doctors, hospitals and related teams are covered by the term alternative medicine. There is a broad range of techniques and beliefs, many of which are respected by some doctors. But unfortunately, as thinking develops on the use of methods other than those traditionally observed in Western medicine, the whole subject and practice area is open to exploitation by individuals who have little experience and no qualifications.

The alternative approach to health care undoubtedly has a valuable role in society, with the emphasis on encouraging the body to activate its own natural defences to illness and less reliance on non-essential medication. However, it is important to remember that natural and alternative medicines and methods can be potent and, therefore, potentially dangerous in the wrong hands. Without a thorough knowledge of the medical history of a case, they can offer more problems than solutions.

Before embarking on any course of alternative treatment, it is a good idea to consult your doctor. The informed person will offer a balanced opinion and point out any aspects to be wary of. When finding a practitioner, do not simply extract a name from a telephone directory. Ask about relevant experience and qualifications and check up on affiliation to, or membership of any organizations. Do not take a long line of letters after the name of a practitioner as a sign of experience or competence without investigating what they stand for and their credibility.

In summary, do not try alternative medicine in ignorance of the disadvantages or possible dangers: if you feel it is relevant and helpful to your condition, then find out about the various organizations, their reputation and standing.

IMMUNIZATION

The doctor and health visitor will advise on immunization related to babies and children. You can expect a baby to receive a series of injections or oral immunization during the first year of life, then at intervals during early childhood, including protection against diseases such as diphtheria, tetanus, polio and measles.

In adulthood, tetanus is an important form of immunization to maintain, with a booster following accidents such as cuts or animal bites.

Immunization is also necessary before foreign travel. The exact programme depends on the countries to be visited and the time of year. Your doctor will offer up-to-date advice. Be sure to arrange an appointment to discuss immunization about three months ahead of travel when visiting countries in Africa, India and the Orient. Some immunization is given over a period of weeks or months and the course must be completed by a certain period ahead of exposure to the disease.

Travel companies also provide advice.

Immunization against common illness, such as influenza, may also be offered to groups of the population who are at risk of complications, for example the elderly or very young.

HEALTH AND TRAVEL

Consult your doctor well in advance of foreign travel to discuss the necessary immunization requirements. These change according to the time of year and current conditions, so the doctor may have to check with a specialist body: this relates to protection against malaria as well as to other diseases.

Apart from the importance of immunization against disease (see above), always pack a small first-aid kit when travelling, either in this country or abroad. The kit should include plasters and antiseptic cream, along with a suitable cooling lotion for sunburn if appropriate. Take tablets or medicine to ease diarrhoea – it makes sense to take both a mild type and a more potent type, depending on where you are travelling and for how long. The chemist or your doctor will offer sensible advice.

Changes in diet often cause diarrhoea, as indeed can the sub-conscious anxiety of foreign travel. Adopt a sensible approach to eating and drinking when holidaying abroad.

- Do not drink tap water, instead buy sealed bottles of mineral water. Even if the local water is not contaminated, you may not be used to the chemicals or minerals which are added to it.
- Avoid eating food which is obviously prepared in unhygienic conditions.
- Avoid buying meats, cheeses, seafood and similar items which are obviously stale, displayed in the sun and attracting flies. Do not confuse simplicity

with disregard for maintaining the quality of the food.

- If you drink too much wine or other alcoholic drink and eat far more than usual, then you can expect your digestive system to react adversely!
- Pay particular attention to the diet of infants and toddlers: it is worthwhile taking a supply of suitable canned food for the first few days until they are accustomed to the local food or you find a source of familiar items.
- Sunburn can be extremely painful and is very bad for the skin and, more seriously, sunstroke or over-exposure to the sun is extremely dangerous. Do not stay in the sun for long periods or during the middle of the day, particularly at the beginning of a holiday. Gradually acclimatize yourself and use a protective cream, lotion or oil suitable for your skin type, remembering to re-apply it regularly. When visiting very hot countries it is also worth checking locally on arrival for any sun creams which are particularly suitable for the climate. Do not allow children to spend long periods in the sun; keep them shaded, keep them in the cool during the hottest time of day and make them wear a sun hat.

IN CASE OF ILLNESS

Make sure you find out about the medical care and customs of the country you are visiting and always take out suitable health insurance before departure. Find out about health cover within Europe before travelling (ask the travel company, doctor or local health authority). Up-to-date information on foreign travel is available in a leaflet produced by the relevant government department. This is regularly revised and may be found in post offices, chemists or at the doctor's surgery.

At your resort, make sure you know where to go should an emergency arise, then relax.

In case of mild sickness and diarrhoea, make sure the person is kept as cool as possible and drinks plenty of bottled water. The patient should refrain from eating until the attack has subsided, and then avoid eating fruit and salad ingredients. Plain, fresh bread is always excellent sustenance the day after an attack of sickness. If sickness does not subside within twenty-four hours, then contact a local doctor or visit a hospital for help.

A–Z OF SOME COMMON AILMENTS AND CONDITIONS

Abdominal Pains Pain in the abdomen may be the sign of something serious or may be due to a simple stomach upset. If in doubt, call the doctor; never let a bad abdominal pain last for more than six hours without asking for skilled advice. When the doctor comes he will want to know how long the pain has been present, exactly where it is, whether it is continuous, spasmodic, spreading, helped or made worse by anything – for example, vomiting. If there has been vomiting keep a specimen for the doctor to see, and keep specimens of the urine and motions. Note what position is most comfortable for the patient, and whether he is more inclined to move about or to lie still. A hot-water-bottle will often ease the pain.

Abscess An abscess consists of a collection of pus surrounded by a zone of 'granulation tissue'; it is formed when the centre of an area of inflammation has been set up by bacterial infection, and when it is on the surface of the skin the abscess is called a boil. Normally the abscess bursts and the pus escapes – a process which can be helped by the use of a poultice. But a bad infection may have to be treated by antibiotics or even a surgical operation.

Do not squeeze a spot or boil because you will force the pus through the protective wall of granulation tissue and spread the infection.

Acne This is a chronic disease of the sebaceous glands which secrete sebum, the fatty substance which normally lubricates the skin. It usually runs a fluctuating course until the patient is about twenty-five years old, and in girls it tends to be worse before their periods. The most common sort is called acne vulgaris, and affects the sebaceous glands of the face, chest, and back at about the time of puberty. It is a distressing disease and can cause permanent scarring and disfigurement; nobody can tell how a given case is going to progress, therefore all cases should be taken seriously. The disease shows itself by the development of blackheads and pimples and may go on to the formation of cysts under the skin and infection with subsequent scarring.

The treatment is simple but has to be continued for a long time: sulphur ointment is recommended to promote drainage of the affected glands, the strength of the ointment depending on the reaction of the skin. Before the ointment is put on each night, wash the face thoroughly and express the blackheads with a special 'comedo extractor' which can be bought at a chemist's; do not try to squeeze the blackheads with the fingers because this can lead to infection. The process is often made easier by putting a hot flannel on the skin for a minute or two beforehand, or wetting the skin with surgical spirit before using the comedo extractor. The sulphur paste is left on all night, and washed off in the morning.

A great number of preparations are sold for the treatment of acne vulgaris but are only suitable for mild cases. More severe cases need a doctor's advice, for the strength of the sulphur ointment may have to be varied, and there are other types of acne treatment available only on prescription.

Allergy Foreign matter introduced into the body provokes a reaction designed to get rid of it; alteration of this natural defensive reaction is called allergy, a condition invoked to explain a large number of diseases. Essentially, the development of an allergy depends on the presence in the body of an antibody, a substance which reacts with the antigen, the matter to which the body is allergic.

- *Allergy to foods* Common causes of allergy are shellfish, milk and wheat. These may bring on an attack of asthma; weals (urticaria) or eczema may break out on the skin. Certain substances such as penicillin or the derivatives of benzoic acid which are sometimes found in food, may set up an allergic reaction. If the cause of the allergy is not easily detected, foods which cause reactions can be tracked down by implementing an elimination diet under medical supervision. Once a patient finds he is allergic to a certain food he should avoid it and if he suffers an allergic reaction after taking penicillin or any other drug he must inform his doctor, who will enter the fact on his notes to prevent the same thing happening in the future.
- *Skin allergy* The skin reacts to allergic stimulation by developing dermatitis. First it becomes red, then it itches; blisters form and weep; finally the surface becomes scaly and thick. Infection may occur and obscure the basic pattern of the reaction. Substances which may set up dermatitis include house dust, cosmetics, deodorants, cloth and the dressings used on it, perfumes, rubber, nickel, soap powders, enzyme detergents, oil, petrol, dyes, and a long list of chemicals. The identification of the cause of an allergic dermatitis needs close co-operation between the doctor and the patient.
- *Allergy affecting the nose* There are two types. One is hay fever, which occurs in the early part of the summer, while the other occurs all year round. In both, the precipitating factor is dust, either from plants or animals, feathers, mould, and so on; there is a watery discharge from the nose, sneezing, and irritation of the eyes. Treatment depends on the doctor's advice.

Amenorrhoea This means absence of the periods. Menstruation usually starts between the ages of twelve and fourteen, and continues at least until the fortieth birthday. The periods always stop before the sixtieth birthday. The commonest cause of amenorrhoea is pregnancy, but there are a number of others; in any case it is best to ask the doctor for advice if menstruation has not begun by the sixteenth birthday or if the pattern of menstruation alters.

Anaemia This condition is frequently, but usually wrongly, blamed for tiredness, nervousness, and lack of appetite. With anaemia, the number of red blood corpuscles is too low, or the amount of haemoglobin in the blood is too small to supply enough oxygen to the tissues in order to support normal function under stress. The existence of anaemia is therefore determined by simple examination of the blood. There are a number of different types of anaemia for which various treatments are needed, but the commonest type is caused by deficiency of iron, either because the diet is deficient or because there is a loss of blood, for example from a bleeding gastric ulcer or excessive menstrual loss. It is important to consult your doctor in such cases.

Angina A word meaning choking, commonly used to describe a condition (angina pectoris) in which a suffocating pain is felt behind the breastbone, in the root of the neck, and down one or both arms. It is brought on by effort, large meals or exposure to cold, and is caused by the narrowing of the coronary arteries of the heart which interferes with the free supply of blood to the heart muscle. Waste matter produced by exertion of the heart muscle builds up and pain develops which acts as an alarm to stop over-exertion. People who suffer from angina have to live within the limits set by the state of their circulation.

Appendicitis This condition is most common in children and adults under thirty. Pain is at first felt round the navel, but after a few hours usually travels to the right lower part of the abdomen. It is accompanied by diarrhoea, nausea – the patient may vomit once or twice and then constipation. The appetite is lost, the tongue dry. If you suspect appendicitis call the doctor, for the best treatment is surgical operation as soon as a firm diagnosis can be made.

Arthritis Over 80% of people between the ages of fifty-five to sixty have changes characteristic of osteo-arthritis present in their joints, and about one-fifth of them have symptoms. Pain in the affected joints varies from time to time, but does not seem to be related to the degree of stiffness. Treatment includes measures to reduce the weight in cases where it is necessary, and encouragement of movement and active exercise. It is best to try to reduce the load falling on the affected hip and leg joints by using a stick on the opposite side.

Aspirin is the drug most commonly found to relieve pain. Unfortunately aspirin may cause irritation of the stomach and even bleeding, while some people are sensitive to the drug, so that it must be used with caution. Paracetamol and Ibuprofen are safe, alternative analgesics that can be bought over the counter.

Athlete's Foot This is a fungal infection of the webs of skin between the toes, usually the fourth and fifth and to a lesser extent the third and fourth. The skin becomes soggy and irritated. Treatment is by application of ointment: Whitfield's or zinc undecenoate. When the infection has died down, the feet must be kept clean and dry. A dusting powder is useful and cotton socks which can be changed once or twice a day are recommended in bad cases.

This very common disease is picked up from the floors of showers, swimming-baths, and other places where people walk about with bare feet.

Backache This is a common symptom of many conditions ranging from arthritis of the spine to pelvic disease in women. Most backaches are simply caused by muscular strains, and they will respond to rest, heat, and local massage with or without liniment; if the pain persists, however, a doctor's advice is necessary. (See also *Lumbago*.)

Blood Pressure As the heart beats, pressure in the arteries rises and falls. When the heart contracts the pressure is highest; it falls as the heart muscle relaxes. The point of highest pressure is called the systolic pressure, the lowest point the diastolic pressure. Actual figures vary from person to person, and increase with age, but there are limits beyond which the pressure can be said to be too high or too low. High blood pressures are dangerous, for they can lead to heart disease, failure of the kidneys, loss of vision, and strokes. In its early stages a high blood pressure produces little in the way of symptoms, and although it is often thought to be responsible for headaches, dizziness, fatigue, and other troubles, doctors most often detect a high blood pressure on routine examination of patients who complain of none of these things. An increasing number of drugs are used in the treatment of high blood pressure, and one thing they have in common is the need for routine regular use. You may not feel very different when your doctor starts you on treatment to lower your blood pressure, and you may wonder if there is any point in taking pills day after day; but remember that the treatment is meant to prevent serious complications rather than alter your present state of health. Keeping your weight down can often reduce a blood pressure on the high side to within normal limits.

Boils Boils are small abscesses in the skin (see page 156).

Breasts The breast is the site of a number of diseases but the most important is cancer, and any lump in the breast always raises the question of malignant growth. A potentially dangerous lump is hard, relatively immovable, and is usually in the upper part of the breast nearest the armpit. Women should check their breasts for lumps every month, about a week after menstruation. While it is true that the vast majority of lumps in the breast are simple and not cancerous, show any lump to the doctor as soon as possible.

Bronchitis This often follows a winter cold in the middle aged and elderly, and shows itself by pain in the chest, shortness of breath, cough, and a fever. Antibiotics are the usual treatment. Smoking is forbidden and should not be allowed near the sick-room, where the air must be clean and at as even a temperature as possible. There is a form of bronchitis affecting children, usually in the winter, which may progress so rapidly that a child with a mild cough in the morning can, by the end of the day, be fighting for breath. Call the doctor at once if a child has the slightest difficulty in breathing.

Bruise This is damage to the tissues by direct violence that does not break the skin but crushes the underlying fat and muscle. The blood which escapes from the small damaged vessels first colours the area red, then as the pigment breaks down the bruise turns blue and finally yellow. The pain can be helped by cold compresses. If the swelling does not go down soon, see the doctor.

Chicken-pox This is a disease of childhood caused by a virus infection. The incubation period is fourteen to twenty-one days, and the patient feels ill a day or two before the spots develop. They start as small red dots on the part of the body covered by a vest, and as the rash develops outwards to the limbs the small red bumps become blisters which eventually scab over. The patient is best kept in bed as long as he feels ill; aspirin will help the headache and calamine lotion the rash, which must be kept clean to prevent infection and subsequent scarring. The period of infectivity lasts for a week after the appearance of the rash, but the disease is very rarely severe and strict quarantine is not needed. Children are usually ready to go back to school about two weeks after the beginning of the disease. The same virus that causes chicken-pox in children causes herpes zoster (see page 166) in adults, commonly known as shingles, but the relationship between the two diseases is not quite straightforward, for while a patient with herpes can pass chicken-pox to a child, herpes does not follow exposure to chicken-pox.

Chilblains These are red itchy swellings on the fingers or toes, nose or ears, which develop in cold weather. If you are susceptible, wear gloves, thick boots, and thick stockings or tights, and do not heat the fingers and toes up too quickly by plunging them into hot water, for example, when you come in out of the cold.

Pay attention to general foot care, massaging foot cream in and around the toes every day after bathing and thoroughly drying the feet. Use a medicated cream intended to promote good circulation. Keeping the feet warm and exercising are helpful preventatives.

Apply a chilblain cream (available from chemists' shops) at the first sign of redness and itching; broken chilblains or infected feet should be examined by a doctor.

Common Cold This is a disease caused by a virus. In itself more of a nuisance than a danger, it is often complicated by bacterial infection of the sinuses, ears, windpipe and lungs which can turn it into a more serious disease. It is, therefore, sensible to stay at home for a couple of days when you catch a cold, for by staying in the warm in a fairly controlled atmosphere you have a good chance of avoiding extra infection – and you will not spread the cold to other people.

Concussion This is injury to the brain caused by a blow on the head which results in a loss or diminution of consciousness. The patient will usually recover within twenty-four hours. The state is not properly understood but, from a practical point of view, it is important that everyone who suffers a blow on the head grave enough to make him unconscious should be seen by the doctor. No lasting damage follows simple concussion, although the patient often cannot remember exactly how the accident happened. Any persisting headache or pain should be reported to the doctor.

Conjunctivitis Also called pink-eye, this is an inflammation of the conjunctiva, the membrane covering the front of the eye, usually due to infection by microorganisms but sometimes caused by mechanical irritation, e.g. an eyelash growing inwards. If there is no obvious cause of irritation, the eye should be bathed with a bland solution such as sodium chloride eye lotion. If the redness persists, ask the doctor for advice.

Constipation A condition in which the motions are infrequent, hard and difficult to pass, constipation usually relates to diet, or changes in diet, lifestyle and stress. Suggested methods of cure are increased physical activity and the consumption of foods with a high fibre content such as raw vegetables and fruits, whole grain products, and bran. Drinking liquids aids the effect of fibre. A person with persistent constipation should see a doctor.

Diabetes This is a disorder related to insulin, a hormone released by the pancreas. Insulin plays a vital function in promoting the absorption of sugar from the blood for use in the body and, without sufficient supplies, the body is unable to change the digested carbohydrates (present in the blood as sugars, referred to as the blood sugar level) into energy.

There are two types of diabetes: the first is referred to as insulin dependent diabetes (type I), the second is non-insulin dependent diabetes (type II).

Type I is also known as juvenile diabetes because it is found in children and teenagers. In this case, the pancreas produces little or no insulin, therefore the body is dependent on receiving controlled and regular doses of the hormone.

Type II diabetes develops in later life, from middle age onwards. It is more common than type I and is caused by reduced hormone production. Insulin is not given for this type of diabetes; however, medication is prescribed to assist in the control of blood sugar levels.

Frequent, severe thirst and a dry mouth, the passing of large amounts of urine, weight loss, tiredness, itching in genital regions and blurred vision can be symptoms of diabetes. The severity varies considerably and, in type II, the symptoms may go unnoticed for some months (if not longer) in adults. Type I diabetes develops fairly quickly, usually over a period of weeks or even days. This results in drastic symptoms, including vomiting, dehydration, drowsiness and diabetic coma, in addition to the above list.

Once the disorder has been diagnosed and the sufferer's condition stabilized, life-long treatment and monitoring is necessary; however, the person can lead a normal, active and healthy life. Diet is vital in the control of both types, with more rigid restrictions applied to type I or severe diabetes.

Diarrhoea This is a state in which the motions become more fluid and frequent than normal. It may be due to an infection of the bowel related to illness, or to food poisoning. It may also result, although in a milder form, from sudden and severe changes in diet or from eating unusual foods which disrupt the digestive system. In some cases, usually comparatively mild, it may be related to stress or anxiety.

For the majority of adults, where the condition can usually be explained by diet or other causes as above, the treatment is fairly straightforward. The modern approach is to let the condition run its course when mild. However, there are many products for controlling the condition, some mild and others which are more potent for speedy relief. Kaolin or kaolin and morphine is available in liquid or tablet form and should be kept in the first-aid kit as a means of easing diarrhoea. At the same time, the person should avoid eating and drink plenty of water.

When the condition is accompanied by vomiting, particular attention must be paid to the likelihood of dehydration and a little salt should be taken in water. Proprietary rehydrating compounds are available from chemists and flavoured varieties are suitable for children, both during and after an attack. If the condition does not ease within one or two days then the doctor should be consulted.

When infants or young children suffer from diarrhoea, more attention must be paid to the condition as young children can quickly become dehydrated. Unexplained diarrhoea in babies or toddlers should be brought to the attention of the doctor, particularly when combined with sickness or loss of appetite. Children must be encouraged to drink plenty of water after an attack.

Earache Earache should be attended to by the doctor, especially in the case of children. Exceptions to this rule are when the pain is caused by pressure changes, for example as when taking off or landing in an aircraft or when driving up or down a steep mountain road; this can be eased by yawning or sucking a sweet.

If someone has a foreign body in the ear, then they should be taken to hospital for its removal. The ear is easily damaged and you should never poke anything in beyond the outer lobe. If an insect flies into the ear, this may be washed out; if it does not float out easily, consult the doctor or hospital.

Mild earache caused by very cold weather or draught usually subsides with warmth. Do not pour anything into the ear; resting the head on a warm pillow or cushion usually helps.

Flatulence This is caused by the gas resulting from digestion and can sometimes be extremely painful. It may be brought on by eating certain types of foods, for example beans and pulses, by overeating or by sudden changes in diet. If someone frequently suffers from flatulence, then the diet should be examined first and thought given to the variety of foods eaten, the cooking methods and overall selection of ingredients. The flatulence may result from eating too much of one type of food, which is not good for providing a broad range of nutrients. Smaller amounts, longer cooking and more variety sometimes solve the problem.

If the flatulence is related to other digestive disorders and problems, with no apparent dietary cause, then the doctor ought to be consulted.

Food Poisoning The symptoms of this begin between four and forty-eight hours after ingestion, and include stomach cramps, vomiting, diarrhoea, chills, headache, and fever. The patient should get plenty of bed rest and refrain from eating until the vomiting stops. Water should be taken, if possible, to prevent dehydration. A doctor should be consulted to watch for dehydration and to monitor the illness. The symptoms should disappear in one to five days.

German Measles Otherwise called rubella, this is a virus infection with an incubation period of two or three weeks, infective until the acute phase is over. It begins with a running nose, headache, and enlargement and tenderness of the glands behind the ears. A rash of small pink spots develops in a day or two over the face and trunk; the spots run together and fade in about two days, leaving a slight peeling of the skin.

The disease is virtually harmless to children, but if a woman in the first four months of pregnancy comes into contact with a case, she should consult her doctor because it can have an effect on the baby she carries. As one attack confers immunity it is sensible to try and make sure that all girls catch the disease in childhood. Women who have not had the disease can be given a vaccine when they are of childbearing age, but once pregnancy has started the vaccine is dangerous.

Growing Pains It used to be thought that pains in the limbs were normal while a child was growing, but the truth is that growth does not cause pain and such pains are never normal. A doctor should be consulted.

Gumboil This is an abscess (see page 156) at the root of a decayed tooth which produces swelling of the gum and the skin around it. The local application of heat, hot salt water gargles and a visit to the dentist are recommended. Antibiotics may be required to clear the infection.

Haemorrhoids These are small enlarged or varicose veins near the anus, otherwise called piles. They vary from mild to quite serious, and usually start to show themselves by irritation. The best treatment is to wash the area three or four times a day with cold water and cotton wool and to avoid standing for long periods. If there is pain or bleeding, it is much better to ask the doctor for advice than rely on proprietary remedies, for very occasionally haemorrhoids are the sign of an underlying disorder. In severe and very painful cases, the haemorrhoids may need surgery.

Hay Fever See *Allergy.*

Headache This may be caused by disease, worry, over-indulgence in smoking or alcohol – but 90% of headaches have no obvious cause. If rest and a proprietary medicine from the chemist do not relieve a headache, and particularly if it recurs, see the doctor. (See also *Migraine*.)

Heart Disease The symptoms of heart disease do not bear a direct relationship to the anatomical position of the heart, and pain over the heart on the left-hand side of the chest is more often due to indigestion than heart disease. The pain of angina (see page 158) or coronary thrombosis is usually felt in the centre of the chest, in the root of the neck, or down the arm. Palpitations tend to be a sign of anxiety and tension, and in general it is found that patients who are certain there is something wrong with their heart are wrong, and it is those who do not suspect it who have heart disease. Symptoms of importance include breathlessness, swelling of the ankles, tiredness, headaches, and giddiness. The patient with heart disease has to live within limits set by the onset of such symptoms. The doctor should provide clear guidelines and the patient should check on his or her personal condition in relation to everyday activity.

Hernia This is a rupture. Although the term strictly means protrusion of any organ from the compartment of the body in which it is normally contained, it is commonly used to mean the protrusion of part of the intestine from the abdominal cavity at the site of a weakness in the muscular walls of the abdomen, particularly at the groin. Do not wear a truss to try to control a hernia without taking advice from the doctor. If you suffer from a hernia, and it will not go back or becomes painful, go to the doctor at once.

Herpes *Herpes simplex* is the name given to the blisters or cold sores that form at the corners of the mouth or on the face. The treatment is to keep the area dry and clean, and to apply cold sore lotion, available from the chemist, at first signs of a blister.

Herpes zoster, or shingles, is a virus infection related to chicken-pox in which painful blisters form along the course of a sensory nerve in the skin, most often running round the chest wall. The blisters must be protected, and the best way to do this is to paint them with flexible collodion (a liquid mixture of ether, alcohol, pyroxylin, and caster oil). This also reduces the pain.

Hiccoughs These are usually irritating rather than worrying in a medical sense. They are the result of a sharp air movement in the diaphragm, resulting in a click from the vocal chords. Usually a symptom of poor digestion (including hurried eating) or anxiety, there is no need to bring the condition to the attention of the doctor unless it has lasted for several days.

Suggested cures include holding the breath for the count to ten, having a drink of water, breathing through the mouth into a paper bag several times, keeping the bag tight around the lips, drinking peppermint tea, eating a slice of lemon and holding the nose and mouth closed for a minute (but no longer).

Influenza This is an acute infectious disease caused by a virus. It starts with a high temperature, shivering, headache, a dry cough, and aching in the bones and muscles. It lasts for about a week but is often complicated by bronchitis or pneumonia, especially in the elderly, and then the illness may take much longer to disappear. People often become depressed after influenza, and the feeling of tiredness and lassitude may last up to three weeks. For injections, see *Immunization* (page 153 –4). No specific treatment for influenza is known, and the symptoms must be treated as they arise. Aspirin is the most generally useful drug.

Ingrowing Toe Nail As it grows towards the end of the toe, the great toe nail sometimes catches in one of the folds of skin at each side and sets up an inflammation. The skin folds may become infected, and the toe is often painful. The nailfold has to be kept away from the edge of the nail until the nail has grown out to its proper length, and then the nail should be cut straight across the end to prevent the same thing happening again. Make sure that shoes are not too narrow, as they can pinch the skin folds inwards. Seek medical advice if infection occurs.

Insomnia This means inability to sleep. The cause is generally undue anxiety, and it is easy to set up a vicious circle in which the patient worries about not going to sleep and is consequently unable to do so. On the whole, it is true that people sleep as much as they need, and that many complaints about 'not being able to sleep a wink' relate to an hour or so at the beginning of the night, after which sleep is normal, or to an hour awake in the small hours – when everything assumes the worst possible aspect. If you suffer from insomnia, remember that worry is the chief cause, and that while sleeping tablets can help to regain the habit of sleep, indifference to loss of sleep is the best way of ensuring that it does not occur.

Irritable Bowel Syndrome This is a common cause of symptoms referable to the large bowel – discomfort in the abdomen, bloating, diarrhoea or constipation, and the passage of thin or hard, round stools, or even mucus. The condition is not dangerous, and is often found in younger people subject to anxiety or emotional disturbance. Treatment is usually designed to relieve the psychological trouble, but the response may not be immediate. In certain cases anti-spasmodic drugs may be prescribed. It is essential to stop smoking and to be very moderate in the use of alcohol, for both these habits exacerbate the disease.

Lumbago This is a term commonly used to mean a pain in the lower part of the back for which no obvious cause can be found. It is often due to trouble in the muscles at each side of the spinal column, and may come on during an attack of influenza or after uncommon exercise or strain. The treatment is rest on a hard bed; local heat may help, and aspirin is well worth trying.

Measles This is a virus infection usually affecting children and occurring in epidemics. The incubation period is about fourteen days, and the disease starts with a running nose, red eyes, and a cough. There is headache and fever, and on about the fourth day a rash of small red spots breaks out on the skin behind the ears and on the face. Before this, white spots may be seen inside the mouth. The spots join up and spread all over the body; after about three days they fade to leave a brownish stain. During an attack of measles the lungs, ears, and eyes are all liable to become infected with bacteria which have nothing to do with the measles virus. The secondary infection may be damaging unless it is treated, usually with antibiotics. While a child is in the acute stages of measles, he has to be kept quiet in bed and is best given a light diet with plenty to drink. Other children should be kept away. Immunization against measles is possible, and is carried out in the second year of life. Ask your doctor for his advice.

Meningitis This is an inflammation of the membranes covering the brain. A severe and dangerous disease, it starts with a bad headache, confusion, vomiting, a stiff neck, and dislike of light in the eyes. There may be a skin rash that doesn't fade when pressed with a cool glass. Medical treatment has to be quick if it is to succeed; if you have any suspicion that the disease is present, call the doctor at once.

Menopause This is a term to describe the cessation of the monthly periods, which normally happens any time between forty and fifty-five. Many women are frightened of the 'change of life', but trouble need not necessarily arise. If you are worried, go and talk to your doctor. You can be sure that the disturbances, which include hot flushes, insomnia, joint pains, increase in weight, and general irritability, will pass. In a number of cases the emotional upset is made worse by domestic strain or by loneliness. Many women find it easier to cope with symptoms of menopause by paying more, or renewed, attention to their personal life, level of activity and social interests or hobbies. Although hot flushes are unpleasant they go unnoticed by other people, and there is no reason to worry about how you look in company. As for sexual activity, the menopause need make no difference except, obviously, that there is no longer the possibility of pregnancy. Hormone replacement therapy is now available to ease the symptoms. It can be a very successful treatment for some women.

Migraine Sometimes used to describe a severe headache, the term strictly means a particular sort of headache which starts with disturbances of vision, sensation or speech, is felt on one side of the head, and is accompanied by nausea or even vomiting. Migraine may run in families, and the frequency of attacks varies. The patient is best put to bed in a darkened room; there are a number of drugs which can be prescribed, but the doctor will treat each case individually. There is no one specific remedy. Attacks are often precipitated by known factors such as flashing lights, anxiety or certain kinds of food, e.g. chocolate or cheese. Some sufferers find that red wine and sherry are best avoided.

Mumps This is an acute infective illness, usually of childhood, caused by a virus. The incubation period is between fourteen and twenty-one days, and the disease starts as a swelling in front of, and below the ears. In children mumps is virtually harmless except in rare cases, but in adults it may progress to involve the sex glands and may prove a fairly serious matter if the testicles or ovaries are infected. It is, therefore, important that no attempt should be made to prevent children, particularly boys, from catching mumps. All patients should be kept quiet while the disease is active, but there is no known specific treatment. The swelling over the angle of the jaw is usually uncomfortable rather than painful; there is a fever but it is mild, and the disease lasts between one and three weeks.

Nappy Rash In some cases the urine of infants is broken down by bacteria into irritating ammoniacal compounds which redden the skin under the nappy and make it sore. Frequent changing of the nappies which if not disposable should be thoroughly rinsed and boiled to ensure sterilization, and the use of zinc compound paste on the skin is recommended. The infant should be left without a nappy whenever possible, to allow air to circulate around the affected area, and plastic pants should be avoided.

If the rash persists, consult the doctor as it may be due to a fungal infection and need a special cream.

Palpitations Sometimes the usually imperceptible action of the heart is felt or heard, especially when the heart is under stress or when all is quiet, as in the night. The heart beats more strongly under the stimulus of strong emotion, and the vast majority of cases in which the patient complains of palpitations are found to be examples of anxiety; only very rarely do they mean that there is anything wrong with the heart.

Phlebitis This is inflammation of a vein, usually associated with varicose veins (see page 173). There is pain and local tenderness, with redness and perhaps swelling over the affected vein. It is treated by support with an elastic stocking or bandage, and while there is no need for the patient to rest more than normal (indeed, movement will help to maintain circulation), the leg is less painful if it is kept up when he or she sits down.

Piles See *Haemorrhoids*.

Pink Eye See *Conjunctivitis*.

Pneumonia This is inflammation of the substance of the lung. The disease may mainly involve the lobes of the lung, when it is called lobar pneumonia and is usually caused by the pneumococcus; or it may spread from the wind passages in the lungs when it is called bronchopneumonia and occurs during an attack of bronchitis, influenza or other infection of the respiratory system. Often the first symptoms of pneumonia do not suggest trouble in the lungs; the patient may complain of violent headache and feel very ill indeed without having any cough or pain the chest, making it difficult to diagnose the disease in its early stages. Pneumonia is a disease which responds well to antibiotics and can, therefore, be treated at home with success. The patient should be kept in a room at an even temperature, not too hot, well-ventilated but free from draughts. He must be encouraged to drink fluids freely, although his appetite will be poor and he will not want to take more than a very light diet.

Pregnancy The first sign of pregnancy is usually the cessation of menstruation. Other indications include swelling and tingling of the breasts, sensitive nipples, frequent urination, and tiredness. Two-thirds of pregnant women suffer 'morning sickness', i.e. a mild nausea upon rising, between the third and sixth weeks.

The average duration of pregnancy in the human being is 274 to 280 days. Although the vast majority of pregnancies are quite normal and free of trouble, it is important to consult the family doctor as soon as you think you might be pregnant, so that he can make sure that everything is as it should be and arrange for a bed to be booked at the hospital for your delivery. Regular visits to the ante-natal clinic will enable him to keep in touch with your progress.

Pulse Rate As the heart beats the arteries expand and contract. The change in volume and pressure can be felt particularly in the radial artery that runs across the bones of the wrist at the base of the thumb, and is called the pulse. The normal pulse rate is between about seventy and eighty beats a minute at rest.

Rash This is a temporary eruption on the skin which occurs very often as part of an infectious fever. Common rashes are measles, in which small raised spots start behind the ears, on the forehead, and the face, and spread over the whole body, running together to form large patches (see page 167); chicken-pox, where the rash starts on the trunk and spreads to the limbs (see page 160), unlike the rash of small-pox which starts on the face, hands, and feet and spreads inwards to the trunk; German measles (rubella) where small red spots start on the face and spread to the trunk, but do not run together (see page 164); scarlet fever (scarlatina) where the rash is irregular and consists of red patches especially at the groin, armpits, and elbows; and nettlerash (urticaria) with red patches and raised weals on the skin.

Respiration The rate of breathing is normally about eighteen to twenty breaths a minute at rest. It is raised in fevers and maladies of the lungs.

Ringworm This is a fungal infection of the skin. The infection spreads outwards from the centre so that the active edge is at the periphery of a circle; this gives the condition its name. It is found in the scalp, where it makes the hair brittle, and elsewhere on the body. It occurs in cattle and domestic animals, especially cats, and may be caught from them. The treatment is local application of suitable ointment or dusting powder. The patient must use his own separate washing things, comb, and towel to avoid spreading the infection.

Shingles See *Herpes*.

Sinusitis The bones of the face contain air spaces above and below the eyes which are called sinuses. They connect with the inside of the nose, so that infections, such as a cold, which involve the nose, can lead to infection of the sinuses.

The symptoms of sinusitis are pain above or below the eyes, headache, a blocked or running nose, and a slight fever. In mild cases rest, inhalations of plain or medicated steam, and the sniffing of a solution of 1 x 5 ml spoon salt in 600 ml water will resolve the inflammation, but in severe or chronic cases the doctor's advice will be necessary.

Sleep See *Insomnia*.

Slipped Disc Between the vertebral bones of the spine are flat circular pads of gristle which let the bones move to a certain extent upon each other and act as shock absorbers. Occasionally, part of one of these pads protrudes from its proper place as a result of injury or disease, and presses on a nerve root as it passes outwards from the spinal cord. The protrusion is usually in the lower part of the spine and the 'slipped disc' presses on one of the roots of the sciatic nerve to cause sciatica. Treatment in mild cases is rest on a hard bed; graduated exercises to strengthen the muscles of the spine are useful. In more severe cases treatment may involve surgical operation.

Sprain This is an injury to a joint in which the ligaments are damaged. The joint is stiff, swollen, and painful, but will recover with rest, cold compresses, and a supporting bandage. Severe sprains should be seen by the doctor, because damage to the ligaments is sometimes accompanied by damage to the bones of the joint.

Squint Usually a new-born baby has a squint, but it should have gone by the sixth month. If it persists, expert advice is needed because the earlier treatment starts, the more likely it is to be successful.

Stammer This is a defect of speech in which there is hesitation in the free flow of words, resulting from lack of co-ordination related to control of the muscles of the voice-box. If it is present in early life it is usually due to physical causes, while its development later is likely to be due to psychological reasons. Treatment is by speech therapy and training in breath control, accompanied by a search for complicating psychological factors.

Stroke If a blood vessel in the brain is blocked by a clot, or bleeds through a part of its wall weakened by disease into the substance of the brain, the patient becomes weak or paralysed in an arm or leg or one side of the face, and in severe cases lapses into unconsciousness. If the damage is to the right side of the brain, the left side of the body is affected, and if it is on the left, the right side of the body is weakened, and in right-handed people the power of speech is upset. The patient may lose vision on one side, and be unable to read because writing has no meaning for him. Similarly, he may be unable to write, or to understand what is said to him.

The immediate treatment in a severe case is to make sure that the patient can breathe easily. Pull the tongue forward and turn him half on his front so that he cannot inhale vomit. Keep him warm and call the doctor. In less severe cases, when the patient is conscious or partly conscious, get him into bed; watch his progress carefully until the doctor comes, because he may slowly become unconscious. Home nursing after a stroke is difficult, hard work. Dangers are bedsores and pneumonia; if the limbs are allowed to become stiff, recovery is impossible, and the paralysed parts must be moved through a full range of movement at least four times a day. Both patient and attendants need great courage during convalescence from a stroke, for it is easy to become demoralized and depressed.

Sunburn If the skin is exposed to strong sunlight it develops a brown pigmentation but, before enough pigment is formed to protect it from the sun, there is a risk of burning from short-wave ultra-violet radiation. The burnt skin becomes red and swollen and on the second day blisters form which are followed by scaling. The patient may feel quite ill, run a temperature, and have a bad headache. Remember that you cannot tell how badly your skin is being burnt – it does not hurt while it is happening – so do not expose your skin to the direct rays of a strong sun for more than thirty minutes on the first day. If there is no reaction, increase the period day by day, but if you get burnt do not, obviously, expose your skin again until the burn is healed. Always use a suitable suntan cream to prevent burning. Children and fair-skinned people should use a sun block cream to cut out the harmful rays.

Teething Milk teeth, which are later replaced by the permanent teeth, begin to develop in the sixth month of life and should be completely erupted by the end of the second year. Although 'teething' in babies is commonly held to be responsible for a large number of troubles ranging from diarrhoea to skin rashes, eruption of the teeth rarely causes anything but local irritation of the gums and dribbling.

Tonsillitis This is an inflammation of the tonsils – two small masses of tissue that lie on each side of the throat. Their function is to filter off germs which might enter the wind passages and set up infection, so it is not surprising that they themselves are sometimes infected. When this happens they swell up and become painful; the patient has a sore throat, fever, a headache, and the lymph glands associated with the tonsils (which lie just behind the angle of the jaw) are enlarged. Treatment should be quick, for scarlet fever or kidney damage may follow infection of the tonsils; a sore throat should never be neglected.

Removal of the tonsils is only advised when there have been repeated attacks of tonsillitis, and enlargement has led to complications such as choking or difficulty in swallowing. Such cases are rarely found.

Varicose Veins The veins which run superficially in the legs are, in the course of time, liable to become distended and painful, and are then called varicose. The condition is present in one out of two women, and one in four men after the age of forty. In severe cases there is pain and a heavy feeling in the legs (made worse by standing), swelling of the ankles, and skin trouble, usually above the ankle. Mild cases are helped a great deal by putting the legs up when possible, but more severe cases may need a surgical operation. Elastic stockings can be worn to give support, but where ulcers form in the lower part of the leg the skilled application of special dressings and bandages may be necessary.

Warts Otherwise called verrucae, warts are very common, small, moderately hard outgrowths on the skin, usually on the hands or the soles of the feet. They are thought to be caused by virus infection picked up in schools, swimming-baths, and other public places. They can be treated by the application of carbon dioxide snow (dry ice) or other mild caustics such as glacial acetic acid or silver nitrate; but they often disappear spontaneously.

Whooping Cough This disease is less widespread than it used to be, for it has been partly controlled by the immunization of children. It is very infectious, the incubation period being seven to fourteen days. Children cough as if they had an ordinary cold, but the coughing grows more severe and spasmodic until at the end of an attack the child draws breath with the characteristic whoop. This is first heard about ten days after the beginning of the illness. Complications such as bronchitis or pneumonia, or infection of the ear are prevented by antibiotics. Some doctors question the wisdom on immunizing all children against whooping cough, for there appear to have been a few tragic complications of the immunizing process. Nevertheless, it is a difficult matter to judge, and each mother should discuss the matter with her family doctor.

Worms The most common sorts of worms to inhabit the human body are threadworms and roundworms. Flat worms are also found, e.g. the tapeworm. If worms are seen in motions, visit the doctor. Signs of infestation with worms are itching and redness round the anus, loss of general health and colour, anaemia, and loss of weight. Threadworms, which come out to lay eggs at night, may cause bed-wetting.

Wounds Whether the wound is an abrasion, cut or laceration, make sure that it is cleaned by washing it well, in running water if possible, and then put a clean dressing on it. If bleeding is troublesome, stop it by direct pressure on the dressing; when it has stopped, change the dressing. If the wound is large or needs stitching, do not put any disinfectant or ointment on it before the doctor sees it. Antiseptics are best avoided even in small wounds if they can be washed clean, and dressings should be light and only just thick enough to exclude dirt. There are a number of good dressings sold in sterile packages; they must not be bound on with heavy bandages, but kept in place with the minimum of sticking plaster. If dressings stick, soak them off in water.

Take any infection seriously, particularly the formation of yellow pus or redness round the wound, and ask for skilled advice; wounds caused by animal bites are particularly liable to infection and should always be shown to the doctor. All puncture wounds made with thin knives or instruments in the region of the chest or abdomen must also be shown to the doctor, for it is impossible to tell how far they have gone in by looking at the entry wound.

BABIES AND CHILDREN

The relationship with the family doctor, or general practitioner, is most important once you have children.

PREGNANCY AND POST-NATAL CARE

It is important to visit the doctor as early as possible in pregnancy for many reasons, including the founding of a good patient/doctor relationship. Most mothers-to-be have the option of either attending a local hospital for all regular checks or of 'shared-care', which means visiting their doctor for most check-ups, with periodic visits to the hospital for various tests, scans, and so on.

Getting to know your local surgery or clinic early in the pregnancy is important, as it gives you an opportunity to find out how well you get on with the doctor and his back-up team. You can also assess the level of support the surgery offers in addition to their medical commitment. At this stage you may decide to change doctors if there is a choice, but leaving this until late in the pregnancy or until the baby is born is not a good idea.

Hospitals are more anonymous than your doctor and you may not see the same person on every visit, so continuity and encouragement can be lacking.

Ante-natal Information Doctors and/or hospitals organize classes to provide practical information and moral support for both parents and it is important to take full advantage of all the information available.

Post-natal Information This is where a good relationship with the doctor is a real plus. The doctor, community midwives and health visitor provide invaluable support during the first months of parenthood. When you may have frequent doubts about your own judgement as to the health care of a young baby, knowing your doctor personally is especially helpful – not only is it easier for you to relate to the doctor, but he or she will be able to relate to you.

On a formal basis, reminders about health and progress checks and immunization information are sent by the health authorities.

CHILDREN

Once infants are old enough to tell you when they feel ill and what is wrong, they are less of a worry health-wise. Young children can deteriorate rapidly from being bright and breezy to being quite ill and it is important to seek your doctor's advice when in doubt. If a child is feverish, disinterested and obviously poorly, then you should not hesitate to call the doctor.

Children are prone to accidents and they may occasionally need urgent medical attention. Depending on where you live, visiting the casualty department of the local hospital may be quicker than going to the doctor when the problem is a bad cut or fall, particularly at weekends.

Older children and teenagers can develop a different set of problems, often linked with an awkward stage in their development. Although minor health problems, such as cold symptoms, are of less concern at this stage, problems related to menstruation and social difficulties often require medical back-up.

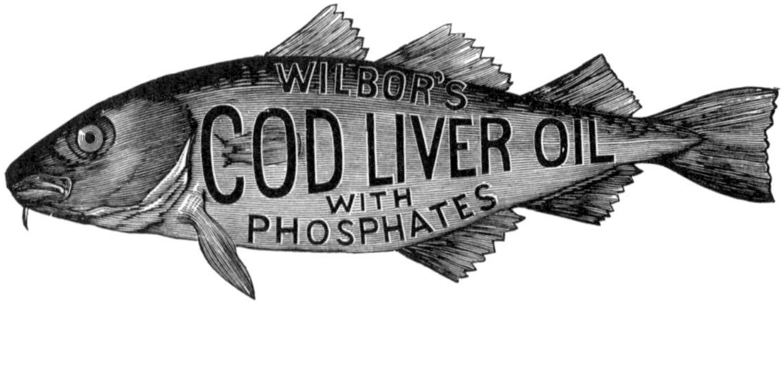

Cleaning

A chapter of useful reminders and guidelines for easing household chores, with organization being the key to efficiency.

Cleanliness has always been considered indispensable to health and therefore it must still 'be studied both in regard to the person and the house, and all it contains'. Having a clean home is as important for hygiene and safety as it is for comfort and appearance.

Everyone in the household who is fit to do so should play their part in keeping the home clean and tidy. Establish a routine for all cleaning, from simple tasks like washing-up to major jobs like cleaning carpets or curtains. The easiest way of organizing the cleaning is to make sure that some jobs are automatically dealt with on a daily basis and other tasks are attended to every week. The extent of housework depends on individual homes, the type of furnishings and so on. However, it is vital that basic standards of tidiness and cleanliness are observed; an untidy home is difficult to keep clean, so the two are closely linked.

Dirty and dusty chores should be finished first. For example, clean a fireplace or shake out the bed before dusting. Clean the floor last, unless it involves vigorous brushing which will cause dust to rise. Rugs should be taken outside to be shaken, if possible. A carpet beater should be used to beat the dust out of a rug or mat, or it may be beaten against a clean area of wall.

When washing a floor, always work methodically so that you finish at the door of the room, then leave the floor to dry before walking on it.

DAILY CLEANING

Daily cleaning, concentrating on essential hygiene and tidiness, should be largely automatic. Getting into the habit of doing a certain amount of basic tidying in every room, every day, is very important to avoid a major clearing-up session and to ensure that the home is a pleasant place to be in.

KITCHEN

Washing-up should be completed after every meal and the sink area should be rinsed and wiped after use. Work surfaces should be cleaned immediately after use, wipe up crumbs and quickly clean with a suitable agent and hot water. The hob should be wiped clean after every major cooking session. Any spills should be cleaned up immediately.

The dishwasher should be stacked promptly after meals and the contents put through a rinse setting if the machine is not put through a full programme immediately. Dishes, cutlery and equipment should always be put away promptly after washing and drying has been completed.

Blinds or curtains should be drawn back neatly every morning and, except in extreme weather conditions, the window should be opened daily or a ventilator used to change the air. The bin should be emptied, rinsed and lined.

BATHROOM AND TOILET AREAS

Washing and toilet areas should be checked after use every morning. Towels should be folded or, if wet, opened out to dry. Curtains or blinds should be drawn back and the window should be opened.

The bath or shower should be rinsed after every use and the wash basin should be cleaned frequently. Keep a suitable, mild cleaner and disposable cloth in the bathroom for this purpose. Tooth mugs should be washed every day. Bleach or a suitable cleaning and disinfecting agent should be used in the lavatory pan on a few occasions each week.

BEDROOMS

Fold back sheet and blankets or duvet first thing in the morning. The coverings and pillows should be given a good shake, the bottom sheet straightened and the bed left to air for a while before it is made. The daily habit of opening, shaking and neatly folding back bedclothes is most important – even if the bed is not made later it will be well-aired and fresh.

Curtains and blinds should be drawn back. Clothes should be put away or put in the laundry basket. The room should be tidied and the window opened.

LOUNGE AND LIVING AREAS

Curtains should be drawn back. Shake and plump up cushions, neaten sofas and chairs and tidy away newspapers and so on. If the rooms have open fires, the ashes should be removed and grate cleaned.

WEEKLY

These are the tasks that keep the house clean throughout and, depending on your lifestyle, some of these jobs may have to be done more often than once a week. Carpets should be vacuumed frequently to keep them in good condition and, in a busy family home, living areas may well need vacuuming daily.

KITCHEN

Check oven and clean as necessary; clean the hob thoroughly, removing washable parts. Clean all surfaces and splashbacks and ensure the kitchen area is tidy. Check the refrigerator and wipe the area near the door. Clean other food storage areas, such as the bread bin.

Brush and wash the floor, or clean as appropriate to the material. Wash the indoor bin, check the outdoor bin and wash with disinfectant as necessary (more frequently in summer than winter).

BATHROOM AND TOILET

Thoroughly clean the toilet, bidet, wash basin, shower, bath and all accessories, such as toothbrush holders. Clean windowsills, mirrors and floor.

BEDROOMS

Change bed linen – sheets, pillow cases and duvet cover, if used. Brush or mop the edges of the floor and vacuum. Dust and polish.

REST OF THE HOME

Dust and polish throughout. Clean all floors by brushing and washing or vacuum-cleaning. Floor edges, corners, cupboard floors and stairs should be cleaned with a pipe attachment or by using a stiff handbrush. Dust surrounding woodwork.

REGULARLY

Work through these chores on a rota system so that they are attended to regularly: defrost (if appropriate) and clean refrigerator; clean windows inside and out; polish brass and silver, including door furniture; wash and dry ornaments; dust pictures, pelmets and door tops and wipe paintwork.

SEASONALLY OR ANNUALLY

Spring or early summer is the best time to give the home a thorough clean. The following tasks should be done at least once a year.

- Sort and clean all cupboards and drawers, from linen cupboard or airing cupboard, wardrobes and clothes drawers down to kitchen units; remember to turn out hall cupboards and areas under the stairs. Sort out cupboards before cleaning the rest of the room, thoroughly washing and drying kitchen and bathroom cupboards, replacing lining papers in clothes storage areas and polishing display cabinets. When the inside of the furniture is fresh, progress to the rest of the room.
- Open all the windows to air the rooms well and move all furniture. Clean carpets and check the condition of sealed floors. Clean light fittings.
- Wash or clean curtains, blinds and upholstery. Upholstery which is not removable should be brushed with a clothes brush and a suitable dry cleaning agent should be used on any soiled areas.
- Wash skirting boards, window frames and similar paintwork and check its condition, noting any areas that need decorating. Kitchen walls, particularly in small, confined areas, may need washing; however, it is not a good idea to wash other walls as this can result in marking and fading.
- Turn carpets which are not fitted so that they wear evenly. Turn mattresses on beds.
- Check for any damage that needs attention. For example, look at flexes on electrical appliances for signs of wearing and check that plugs are not loose.
- Defrost the freezer.

CLEANING EQUIPMENT

You will need a few basic items of equipment in addition to a vacuum cleaner or carpet sweeper.

CLOTHS AND DUSTERS

Disposable washing cloths are by far the most hygienic for kitchen use. Use separate cloths of the same type for cleaning the bathroom and toilet. Thoroughly rinse cloths in very hot water after use, then shake them out and leave them hanging to dry.

Keep a polishing cloth for rubbing windows dry after washing. Dusters for general household use should be washable (and washed regularly) and it is a good idea to keep separate dusters for wax polish used on furniture and for spray surface polishers for use on mirrors, tiles and so on. Keep separate cloths for polishing brass – old pieces of rag are ideal for rubbing on the polish, with dusters to clean it off and buff the metal.

BRUSHES AND MOPS

Keep a long-handled, soft floor brush for hard floors and wash it occasionally, leaving it to dry outside. A short-handled soft brush for use with a dust pan is handy for cleaning corners; a stiff, short-handled brush is useful for stair carpet or carpet edges. Keep a separate soft brush for cleaning ashes from the fireplace.

A scrubbing brush is not necessarily vital – it depends on your flooring – but it can be useful for doorsteps. A washing-up brush is essential for scrubbing around the sink as well as for cleaning boards and baking dishes. A toothbrush is useful for scrubbing around awkward sink areas and behind taps.

A good mop is essential for washing floors, unless you intend getting down on hands and knees! There are several types available. A sponge-top is the most effective for rubbing off dirt and it is wise to buy a mop handle on which the heads can be replaced when they wear out. Always thoroughly rinse and dry the mop after use.

OTHER USEFUL EQUIPMENT

A few minutes in a hardware shop will reveal a host of gadgets, many types of brushes, different mops, dusters and products which mayor may not be useful. depending on your patience with such items. Generally speaking, these gimmicky products, have short-lived value which will not beat the basic items above. You may, however, find the items below useful.

Invest in a strong pair of rubber gloves with a surface designed for gripping so that you can use very hot water for washing-up and cleaning – this is more hygienic than hand-hot water. Gloves are also essential when using strong oven-cleaners.

A window cleaning blade (rather like a windscreen wiper on a car) is useful for achieving a good finish when washing the inside and outside of windows, glass doors or mirrors.

Feather dusters, or similar, are ideal for cleaning dust from high ledges and for dusting away cobwebs.

CLEANING MATERIALS

There is a vast selection of cleaning products available today and this can be confusing when deciding which product to buy. The choice depends on the chore, so before buying consider what job you want the preparation to do and the type of surface it is to be used on.

There are products available for:

- Cleaning off dirt, whether food and cooking deposits or grime on the floor
- Killing germs, or bacteria and other unwanted micro-organisms
- Achieving a good finish on a surface
- Giving the room a pleasant smell

Note Never mix different cleaning products as they contain chemicals which can react together to give off noxious fumes. Combined products can also have adverse effects on surfaces or materials.

CLEANING PROPERTIES

As mentioned above, it is important to distinguish between products which will actually remove dirt and others that add a finish, or shine to the surface. Thorough cleaners are vital in the kitchen where bacteria, or germs, can survive in cracks and crevices to contaminate food. Bleach is the most basic, practical and adaptable example of a cleaner which can be used throughout the home. However, always check that the surface or appliance does not have a finish which must not be bleached. Bleach is also useful for drains and toilets.

ABRASIVES

Abrasive powders and the more popular creams are useful for cleaning ceramic washbasins, some baths and some sinks, also for work surfaces. However, they are unsuitable for surfaces which mark or scratch easily.

LAVATORY CLEANERS

There are many brands, all claiming to kill germs, smell fresh and clean away scale. Any good bleach will act effectively to clean the toilet thoroughly if left to soak for a few hours.

There are cleaners which can be placed in the cistern to work on a continual basis. These are useful but should not be seen as an alternative to a thorough weekly clean.

NO-RINSE CLEANING AGENTS

These are useful for floors and cupboard fronts, also for bathroom surfaces and windowsills. Kitchen work surfaces should receive more thorough attention however, involving a good wash with very hot water, as a spray and wipe is not adequate protection against possible food contamination by bacteria.

POLISHING AGENTS

There are many types of polish available, from traditional beeswax polish to non-greasy sprays.

Traditional polished furniture should be dusted, then polished with a wax polish, working in the direction of the grain and rubbing the wax into the wood. This protects the wood and emiches it, as well as giving a good shine.

Spray polishes containing wax are easy to use but they build up on the surface of the wood, creating an unwanted film over the years. Spray polishes are fine for sealed furniture, but it is better to use ordinary wax polish for valued wood which has been French polished.

Non-greasy sprays are suitable for laminates, mirrors, cupboard doors, tiles and so on. They give the surface a good finish and remove small deposits of dust. However, they do not give the surface a really good clean in the same way as hot water.

AIR FRESHENERS

There are many types available, from room sprays to gadgets which give off questionably pleasant aromas and, if you like the smell of an air freshener, there is no harm in using one.

However, a clean, well-aired home should not need an air freshener. These products must not be used to hide unpleasant smells which are the result of poor cleaning or bad ventilation.

TRADITIONAL CLEANING POTIONS

These mixtures may not be valuable for cleaning modern furniture, but they are of historical interest and may be helpful when restoring old and neglected items. Chemists' shops and a good hardware store are sources of information on ingredients, as well as upholstery suppliers and furniture restorers who are often aware of old-fashioned cleaning agents. The quantities and exact wording have been updated.

POLISH FOR STOVES AND STEEL ARTICLES

Mix 1 spoonful of turpentine and 1 spoonful of sweet oil, then stir in enough emery powder to make a paste. Rub the paste on a small area, then rub it off quickly with a clean piece of soft cloth. Polish with dry emery powder and a clean leather (or cloth).

The above would have been used on iron stoves or grates. Emery paper and paste are certainly obtainable from plumbers' merchants.

FURNITURE POLISH

Mix equal proportions of linseed oil, turpentine, vinegar and spirits of wine. Shake the mixture well and rub on the furniture with a piece of linen rag. Finish by polishing with a clean duster.

Note Vinegar and oil, rubbed in with flannel or tough cloth and then polished with a clean duster also produces a good finish.

FURNITURE PASTE

Mix 75 g/3 oz common beeswax, 25 g/1 oz white wax, 25 g/1 oz curd soap, 600 ml/1 pint turpentine and 600 ml/1 pint boiled water (cooled) in a screw-topped bottle or jar and shake well from time to time over a period of 48 hours.

TO CLEAN MARBLE

Take two parts of soda, one of pumice-stone and one of finely powdered chalk. Sift these through a sieve and mix to a paste with water. Rub the paste all over the marble and the stains will be removed. Wash with soap and water for a beautiful bright finish.

TO CLEAN DECANTERS

Roll up some small pieces of soft brown paper or blotting paper. Wet them and soap them well. Put them into the decanters about one-quarter filled with warm water, shake for a few minutes, then rinse with clear cold water. Wipe the outsides with a dry cloth and put the decanters to drain.

As a modern alternative to the above, tablets sold for soaking dentures are an excellent cleaner for glassware. Leave the dissolved tablets to soak for several hours or overnight.

TO BRIGHTEN GILT FRAMES

Take sufficient flour of sulphur to give a golden tinge to about 900 ml/1½ pints water. Place the mixture in an old pan and add 4–5 bruised onions or a head of garlic. Bring to the boil. Strain off the liquid and cool. Use a soft brush and some of the liquid to wash any gilding that requires restoring and, when dry, it will appear as bright as new.

LAYING AND LIGHTING A FIRE

In winter, in a room with a traditional coal fire, the final task when cleaning on a daily basis is to lay the fire ready for lighting.

First place a few cinders or small pieces of coal in the grate to part cover the fire basket. Add a layer of loosely crumpled paper, then arrange some thin, dry sticks on top. The sticks should be neat and stable enough to support the coal. Carefully place large cinders and medium-sized pieces of coal or smokeless fuel on the sticks. The laid fire should not be too high nor too far forward in the grate. When lit, the paper must be loose enough, and the sticks and coal small enough, to allow a good draught to pass through. This will ensure that the fire burns well.

PAPER BOYS

Old-fashioned kindling, made by rolling up a sheet of newspaper very tightly, then knotting it. Several of these were placed on top of the loosely crumpled newspapers when dry sticks were in short supply.

FIRELIGHTERS

Flammable cubes or fingers which are placed between the coal or smokeless fuel. Always follow the manufacturer's instructions.

SMOKELESS ZONES

Many towns and some rural areas are smokeless zones. Only smokeless fuel may be burnt in these areas.

Laundry

Simplified by modern fabrics, detergents, washing machines and steam irons, today's laundry procedure is far removed from the week-long event of a century ago.

The secret of successful laundering is good organization and the first step is to sort the laundry according to whether it is washable or only suitable for dry-cleaning. Check garments for washing or cleaning instructions before buying them. Do the same when buying fabric and note the details for future reference, otherwise expensive curtains or a home-made garment may shrink or run when washed.

All washable items must be further sorted and, as most households have an automatic washing machine, hand-wash items must be separated from machine-washable goods. The laundry for machine-washing should then be divided into piles according to the fabric type and washing code.

FABRIC TYPES

Fabrics are made from one or more of a few basic types of fibre, either natural or man-made. In addition, various finishes may be applied to the fabric or used in the making of household goods and clothing. Prints, dyes and surface finishes are used in the manufacture of fabrics and then, as the garments or goods are made up, a variety of additional materials may be included, for example, linings, fastenings, tapes, braiding, trimming and so on. Therefore, identifying the main fabric type is not necessarily a clear indication of laundry method, so the specific instructions provided by the manufacturer should be followed as these take into account the whole garment or item.

NATURAL FIBRES

Cotton Absorbent, strong and hard-wearing, cotton can usually withstand repeated washing at high temperatures, depending on the finish or colour applied. Cotton is often combined with man-made fibres to give a material with greater resistance to creasing. Pure cotton fabric is available in a wide variety of weights and textures; it may be fine and used in light clothing, or thick and tough and used for sheets, pillowcases and so on. Cotton-polyester mixtures are commonly used for tablecloths, bedcovers and other household 'linens'.

Linen Heavier than cotton but with similar properties, the fabric often has slubs or thick threads running through the yarn to give a characteristic texture. Linen and cotton are combined to produce a fabric known as linen union.

Wool Used alone or in combination with man-made fibres, wool features in many different types of clothing and also in upholstery fabrics. Wool is soft, springy, warm and bulky, producing absorbent fabrics which require careful laundering to avoid shrinkage. Wool should not be washed at high temperatures and the majority of woollens should be handwashed, although some are machine-washable on a special delicate or woollen programme. However, many fine woollen fabrics have to be dry-cleaned.

Silk Silk may be fine or heavy, with a slub, or with a variety of finishes, including satin or sand-washed. Some silk garments should be dry-cleaned but the majority of silk fabrics can be washed with care.

MAN-MADE FIBRES

These may be roughly grouped into cellulose-based fibres, which are generated from naturally fibrous materials of plant origins (such as wood) and synthetics, which are generated from oil-based materials. A combination of these fibres, or of man-made and natural fibres, is used in the majority of fabrics and clothing.

Acetate With aesthetic characteristics associated with silk, this is frequently used for evening wear and similar fashion clothes. It is also used in light furnishing fabrics, such as cushions.

Tri-acetate More robust than acetate and suitable for permanent creasing by heat treatment, this fibre is used in clothing and furnishing fabrics.

Acrylic Similar to wool in appearance and bulk, acrylic is 'easy-care' but will be distorted by heat. Widely used in furnishing, upholstery and clothing fabrics as well as flooring.

Nylon Strong and easy to care for, this is used in many household fabrics as well as for clothing.

Polyester Strong, 'easy-care' but heat-sensitive, polyester is popular for household and clothing fabrics and is often found mixed with cotton.

Vinyl This is used to give a leather-like appearance to fabrics.

Viscose (rayon) Widely used in a variety of fabrics both household and clothing, viscose has many of the properties associated with cotton but it does not have the same strength and resilience when wet.

LABELLING

Always check the manufacturer's label before laundering an item. The following international symbols are typical:

- The washing tub indicates that the garment may be washed and gives the maximum water temperature.
- The bars underneath the tub tell whether the minimum, medium or maximum wash may be used in terms of length and degree of agitation.

FABRIC CARE SYMBOLS

WASHING SYMBOLS

Textile/ Machine Code	Machine	Handwash	Examples of Application
	MAXIMUM wash in Cotton cycle.	Hand hot (50°C/122°F) or boil. Spin or wring.	White cotton and linen articles without special finishes.
	MAXIMUM wash in Cotton cycle.	Hand hot (50°C/122°F). Spin or wring.	Cotton, linen or viscose articles without special finishes where colours are fast at 60°C/140°F.
	MEDIUM wash in Synthetics cycle.	Hand hot (50°C/122°F). Cold rinse, short spin, or damp dry.	Polyester-cotton mixtures, nylon, polyester, cotton and viscose articles with special finishes. Cotton-acrylic mixtures.
	MAXIMUM wash in Cotton cycle.	Warm. Spin or wring.	Cotton, linen or viscose where colours are fast at 40°C/104°F but not at 60°C/140°F.
	MEDIUM wash in Synthetics cycle.	Warm. Cold rinse, short spin, do not hand wring.	Acrylics, acetate and triacetate; including mixtures with wool; polyester-wool blends.
	MINIMUM wash in Wool cycle.	Warm. Do not rub. Spin. Do not hand wring.	Wool, wool mixed with other fibres; silk.

Textile/ Machine Code

Articles labelled should be washed in the appropriate MEDIUM or MINIMUM cycles or handwashed.
The terms MINIMUM, MEDIUM and MAXIMUM wash refer to the washing time and agitation required. Follow the manufacturer's instructions.

Handwash only (see garment label).

Do not machine or handwash.

Mixed Load Washing Advice
Select lowest wash temperature indicated on the labels.
Where load contains labels with and symbols use the MEDIUM wash cycle at your selected temperature.
Where appears always use the MINIMUM wash cycle.

DRYING SYMBOLS
The square wash code symbols relate to drying.

Means tumble-drying is the ideal method (not essential, of course). Tumble-dry synthetics at lowest possible heat – follow recommendations in machine booklet for other fabrics.

The other drying symbols below are no longer in general use, but are still found on some garments.

Means drip-dry. Hangers are easiest for shirts, blouses, etc., but make sure they do not stain. Final rinse is cold.

Means dry flat – spread a towel on a table or on a rack or piece of hardboard over the bath for heavy garments.

IRONING SYMBOLS
Match the dots on your iron controls to the dots on the iron symbols on the garment label, which are explained below.

hot (210°C/410°F) cotton, linen, viscose, rayon

warm (160°C/320°F) polyester mixes, wool, silk

cool (120°C/248°F) acrylic, nylon acetate, triacetate, polyester

do not iron

DRY-CLEANING SYMBOLS
Again, as always, look for the label. The circular dry-cleaning symbol is commonly misunderstood. The letters inside the circles stand for the dry-cleaning fluids to be used.

(A) Any solvent can be used – so you can go to any dry-cleaner or coin-op.

(P) Various solvents can be used; in practice you can go to any dry-cleaner or coin-op machine.

(P) This tells the dry-cleaner to take certain precautions, so do not use coin-op machines.

(F) This indicates a special cleaning fluid for delicate fabrics or graments. Do not use a coin-op. Not even all dry-cleaners have this. It is best to draw attention to this symbol when you take in your clothes.

SELECTING A PRODUCT

A heavy-duty product is necessary for the bulk of household laundry, but the choice of an enzyme-rich (biological) product or 'nonbiological' liquid or powder is open to personal preference.

The majority of leading brands are designed to give good results in the medium temperature range of 40–60°C/104–140°F, which is particularly suitable for the many mixed fabrics which include some man-made fibres.

Fabric Conditioner This is added to the final rinsing water. It contains agents to give the fabric bulk and a soft feel, to impart a pleasant smell and to reduce static which can be a problem with man-made fibres, especially when tumble-dried. Fabric conditioning pads are also available, for use in the tumble-dryer.

Water Softener Water softener may be purchased for use in areas with very hard water. When it is added to the washing water less washing agent will be needed.

Stain Removing Agents There is a cleansing product available for almost every type of stain, from felt-tip pen marks to oil. These should be used exactly according to the manufacturer's instructions.

There are also products for soaking heavily soiled fabrics before introducing them to the normal laundry process and others for rubbing on dry stains before washing.

Starch Traditional hot-water starch and cold-water starch are both ideal for household linens and they are used as a final rinse for the clean laundry. They should be hand-mixed in a bowl and the items rinsed individually in the solution. Spray starch is for use as you are ironing and will give less stiff results but a pleasant sheen and aroma to laundry. Spray starch is most suitable for cotton garments which require light starching and items such as pillowcases; it may be used on table linen, but does not give a finish which is as crisp or smooth as that obtained with traditional starch.

Dry Cleaning Spray and Fluid These are ideal for removing small spots and stains on certain fabrics; however, they are not intended for all-over use or for major cleaning jobs.

LAUNDRY PROCEDURE

By following this simple step-by-step guide to efficient laundering, it is possible to avoid many common washing problems.

- First check the fabric for any damage which should be repaired before laundering.
- Separate washable items from those to be dry-cleaned. Then separate hand-wash items (delicate fabrics, some woollens and items which are not dye-fast) from machine washable goods. Finally, sort the machine washing into piles according to the wash programme.
- Remove any trimmings which cannot be washed or cleaned, such as belts, buckles, buttons (leather, wood or other decorative types), some shoulder-pads and trimmings such as sequins, fur or feathers.
- Close fastenings and empty pockets.
- Check for any stains and deal with these first.
- Tack any pleats in place with several large stitches so that they are easy to press after washing.
- Hand-wash delicate items in lukewarm water using a mild detergent or soap flakes. Keep coloured items separate at all times until completely dry.
- Soak heavily soiled fabrics in cool water and washing agent for several hours before washing. Do not put heavily soiled or stained fabric into very hot water as this tends to 'set' the stain.
- Follow the recommended washing and drying procedure for the particular wash load.
- Never leave wet washing in a machine or folded in a bucket for long periods, particularly in warm conditions as this results in washing mould and foul-smelling fabrics.
- Prepare wide plastic coat hangers for delicate clothing or items which should be drip-dried.
- Prepare a clean surface and white linen or towel for items which have to be dried flat (for example, woollen jumpers).
- Wipe the washing line with a clean damp cloth before hanging out clean washing.
- Turn bright clothes inside out on sunny summer days as bright sunlight can cause some coloured fabrics to fade.
- Hang garments neatly and appropriately so that they do not stretch while drying. For example, hang T-shirts across the back, with the washing line running under the arms and pegs in the underarm seam.
- Hang long garments which are fairly weighty evenly over the line to reduce

the pull on the fabric. For example, some dresses should be hung over the line at the waist rather than under the arms.
- Fold trousers and shorts into their crease marks before hanging them out, for ease of ironing.
- If you use a tumble-dryer, sort the laundry into fabrics of similar weights and types for drying together. Remember that a tumble-dryer does not take as much laundry as a washing machine of the same size.
- Never leave washing unattended on the line for long periods; always take it in on the same day as it is put out to prevent soiling.
- Open out damp or just dry washing to air if you are not going to iron it immediately. Use a clothes airer, hang items or tumble-dry them briefly.

BOILING

Boiling can still be a useful way to ensure that tea-towels and other kitchen cloths, kitchen hand-towels, towelling nappies and white linens are really clean.

Heavily soiled items should be washed first, then rinsed and brought slowly to the boil in cold water with a little washing soda added, then boiled for about two hours.

Items which are not so badly soiled need not be pre-washed. They can be placed in cold water, with a little washing soda and soap or mild detergent added. They should be heated very slowly with frequent stirring, then brought to the boil.

IRONING

- The majority of fabrics benefit from being ironed while still slightly damp, particularly cotton or linen. Follow the manufacturer's instructions for the heat setting on the iron.
- Put the iron to heat and do not begin to use it until the indicator light shows that it has reached the desired temperature setting. This is important as the iron may well peak at a slightly higher temperature before the temperature levels out as the heating element automatically turns off, then it is indicated that the desired setting has been reached.
- Always iron on a clean, padded but firm surface. Wash the ironing board cover frequently and replace or repair it when damaged. The cover should

be firmly fitted to the surface, otherwise it will slip as the clothes are ironed.

- A sleeve board, rather like a miniature ironing board without the stand, is useful for achieving a smooth finish when ironing dress or jacket sleeves or awkward, narrow areas of fabric. Alternatively, make a large pad of fabric (such as a folded towel) and cover it with a clean, white tea-towel; hold this under any small, difficult areas of fabric while pressing them, taking care to avoid burning yourself.
- Where a particular crease mark is required, always iron on the right side of the fabric. When ironing on the reverse of the fabric, take care not to press seam marks through to the right side.
- When pressing creases into trousers or similar, lay a piece of clean white cotton fabric over the surface of the garment to prevent the fabric from becoming shiny. If the garment is dry, dampen the cotton and use a slightly higher temperature than recommended for the garment.
- Press difficult areas before ironing the bulk of a garment. For example, press the waistband and closing or pocket edges before the main areas of fabric on a skirt.
- Press collars and cuffs from the right side to avoid any facing from underneath showing. Press the folded collar into place from the collar band side, working along the edge.
- Press pleats neatly in place, avoiding pressing the tacking cotton holding them in place. Remove the tacks once the majority of the pleats are pressed, then press the last part. If the cotton is pressed it will leave a mark on fine fabrics.
- When ironing a lined garment, remember that the lining may require a lower heat setting.
- Lastly, remember to keep the iron clean: use a recommended cleaner to remove any burnt-on fabric finishes. If you do scorch fabric, wipe the iron with a damp cloth afterwards, taking care not to burn your hand.

USING A LAUNDERETTE

The standard of these premises varies enormously as does the service offered. Some establishments with attendants offer a washing service, so that the dirty washing can be left and picked up later.

When you go to the launderette, use one or more large clean bags to carry the washing. It is best to take your own washing agents, as this is far more economical than using the powder dispensers on the premises. Ensure that you have plenty of coins in various denominations as most launderette machinery is coin-operated. Do not leave the washing unattended and always check that the machine has a clean appearance before putting the washing in.

Read the instructions on the machines and follow them, including advice on the volume of washing for the machines and choice of washing agents. This is important as, should your washing suffer damage, you may wish to seek compensation from the owner. This is only possible if you have followed instructions provided and it is obviously a lack of maintenance or malfunction due to negligence which caused the damage. Do not be put off by notices disclaiming responsibility for damage – if a tumble-dryer overheats due to malfunction and consequently damages your washing, then you are entitled to compensation.

Some launderettes have very large machines for washing items such as duvets. Some also have coin-operated dry-cleaning machines.

PROFESSIONAL DRY-CLEANING

The most expensive option, this cleaning method is mainly used for heavy garments such as coats and suits, and specific fabrics which can be harmed by water. Always point out any stains or dirty areas when taking clothes to the cleaners, ask for advice if necessary and enquire about the various services offered.

Always air clothes well after dry-cleaning, as the solvents used give off poisonous vapour.

STAIN REMOVAL

Unfortunately, there is no magic solution for removing stains. If possible, rinse washable fabrics in warm water as soon as you can. Depending on the fabric and the type of stain, the mark may wash out with soap or detergent; other stains may be removed by a soaking in warm water and heavy-duty washing powder or bleach. In some cases special solutions and methods should be used. There are many specific stain removal agents on the market and these should be used exactly according to the manufacturer's instructions. Remember to test a small, discreet area of fabric for colour fastness before using any stain removal solution.

STAIN REMOVING TECHNIQUES

If the stain is to be soaked out, then use lukewarm or cold water; boiling or very hot water will 'set' the mark. Heavy-duty detergents work best at a lukewarm or cool temperature as this promotes enzyme action on protein-based stains (egg, milk, blood and so on).

When applying a stain removal solution to a small area of fabric, hold a pad of absorbent white cotton fabric or white absorbent kitchen paper underneath the stain. Work from the outside of the stained area toward the centre so that the mark is not spread. If the fabric should be washed after applying a special treatment, then do this at once, before the stain has time to set again.

Work in a well-ventilated area when using solvents to remove stains. Never mix different types of stain remover, detergents, bleaches and solvents. Do not smoke or use solvents near a naked flame as many are highly flammable.

USEFUL TREATMENTS

Glycerine This softens dried-on stains and lubricates the dirt. Mix with double volume of water and dab generously on the stain. Leave for at least an hour, then soak and wash in detergent.

Washing Soda Dissolve about 15 ml/1 tbsp crystals to each 600 ml/ 1 pint water and use for soaking or sponging. A strong solution may be used on white cottons or neat soda may be placed on the stretched fabric and boiling or very hot water poured through. The most practical way of doing this is to stretch and secure the fabric over a basin or bowl placed in the sink.

White Vinegar Diluted in the proportions 5 ml/1 tsp vinegar to 300 ml/½ pint water, this may be used for removing perspiration stains; however, vinegar and acetic acid must not be used on acetate fabrics.

Ammonia Diluted in the proportions 30 ml/2 tbsp ammonia to 90 ml/6 tbsp water, this may be sponged on acid-based stains. Use only in a well-ventilated room and avoid breathing in the fumes.

Surgical Spirits White spirits may be applied neat to some stains such as permanent ink, ballpoint pen ink and some felt-tip pen marks.

Hydrogen Peroxide Available as ten-part solution from chemists, this may be used as a bleach. It should be diluted with four parts water.

Grease Solvents A variety of brands are available, including dry-cleaning spray or solution for dabbing on stains.

COMMON STAINS AND SUGGESTED TREATMENTS

Blood Heavy-duty detergent will usually remove blood and other protein-based stains. Soak in a warm-water solution for several hours or overnight, then wash according to fabric type.

Candle Wax Gently scrape off the wax without harming fabric. Place the item on a thick layer of absorbent kitchen paper and cover with a double thickness of paper, then apply a warm iron to melt the wax; the paper absorbs the molten wax. Move the paper and apply heat to clean paper each time until the wax is completely dissolved and absorbed. Finish with a solvent stain remover.

Chewing Gum Chill the gum to harden it, placing the fabric in the freezer for speed, then pick as much as you can off the fabric. Use a grease solvent fluid or rub in a strong hand cleaner, such as Swarfega, before washing.

Creosote or Tar Treat with grease solvent over a pad of cloth, then wash.

Fat and Grease Any surface fat should be scraped away. A warm iron and paper may be used to melt and absorb fat as for candle wax. Finally, use a grease solvent or dry-cleaning spray.

Inks Washable ink should be removed by washing or soaking in heavy-duty detergent. Surgical spirit should be dabbed on permanent inks and ballpoint pen ink. There are also proprietary brands or stain removers for specific inks.

Moulds Heavy-duty detergent usually removes mould stains; however, old stains should be treated with a weak solution of bleach (on suitable fabrics), 1 part bleach to 100 parts water. Alternatively, hydrogen peroxide may be used to soak away stains (1 part hydrogen peroxide to 4 parts water).

Perspiration Soak or wash in a weak household ammonia solution. Alternatively, white vinegar solution is also successful.

Scorching Soak in washing soda or rub gently with hydrogen peroxide solution.

Urine Thoroughly rinse in cold water, then soak in heavy-duty detergent. Persistent stains should be soaked in a solution of hydrogen peroxide and ammonia diluted as given. All treatments should be followed by washing in heavy-duty detergent, which is usually sufficient treatment for fresh staining.

Wine Soak in heavy-duty detergent, then wash at high temperature. If the fabric cannot be washed at high temperature, use a solution of hydrogen peroxide.

Help in the Home

From employing a full-time nanny to engaging occasional assistance with household chores or entertaining, this chapter offers guidance on key points to consider.

Households employing full-time, residential staff are rare; however, the increase in the number of women who work outside the home has resulted in greater dependence on some form of household assistance, ranging from a live-in nanny to weekly help with the cleaning. As those with experience will know, there are positive and negative aspects to employing help in the house. This chapter outlines key points to consider when looking for and employing people to come and work in your home and offers suggestions on how to avoid some of the pitfalls.

FINDING HELP

This is not necessarily as easy as it may at first appear; domestic helpers come into a highly personal environment, quite unlike the usual workplace. Therefore, it is not simply a question of finding the person who is 'qualified' to do the job, but of finding someone who will be suitable for your home, even if they only come in for a few hours a week.

RECOMMENDATIONS

Personal recommendations from friends, neighbours or colleagues are by far the best way of finding an employee in terms of practicalities such as reliability and honesty.

If you are looking for any part-time domestic help, then it is well worth asking around; many people who work part-time in one household visit a number of other homes on the same basis.

ADVERTISEMENTS

Check the local paper and shop windows for people advertising their services.

ADVERTISING

Local shop windows can be a good place to put your own advertisement, depending on the area in which you live. Phrase the advertisement carefully, stating what type of help is required and giving a guide to the number of hours. Remember to add 'references required' and give a telephone number, but not an address. Never give information which may jeopardize your household security; for example, do not mention work arrangements which indicate that the house is empty every day.

The same rules apply if you are advertising in a newspaper, where it is best to use a box number.

AGENCIES

There are agencies which specialize in domestic help, from nannies and cleaners to nursing help for the aged or sick. Agencies charge a fee: always check financial details before getting involved, and find out what come-back you have on the agency if the employee is unsatisfactory.

THROUGH THE DOCTOR

Some assistance, such as home helps, meals-on-wheels or nursing help, can be available through the local health authority network.

Also, the doctor may know of private nursing agencies which offer help with the care of the elderly or sick.

EMPLOYING HELP

Once you are in contact with potential employees, there are certain simple rules which will help you to determine which person is most suitable and to establish the terms of employment. No matter how minimal the help, follow these rules both as a matter of courtesy to the employee and to avoid the possibility of unpleasant pitfalls yourself.

Firstly, make sure you have the candidate's name, full address and telephone number.

REFERENCES

When dealing with telephone replies to an advertisement, it is a good idea to ask for the names and telephone numbers of referees and contact them before arranging an interview. Take the address as well if possible and check that the referee has been warned that you may ring or write, then follow up the reference promptly. If the person prefers to provide written references, these should be sent in advance of an interview if possible.

Dealing with references before arranging an interview will save time being wasted on unsuitable applicants and is some security against giving your address and information about your circumstances to someone with dishonest intentions.

Of course, the exact nature and extent of references depends on the job. If you are employing someone to come and clean for a couple of hours a week, you are simply looking for a character reference and some indication that they are capable of the job. When looking for a part- or full-time employee to take responsibility for children or to care for the sick, the references should be more comprehensive, both in confirming the honesty, stability and reliability of the person and in outlining their qualifications or experience for the work.

If you spend time away from home, so that the person will have to be given keys for access, or if you are employing live-in help, then it is absolutely vital to pay close attention to references.

INTERVIEWING POTENTIAL EMPLOYEES

Make sure you are well prepared for an interview and give yourself time to assess the person and their references before launching into details of your household situation and personal arrangements.

Begin by putting the person at ease, perhaps with some tea or coffee, and by telling them a bit about the house or the work. Make this fairly general at first since they may be nervous and not absorb much information until they have relaxed. During a brief period of general chat you may notice quite a few points about the person; apart from details of their personal appearance you may discover their interests and so on.

Once you have broken the ice, get down to the business of establishing their situation. Find out about:

- Previous experience
- Present employment and reasons for leaving it, if relevant
- Interest in the job; even with a minor cleaning job you can learn a lot about the person's standards by asking for their opinions on certain aspects of cleaning
- Why they want the job (without asking the question directly), although this

may be obvious from their circumstances
- Their own responsibilities and other commitments or employment

List any specific queries you have beforehand, such as whether they drive, any likely transport problems, whether they have brothers and sisters or children of their own, general health and so on. You may want to keep the interview fairly informal, so having a list of points to tick off may not be suitable, but a small pad with a few reminders need not look intimidating.

Use the interview to tell the person about the position they will hold in your household, the type of work, briefly explain relevant family circumstances, planned living arrangements and so on. Having a list of duties to refer to is a good thing. The extent to which you give information at this stage depends on the circumstances. If you have already decided that this is definitely not the person for you, it is pointless going into detail; politely skim the facts, allowing time for the candidate's queries, then bring the event to a close.

When you have explained your side of the relationship, details of salary and other formal arrangements, encourage the candidate to ask questions and answer them honestly. Then, if you think the person is suitable, take them around the house paying attention to areas relating to their duties. This will give them an opportunity to seek further information about the work.

Finish the interview by thanking the candidate for taking the trouble to come and see you. Tell them you will be in touch and follow up quickly. In the case of finding a suitable person for occasional cleaning help, you may simply prefer to make arrangements at this stage.

WRITTEN CONFIRMATION

Follow up interviews either with a polite rejection or, for successful applicants, written confirmation, offering details of the job, duties, pay, agreed trial period and notice period.

Special care must be taken in the case of full-time employees and you should always seek the advice of the Citizens' Advice Bureau with regard to employer's and employee's rights before entering an agreement.

AGREED TRIAL PERIOD

Whether you are employing full-time help or someone to come in for just a few hours a week, having an established period of assessment serves several excellent purposes. Make sure you clearly state an agreed trial period in the written confirmation. Allow time for both you and the employee to settle down and get to know each other and for the employee to become familiar with the job. A month is usually a suitable period.

Prepare a written outline of duties, with notes about your household standards and any house rules (these should all have been discussed at the interview). Go through it with the employee, then use the agreed trial period as the time for ensuring that standards are maintained and rules followed – it is pointless asking the cleaning lady to clean the bath with a particular product, then to overlook the fact she ignores your instructions. She may well have genuinely forgotten and, if you do not point it out, you will be aggravated and she will continue in innocent ignorance. Major and minor points can be cleared up without embarrassment under the canopy of the trial period.

During this time you will find out whether the person's work is satisfactory and, if you calmly and politely discuss problems, either the employee has the opportunity to adjust the work or will be aware that the relationship is not successful.

The agreed trial period also provides the employee with the opportunity of coming back to you with problems. Arrange to have a chat about how work is progressing on at least one occasion before the end of the period.

Review the situation at the end of the agreed period, either to encourage a successful employee, or to suggest that the relationship is not working.

GIVING NOTICE

Never an easy task, giving notice is most difficult when dealing with living-in staff, particularly when the problem may be related to personal differences rather than the actual work involved. Always exercise the trial period as a means of terminating employment if you are unhappy with the relationship: it will be more problematic to do so at a later date.

It is reasonable to try and resolve problems first before giving notice. Explain the shortfalls, give the employee a chance to state their point of view, then suggest that perhaps difficulties can be overcome within a given period. Do not complain about just one thing if there really are a number of problems:

explain how you feel about everything to give the person a fair chance of resolving the situation.

Always sit down with the employee to discuss serious problems, especially those which may result in dismissal and carefully prepare what you want to say beforehand. Do not confuse minor irritations with the core of the trouble – concentrate on the facts. Be calm and reasonable. Do not enter into any argument and avoid making petty comments.

In the unfortunate circumstance of acrimonious dismissal you and the employee may prefer to have monies paid in lieu of notice, terminating the employment on the same day or at the end of the week. This is often better for all concerned.

EMPLOYMENT AND THE LAW

The laws relating to employment, covering the rights of employees and the responsibilities of the employer, are far more extensive for fulltime employment than for part-time help. If you intend employing a part-time childminder for six hours a week, a window-cleaner once a month or a cleaning lady for eight hours a week, you are unlikely to have to fulfil extensive responsibilities. However, it is sensible for prospective employers to check with the Citizens' Advice Bureau. They will guide you towards details of current laws on working hours, agreements with employers, responsibilities for National Insurance or other payments, terminating employment and so on.

As a general guide with regard to full-time help, you must define the work and conditions in writing, agree a notice period, provide minimum holidays, observe current laws relating to matters such as maternity leave and you may be involved in a redundancy situation. You must also be aware of information required for taxation purposes.

Remember that it is against the law for foreign residents to work unless they have the necessary work permits.

TYPICAL HOUSEHOLD HELPERS

The following notes discuss the various helpers you may employ in your home.

NANNY

The nanny may live-in or come in on a daily basis, or on specified days of the week. Nanny-sharing is a useful method of establishing a good relationship with a reliable trained nanny for a certain number of days a week for those who do not want or cannot afford a full-time person.

Anyone who is left to care for children, particularly infants or toddlers, must be trained or fully experienced. References and details of training and/or previous employment and experience are vital. It is a good idea to allow time when you can be with nanny and child during their first week together to ensure that everything works out.

The duties of the nanny and her relationship to child and mother must be clearly defined, understood and observed. Matters such as discipline, children's entertainment, eating habits and manners are typical points to sort out.

The trained nanny is a professional and you must not expect her to wash the kitchen floor or clean the house. However, it is quite usual to expect that she will be able to prepare the child's meals while you are out. Many arrangements do include some minor household duties, or the nanny may enjoy baking or cooking occasionally (if this is to your liking) as an activity to share with the child.

If you have a live-in nanny, she may well be involved in some household duties, such as hanging out washing or generally helping as a member of the family. Goodwill with helping is excellent but must not be exploited. A live-in nanny must have clearly defined time to herself. She should have somewhere of her own to relax and to have visitors. The most practical arrangement is for her to have a bed-sitting room (if the house does not provide space for separate bedroom and sitting-room) with a television, table and easy chairs. In return she should treat your home with respect, keeping reasonable hours when she goes out.

MOTHER'S HELP

Reliable but untrained, a mother's help should be competent with children, trustworthy and sensible. You should be satisfied that the person is capable and that the child is safe in her care.

The mother's help may undertake some housework by agreement, but generally her primary responsibility will be the child or children.

BABY-SITTER

Anyone who baby-sits must be reliable, kind and mature enough to cope with any emergencies in your absence. The age of the child is important in determining the suitability of the baby-sitter. A young baby is more likely to need experienced attention than a six-year-old child.

'Professional' baby-sitters are hired by the hour, but groups of parents may get together to share the job on a return basis. This is ideal as it saves having to pay a baby-sitter every time you go out for the evening.

If you are not linked to a scheme, then try to find a baby-sitter on a personal recommendation basis. It is obviously preferable if the child knows the person well.

Always tell the child who is going to babysit, then prepare them for bed and make sure young children are settled for the night. Leave a telephone number for the doctor and a contact number where you can be reached in case of emergency. Leave instructions about feeding, if required, a suitable drink for baby or child, any helpful advice about a favourite toy and so on. Make sure the sitter is able to make tea or coffee and, if you are out for a long time, you may need to leave some food.

Let the baby-sitter know when you will be home and try to be on time. Telephone if you are delayed. If you do not return until late in the evening, you may need to give the baby-sitter a lift home or money for a taxi.

AU PAIR

An au pair is obtained through an arrangement or mutual convenience, whereby girls from abroad come to stay in family homes and receive free board and lodging in exchange for some help in the house. She has no rights as an employee and should not be treated as such. Her role is to help for about half the day but to spend the rest of the time studying English or as a tourist.

An au pair usually acts as a mother's help, generally assisting with children and with everyday household duties. She should not be treated as a cleaner nor given the responsibilities of a nanny. You should treat the girl as a member of the family, paying her pocket money as well as providing bed and board.

Specialist agencies provide au pairs, or you may find someone through a personal recommendation. An agency will want to know about your circumstances and you should be told as much as possible about the girl who will be visiting you; however, interviews are not usually practical.

It is important to agree any duties, terms or house rules before the au pair arrives, either through the agency or the mutual friend. Avoid any misunderstandings arising from language difficulties by making sure terms are agreed in both languages, if necessary.

Once the au pair has arrived, the main difficulty can be coping with a stranger living as part of your family. This depends on your circumstances and outlook, also on the character of the au pair. Some relationships work well; other fail miserably.

CHILD-MINDER

A professional child-minder is a member of a registered group of people who care for children in their own homes during the day (for up to a period of eight hours, or as currently specified). Many child-minders have children of their own and they may look after more than one extra child, providing care and meals. Sometimes, the mother will provide the food for very young children and infants, delivering it each day with the child.

Personal recommendation is the best way of finding a child-minder and, when deciding on this type of care, think carefully about the standards of behaviour, type of environment, and entertainment or play facilities that you require for your child.

Introduce a young child to the child-minder on a gradual basis, for short periods at first until the infant grows to enjoy the visits and is confident that you will return. Monitor your child's reaction to the arrangement and make the effort to spend a few minutes talking to the minder at the end of the day. You should soon be able to tell if the toddler is happy, even if some morning starts are tearful. Sort out minor problems as they arise, make sure the infant is eating well and make a point of establishing a good relationship with the child-minder.

CLEANER

There are many different ways of obtaining help with the cleaning, from employing a cleaning lady to come in once a week to ease your own workload to hiring a specialist company to do a complete spring clean.

When employing a cleaner, take note of the general information on finding and employing staff. Personal recommendation really is a plus. Compile a clear, comprehensive list of tasks with any specific notes about your requirements and always agree the duties at the beginning of the relationship. You may not want a pan scourer used on the hob fittings, or a particular product used to clean the bath; sort these points out right at the beginning. Show the cleaner around with the list to clarify everything on the first day. Make sure standards are maintained after an initial period of enthusiasm and try to develop a positive, friendly but working relationship with your cleaner, in which criticism is easily given and accepted, and praise or thanks is forthcoming as appropriate.

Cleaning agencies operate in towns and cities. The disadvantage of acquiring a cleaner through an agency is that you may not keep the same person for a long period, makng it difficult to develop a relationship and to have the work done to your specific requirements.

Local companies also offer a 'spring cleaning' service, where a team of people move in to wash paintwork, clean carpets and upholstery, as well as do the dusting, washing and polishing. Before working through any company or agency, always check details of payments, staff reliability and insurance to cover any breakages or accidents which may occur.

WINDOW-CLEANER

Personal recommendation is the best way to find a trustworthy window-cleaner, otherwise look for a reputable company in the telephone directory and ask for references or for evidence of other local contracts. Do not simply admit anyone to your home who arrives carrying a bucket and ladder! Check that window-cleaners are insured against accident and damage, and make sure they bring their own equipment.

Make an arrangement with the windowcleaner on the frequency of visits; once a month is typical although you may not want such a regular service – it depends very much on the area and the speed with which your windows get dirty.

GARDENER

You may want year-round help in the garden, seasonal assistance or occasional help with a heavy job. Alternatively, you may want your garden completely cleared and re-designed. All are possible. Recommendation or the placing of an advertisement in a local shop or paper is the best way of finding casual help for weeding, digging, mowing the lawn or cutting hedges. These are not specialized and there are often reliable odd-jobbers who will provide exactly the service required.

However, if you want experienced help with planting, digging and saving bulbs or plants, cultivating different areas of the garden and paying specific attention to lawns, trees and so on, then you should find an individual gardener or horticultural compnay. Landscape gardeners, nurseries and garden centres also offer services, either on a one-off basis or on a seasonal or long-term contract.

Always make sure you are quite clear about fees and what they cover, so that you will not be landed with unexpected extra charges for plants, compost and other additional items.

HOME HELP

Provided and subsidized by the local authority, the home help service is intended for the elderly and infirm, those restricted by illness and the disabled and is in great demand. Approach your doctor or the local authority for information.

The home help offers a cleaning service and, sometimes, personal help of a friendly, or neighbourly, but unqualified kind. The regular visits of a home help can contribute to the quality of life, allowing someone to maintain their independence.

NURSING HELP

Trained nursing help can be obtained through specialist agencies. Occasionally, such help will be advertised on an individual basis in the local paper. As always, it pays to ask as many personal contacts as possible – the doctor, local centres for the elderly, community or religious groups.

You may require a full-time nurse, overnight assistance or occasional help to ease the burden on the family carer. Remember that a qualified nurse should not be expected to undertake any household duties other than those relating directly to the welfare of the patient.

HELP WITH ENTERTAINING

Catering services vary from area to area and can range from a 'dial-a-dinner' service to comprehensive catering and entertainment for functions such as weddings.

As well as the larger catering companies, it is worth remembering that many individuals operate a catering service on a price-per-head basis for dinner parties, buffets or cocktail-style food. You may want the food to be delivered ready-cooked for you to serve, or you may want it to be prepared in your own kitchen and served to anything from six to a hundred guests. Engaging an individual cook rather than a catering company is often cheaper and the food can be far better quality. Many such cooks have links with assistants and waitresses for serving larger and more formal meals.

You may want to cater for an occasion yourself but hire all the necessary china, cutlery and glassware. Local catering companies hire out everything from folding tables, linen, specialist equipment, tea urns and glasses to vast serving platters.

If you require waiting staff, check the local papers for individual advertisements or ask a local catering supplier for recommendations. There are also agencies which supply catering staff for domestic purposes. A butler can add an air of grandeur to a special occasion.

Children's parties are well served by companies offering a complete package, including food, entertainment and presents.

Cost and Commitment When engaging catering services, make absolutely certain that you are provided with a comprehensive quotation for the cost and that you have agreed on all the details well before the event. With large functions, such as weddings, you may have to book well in advance. You may opt to use an individual cook who will provide waitress back-up, in which case you may need to organize the wine, flowers, marquee, tables and other equipment yourself unless an arrangement can be made with the caterer.

Whether you are commissioning an intimate dinner party or a major function, always start by stating what you want, then ask to discuss a menu and other details of arrangements. Once the arrangements are verbally agreed and the caterer and other suppliers have seen the premises, then you must obtain a written quotation detailing everything involved and the cost. Make absolutely certain that there are no hidden costs, such as flowers, glass hire and travelling expenses.

For large functions, make sure that you agree a date for the number of guests to be finalized. Reducing the numbers at a late stage will not necessarily entitle you to a price reduction, as commitments will already have been agreed to suppliers further down the chain. If you make adjustments after you have agreed the fee, then you can expect to pay for them.

Money Management

Balancing income against outgoings is not always easy, particularly when unexpected expenses occur or the changing economic climate leads to price increases all round. This chapter highlights some of the key points to remember when considering financial commitments.

Managing domestic finance can be a complicated business when there are so many tempting invitations to stretch income and broaden spending power. Caution is by far the safest option when it comes to running a home, especially when providing a stable environment for a growing family. This chapter examines aspects of expenditure, briefly outlining sources, then looks at means by which money can be raised over and above expected income.

INCOME

This is the total amount of money which comes into the household budget. In anticipating income, consider only the regular and reliable amounts that are known to be due and do not speculate on likely prize winnings or possible extra earnings. Salary, various state allowances paid regularly, any dependable income on stable investments and so on can all be included in the budget when planning ahead.

INCREASING INCOME

Income may be increased by a change of employment or by taking on extra work, a second job or by producing and selling something in addition to the main means of employment.

In many cases, long-term predictions can be made about income and this is often an important factor in domestic economics. For example, the young person who follows a course of training or education which leads to positive, long-term career prospects can usually expect to receive increases in salary over a number of years in employment.

After some years' employment this is quite likely to change when career and financial prospects level out. In such cases, although they may expect their salary to keep pace with the cost of living, they will not anticipate any significant improvement in work and related financial status linked to promotion.

REDUCED INCOME

Unfortunately, reduced income is not always easily anticipated or predicted, although it is likely that at the end of their working life most people may expect a reduction in income; for example, their pension may be less than their salary.

Sometimes it is also prudent to take a pessimistic view and consider the possibility of redundancy or early retirement depending on the particular field of work.

PERSONAL FINANCIAL PLANNING

Preparing and keeping to a realistic financial plan is important when setting up home as well as when considering major expenditure at any point in time. When dealing with banks, building societies and so on, such information is used to estimate the credit-worthiness of individuals.

EXPENDITURE

Whereas there is usually little flexibility in income, there can be opportunity for great alterations in expenditure over and above a certain basic amount. So, for financial planning purposes, expenditure can be divided into essentials and non-essentials; in addition, there is some scope for thinking in terms of fixed essentials and flexible essentials.

FIXED ESSENTIAL EXPENSES

These are the monies that have to be paid at the correct time, with the amounts that are due being beyond your immediate control. Here are a few examples.

- Rent
- Mortgage
- Insurance premiums
- Taxes
- Licences (car and television)
- Payments already owed on credit agreements or loans
- Travel (that is, essential travel to the place of work)

Obviously, the only opportunity for changing the above is by making significant adjustments to status – moving closer to work, renting cheaper accommodation, getting rid of the television, selling the car and so on. Under normal circumstances, balancing the household finances should not involve this type of change.

FLEXIBLE ESSENTIAL EXPENSES

These are essentials that have to be paid for, but the amount of expenditure can be varied by adjusting the level of use and economies can be made to a certain extent without undue hardship. Examples include:

- Gas, electricity and other fuels used for heating, such as oil or coal
- Telephone
- Food (reduction depends on the current level of expenditure)
- Essential clothing
- Car maintenance and fuel

NON-ESSENTIAL EXPENSES

These are other outgoings that are not necessarily luxuries but that can be cut out completely if the need arises, if only for comparatively short periods. For example, many people expect to take an initial drop in their everyday standard of living when they increase their mortgage repayments. They may anticipate entertaining less frequently, avoiding eating out or not spending money on entertainment or hobbies. Include anything from non-essential clothing (and keeping up with fashion is not essential) to holidays away from home (excepting visits to relatives or friends).

UNPLANNED EXPENSES

These are the unpredictable bills that crop up when the car breaks down, a tile falls off the roof of the house or a piece of essential equipment needs repairing or replacing. In an ideal world, either your income should allow you to cope with small to moderate amounts or you should have money saved for such an event.

RAISING MONEY

Reasons for wanting money in addition to income vary according to lifestyle and time of life. To simplify the process of finding extra finances, it is convenient to think in terms of small amounts to be repaid in the short term and major financing which constitutes a long-term commitment. One of the main reasons for borrowing money, and involving major finance in domestic or personal matters, is for house purchase.

MORTGAGE

A mortgage is a loan secured against a freehold or leasehold property and building societies, banks and brokers are the main sources. The availability and conditions relating to mortgages vary according to the economic climate and the housing market and factors such as the prevailing government attitude towards housing and social trends towards home-ownership. This may sound like a comment from a lecture on social economics, but such factors deserve consideration as changes can be quite drastic over a few years.

Perhaps the most important point to remember when considering a mortgage application is that there are some unscrupulous companies whose main concern is making money out of the borrower, regardless of the practicalities relating to repayments in the long term. If you are refused finance by the well-known, reputable banks, building societies and similar establishments but offered a complicated deal from another, dubious source, then you really ought to think twice about the offer and your ability to meet all aspects of the arrangement.

TYPES OF MORTGAGE

Traditionally, there are two main types: endowment or repayment mortgage. The majority of mortgage agreements are planned over a span of twenty to twenty-five years for repayment. Variations become available from time to time, such as low-start options and those linked to savings plans.

Repayment This is sometimes called an annuity mortgage. Equal monthly repayments are calculated at the beginning of the agreement; however, these vary during the life of the mortgage according to changes in the interest rate. The interest and capital are paid simultaneously, although during the early years the larger proportion of the payments covers the interest. Towards the expiry, the larger portion of the payments is for capital. In a situation where tax relief is given on interest, the mortgage will be less of a financial burden in early years, which is when most borrowers need help.

Endowment This is linked to a life assurance policy. Two separate monthly payments are calculated; one on the interest and another to a life assurance policy which matures (or from which the money can be redeemed) at the end of the time of the mortgage agreement. When the life assurance is cashed, it yields sufficient to repay the capital and may offer the borrower an extra lump sum from any money accrued in addition to the original loan.

Make sure you understand the implications of different types of mortgage and adopt a realistic approach to your future prospects. With unusual mortgage arrangements, be certain to have a clear understanding of the alternatives at the end of the different repayment stages.

MORTGAGE APPLICATION

Obviously, as they are lending large sums of money, mortgage companies require extensive details about the borrowers. Depending on current trends, the mortgage may only be granted to cover a percentage of the cost of the property, which means you have to find cash or take out another loan (not usually advisable) for the remainder. The amount available is calculated on the income of the borrowers; obviously, income can change, so make sure you are not encouraged to borrow well beyond either your means or your future prospects.

Before considering your application, the mortgage company will require the following information

- Your age
- Employment details and salary (backed by written confirmation from the employer)
- Existing financial commitments
- Health details
- Pension arrangements
- Full details of the property, including a survey (chargeable to you)

Once the company has satisfied itself that you and the property are mortgage-worthy, you will be made an offer. This is based on the personal information supplied and on the valuation of the property.

The Property Value and Conditions For purposes of the mortgage, the property may be valued at less than the sale price. If this is the case, the mortgage will be calculated on that sum, meaning you have to pay the difference between the mortgage valuation and the sale price of the property.

Also, depending on the age and general condition of the property, there may be any number of conditions involved in the offer of a mortgage. For example, it is quite common for a request for rewiring, woodworm treatment, damp treatment or attention to the roof to feature in an offer on an older property. This usually involves work to be done within a given time period. You may be able to negotiate details to some extent.

BANK LOANS

These are loans of an agreed sum, for an agreed length of time . You must have an account with the bank and you will have to provide extensive personal details of other financial commitments and prospects other than those already known to the bank.

The bank will want to know what the money is for and how you intend to repay it. The type of loan will depend on the amount of money and the use. In some cases, if the amounts are large, the bank may require security against the loan.

Depending on the reasons for the loan and current taxation regulations, you may be able to claim tax relief on the interest paid on the loan.

Interest on loans is higher than that on overdrafts.

BANK OVERDRAFT

This is an agreement between you and the bank for your account to be overdrawn by a certain sum for a given length of time. You agree to reduce the amount of the overdraft in stages or to pay it all off by a certain time, depending on the circumstances and amount. Interest is paid at an agreed rate.

An agreed overdraft can be a cheap way of borrowing small amounts of money in the short term. It is far better to negotiate an overdraft with the bank manager than consistently to become overdrawn, incurring higher interest charges and loss of goodwill with the bank.

CREDIT CARDS

Available from banks, financial organizations or major retailers (through their selected credit companies), a credit card allows you to spend up to an agreed amount within a given period. A monthly statement is issued offering you various options . You can pay the amount in full without incurring interest, you can pay the minimum payment quoted on the statement or you can pay any sum larger than the minimum payment, but less than the full amount. If you choose either of the latter options, you will be charged interest on the sum outstanding (which is effectively borrowed). Some budget account schemes are based on the card-holder paying a fixed amount every month, then having a spending allowance.

It is possible to have more than one credit card (indeed, several) and the information sought before providing this service varies according to the establishment.

A credit card can be very useful in managing money by delaying certain payments over a short period with the intention of meeting the monthly statement with full payment. However, the danger of overspending and accumulating high-interest debts, is very real.

CHARGE CARD

Unlike a credit card, the monthly statement has to be paid in full without any opportunity for paying instalments and interest. Charge cards are available for major retailers (rather like an account) and through independent companies.

Note If you use a card for payment, the retailer pays a percentage of the transaction to the credit company, an amount which is larger for charge cards than credit cards. Occasionally, this charge may be passed on to the cardholder, but this must be made clear before the transaction takes place. It is often in the interests of the retailer to pay the percentage on each transaction as the use of a card avoids nonpayment problems and cheques which do not clear when presented to the bank.

It can sometimes be in the interest of the card-holder to agree to pay the fee, for example in a transaction with a foreign retailer, which would otherwise involve foreign currency, exchange rates, bank drafts and fees.

MAIL-ORDER CREDIT

Mail-order catalogue sales can be made on the same basis as a credit card, with a spending limit provided and interest charged after an agreed period.

HIRE PURCHASE

Payments made at agreed intervals over a period of time complete the purchase; with interest charged on the basic price. The goods do not become the purchaser's property until the agreed payments are complete, therefore they cannot be sold until the final instalment has been paid. However, once the purchaser has paid a third of the total amount, the owner cannot reclaim the goods without a court order.

Hire purchase is usually one of the most expensive ways of borrowing. Comprehensive laws cover HP agreements and you should always be aware of your rights in such cases.

CREDIT SALES

These 'buy now, pay later' schemes differ from hire purchase in that you own the goods from the start of the agreement. This means that you can sell the goods while you continue the agreed repayments: an important difference, especially when purchasing expensive items.

STORE ACCOUNTS

Independent retailers and large chains offer accounts to customers. They usually operate on the same basis as a charge card, with an agreed spending limit and monthly statement to be paid in full. There are also accounts, which offer credit on which interest is payable.

OTHER METHODS OF RAISING MONEY

Finance companies offer loans, often at high rates of interest and generally for fairly large amounts. Security may be required against money borrowed.

Finance agents operate locally, usually on a door-to-door basis, either offering loan schemes or offering credit 'checks' for small amounts or vouchers for large amounts. Weekly repayments are made and the checks or vouchers are accepted by some local retailers.

Pawnbrokers operate in some towns, offering cash in return for goods. You should, by law, receive a form in exchange for your goods. This should detail your rights for gaining return of goods within an agreed period for the original amount, then on an interest-payable basis.

PRIVATE AGREEMENTS

Borrowing moderate amounts of money from parents, close friends or relatives can be practical, depending on individual circumstances. The lender may want to help the borrower by offering an interest-free loan, or a loan to be paid back with the same rate of interest that the lender would have received in a bank deposit account or building society account (less than rates charged on loans, so the borrower benefits and the lender does not lose). However, such arrangements should always be undertaken on a formal basis, with regular payments made by standing order from the borrower's account.

This method of borrowing can often be an ideal way for young people to acquire comparatively small amounts for a specific reason, often related to home improvement or buying items such as a second-hand car. Remember, however, that private agreements should always be regarded as a means of paying less interest; they should not be taken on with a view to the possibility of never completing full repayment – this can sour a relationship, causing hardship all round.

SAVING AND INVESTING

If your income is more than you need to live in reasonable comfort, it is wise to save a small amount by means of an easily accessible scheme in case you need money unexpectedly. Building societies and banks offer a number of accounts with a moderate interest on money saved and without penalty for instant withdrawal up to a certain amount.

An investment tends to be longer term and the capital should accrue a higher rate of interest than in a savings account. Some schemes allow for withdrawals without penalty if a specified period of notice is given. Longer-term investments mature after a number of years, sometimes with additional payment of a lump sum. Interest rates usually increase with the sum invested.

There are many alternative savings and investment schemes, often with government backing and tax-related concessions. Although it makes sense to keep your emergency savings in an account which is convenient and readily accessible, before making an investment or saving additional sums always investigate every possibility. The various building societies and banks offer different interest rates, national savings schemes are usually in operation and the Post Office also runs some accounts.

INSURANCE AND ASSURANCE

Insurance provides financial compensation in unexpected emergency situations. Obtaining an insurance policy may form a binding part of an agreement; for example, when taking out a mortgage to buy a house, the financing company will insist on building insurance to cover loss or damage in instances such as fire. Car insurance to cover damage by accident to others is compulsory by law, but the policy does not necessarily have to cover damage to the policyholder's car. There are many other forms of insurance – house contents, health, pet illness and so on.

Assurance policies, on the other hand, are taken out in preparation for a future event, such as death or retirement.

Specialist companies deal with insurance and assurance policies, also most banks and building societies provide advice. Finding the policies best suited to your needs means shopping around in a crowded and confusing market. Make sure you have the essential insurance and assurance cover you need, but do not give up assessing the alternatives. Independent advice is offered by many reputable finance houses and this is often advisable, particularly for those who are self-employed.

PENSION SCHEMES

These are a form of assurance policy, providing a regular income and/or lump sum for the future, usually combined with payment related to premature death.

The state pension is government-run and it provides a minimum income for those of pensionable age. To ensure a comfortable retirement, it is sensible to invest in a personal pension scheme during your working life. At one time, employers were in a position to make membership of company pension schemes a requirement for employment; however, this is no longer the case.

Pension schemes are a complex area and taking professional advice is essential, either from banks or similar organizations or through an independent adviser.

MONEY MANAGEMENT REMINDERS

- List all income and expenditure to assess your financial situation: this is particularly important when you first live alone or run a household.
- Consider all forms of borrowing carefully, making sure you will be able to meet the repayments for the full length of the agreement.
- With major borrowing, such as a mortgage, involving or affecting partners or family, ensure you have some security against death. A pension policy usually covers this.
- Continually assess all financial commitments – credit cards, credit purchases, bank loans and mortgage, as well as household expenditure. Do not extend credit to cover shortfalls in income when economizing in certain areas is an option.
- In case of financial difficulty, always consult the bank or building society immediately and explain the problem. Do not let a problem drift until a substantial amount of money is owed.
- If you anticipate a change in circumstances, temporary or otherwise, make sure you warn the bank and other financial bodies with whom you are involved.

- If you cannot pay essential bills (taxes, fuel and so on), then let the company know and seek their advice.
- Never sign any financial agreements without having spent time considering the implications and reading all the small print. Ask for an explanation of any points which you do not understand.
- Never sign a blank, or part-filled, form.
- Find out about banks and building societies: take the trouble to compare accounts and services. Assess their efficiency and approachability at branch level. Remember you are a customer – they are not doing you a favour.

Social Customs

This chapter serves as an introduction to contemporary social customs, from feeling at ease when entertaining to being aware of the etiquette surrounding sad occasions, such as funerals.

In a society which has abandoned rigid rules about etiquette, customs still hold a place of importance and playa vital role. Their existence facilitates the organization of formal functions and ceremonies. They are also invaluable in easing the stressful procedures related to events such as death.

ENGAGEMENT

Engagements are not as formal as they once were. However, the couple may wish to make a formal announcement through a local or national newspaper and/or hold a celebration party.

Unless the couple are under eighteen, there is no legal obligation for parental consent, and the traditional interview between prospective husband and the bride's father is no longer an essential feature of the occasion. In some families, the bride's father may expect to 'interview' the young man, even if only on an informal basis. More commonly, the couple may prefer to announce their engagement jointly to each set of parents, at the same time seeking their blessing.

Press announcements are traditionally paid for by the bride's family. The wording is usually simple: 'The engagement is announced between (John) son of (parents' name and address) and (Anne) daughter of (parents' name and address).'

It is customary for the man to give his betrothed a ring (traditionally a diamond ring) which is worn on the third finger of the left hand. The man may be given a gift by his fiancee to mark the engagement. Nowadays, however, some couples dispense with the engagement ring.

Cards may be sent and gifts may be given to a couple on their engagement, but this is not essential. Any gifts should be acknowledged promptly.

Once a couple are engaged it is usual for both sets of parents to meet, although this may be postponed until the date for the wedding is set. If the parents do not meet soon after the engagement, then letters may be exchanged.

BROKEN ENGAGEMENT

This is a private affair. If the engagement was announced in the press, then a simple statement that the wedding will not now take place may be sent to the paper. If the engagement is broken off after the wedding plans have been made, these should be cancelled promptly and cards simply stating that the wedding will not be taking place should be sent to cancel invitations. Any gifts should be returned. The engagement ring should be returned, unless the man particularly wants the woman to keep the ring and she agrees.

Family and friends should be supportive, but they should not dwell on the subject of the broken engagement.

MARRIAGE

Organizing a wedding can be a daunting prospect, eased by the contemporary trend towards sharing out the responsibility and cost between the families and couple (where appropriate). Indeed, many couples who are established in their careers may wish to take on the main part of organizing and paying for the wedding.

The couple usually decides where and when to marry – traditionally this is in the bride's home parish – and they decide whether the wedding is to be a grand occasion or a simple affair for close family and friends. The ceremony may take place in church or in a registry office. A registry office wedding may be followed by a church blessing, often attended only by the bride and groom, attendants and immediate family.

The wedding is followed by a reception or wedding breakfast. This may be held at an hotel, in a hall or other suitable venue, or at the bride's parents' home. There are several options and a daytime reception may be followed by an evening party, often an opportunity for inviting friends or colleagues who were not present at the wedding.

There are various customs relating to the organization of different aspects of the celebration and the roles adopted during the day. The traditional procedure is outlined here; however, it may be varied according to the wishes of the couple and their families.

The Bride's Parents organize and pay for the reception, the bride's dress, the wedding cake, cars to the church, flowers for the church and reception, and the photographer. They send out the invitations and receive replies.

The bride's father leads her up the aisle on his left arm, taking her to the groom. He then steps back to take his place next to the bride's mother.

The Groom pays for the ceremony and wedding ring(s). He buys presents and flowers for the bridesmaids and buttonholes and sprays for the other attendants. He also pays for the car which takes him and the best man to the church and the bride and himself to the reception.

The groom awaits his bride at a church wedding, standing before the altar on the right side of the aisle, his best man on his right.

The Best Man and Ushers pay for their own clothes. Ushers greet guests at the church, give them the order of service and hymn books, then show them to their seats. The best man looks after the ring and ensures that the groom is at the church or registry office in good time. The best man and ushers ensure that the wedding party and guests all have transport from ceremony to the reception. The best man acts as a master of ceremonies at the reception.

The Bridesmaids and Attendants may pay for their own clothes, or sometimes the bride or bride's mother may pay. Where there are a number of attendants, there may be a chief bridesmaid; if there are any young children, either bridesmaids or page boys, it may be the chief bridesmaid's job to look after them. A married or older bridesmaid is usually referred to as a matron of honour. The chief bridesmaid or matron of honour takes the bride's flowers during the ceremony.

The bridesmaids greet the bride and her father at the door of the church, then follow them in procession down the aisle.

RECEPTION AND SPEECHES

The bride and groom usually receive the guests, along with best man, bridesmaids and both sets of parents. A welcoming drink is usually provided, followed by the food. This may be a formal 'sit-down' meal, a buffet, or finger-food which is handed around.

It is customary for the best man to act as the master of ceremonies when the time comes for the speeches. The bride's father makes the first speech and toasts the bride and groom. The groom follows with a speech of thanks to the bride's parents and good wishes and proposes a toast to the bridesmaids. The best man thanks the groom on behalf of the bridesmaids. He toasts the parents and reads greetings from absent friends. In a suitable gathering, the best man's speech may offer a light-hearted view of the matrimonial match.

The Bride Although it is traditional for the bride to remain blissfully silent throughout the reception, she may feel inclined to make a speech, often to thank her parents and other friends or relatives who have helped in her preparations. Although her parents may have paid for her wedding dress, she will usually buy her own going-away outfit and may well pay for her trousseau. The bride changes towards the end of the reception, before leaving for the honeymoon. Following a daytime reception, some brides change into evening wear before an evening party.

The Wedding Cake is cut by the bride and groom after the speeches. Everyone's attention should be drawn to this ceremony. The bottom tier of the cake is removed and cut up, then handed around.

Cake is sent in special boxes to relatives, friends and colleagues who could not be at the wedding. It is the custom to keep the top tier for the christening of the first child. But, since many couples do not plan to have a family for some time, this tier may be used for another special occasion, such as the first wedding anniversary.

WEDDING PRESENTS

The couple may draw up a list of suitable presents which should contain a broad range of items, with a selection of small and inexpensive ideas as well as many moderately priced gifts. Often, providing an idea of colours, styles and ranges of goods is an excellent way of compiling a guide to useful gifts.

Usually, the bride's mother will take charge of the list and give a copy to those who ask for it, or provide suggestions. It is important that items are crossed off as they are chosen, to avoid duplications.

Today many couples choose to place their list at a particular shop or department store. Guests can visit or telephone the store and choose their gift, which will then be deleted from the list. Some stores will also wrap and deliver the present.

However, it is worth remembering that many people do not favour lists.

WEDDING ANNIVERSARIES

Although some couples mark each wedding anniversary with some form of celebration (see the list below for the names of anniversaries from one to sixty years), it is customary for relatives and friends to acknowledge silver, ruby and golden wedding anniversaries (twenty-five, forty and fifty years) with greetings and gifts. The couple, their children or close relatives may organize a celebration with a cake.

1 year – Paper	13 years – Lace
2 years – Cotton	14 years – Ivory
3 years – Leather	15 years – Crystal
4 years – Linen	20 years – China
5 years – Wood	25 years – Silver
6 years – Iron	30 years – Pearl
7 years – Wool	35 years – Jade
8 years – Bronze	40 years – Ruby
9 years – Pottery	45 years – Sapphire
10 years – Tin	50 years – Gold
11 years – Steel	55 years – Emerald
12 years – Silk	60 years – Diamond

BIRTHS AND CHRISTENINGS

Immediate family and close friends should be told of the birth promptly, usually by the father. The parents may then send out announcement cards which generally include details such as the baby's name, date and time of birth, and birth weight. Sometimes, a birth is also announced in a local or national paper. Congratulation cards may be sent, and close friends and relatives often send flowers to the mother or give small gifts to the baby.

CHRISTENING

This may take place during a regular church service or separately. Godparents are selected as guardians of the child's Christian upbringing. There may be two godfathers for a boy, and one godmother; or two godmothers for a girl, with one godfather. The gift from godparents to child should be something which will last, and traditionally it is of silver.

Although a christening and the role of godparents is, strictly speaking, a religious one, social custom makes the commitment a special one. Godparents should remember their godchild's birthday and they usually give Christmas presents. They should take an interest in the child and often the special relationship will continue into later life.

Celebration Christening celebrations are not usually formal occasions and they can range from tea and cake after the ceremony to a party for family and friends.

VISITING MOTHER AND BABY

Always check with the partner to find out whether mother and child are ready to receive visitors and the best time to call. Unless you are a close friend or relative, or invited to stay for a specific length of time, keep visits brief. Some parents, particularly with a first baby, may feel pressurized and tired when first coping with a baby awake at night and needing much attention during the day. Never pick up a baby unless invited to do so.

FUNERALS AND MOURNING

Relatives and close friends have to be informed of a death promptly, preferably in person or by telephone. Warn the person that the news is sad and make sure that the elderly or anyone who is likely to be shocked and distraught has a companion to look after them.

An announcement may be placed in the local or national paper and this is one of the tasks handled by the funeral director. The announcement may include information about the funeral and the wishes of the deceased with regard to floral tributes or, alternatively, donations. Requests for a private, or family only, funeral and for donations rather than floral tributes should be announced promptly.

If flowers are sent, they should be delivered to the funeral director or to the house on the morning of the funeral (unless there is an announcement to the contrary). A card or note accompanying the flowers should have a message addressed to the deceased.

Letters of Sympathy Letters or cards may be sent to the next of kin or chief mourners as soon as possible after the death. These should be acknowledged in due course.

FUNERAL SERVICE

The chief mourners usually assemble beforehand at the house and the family sit in the front pews, traditionally on the right of the aisle for the service. There are few rules and guidance is usually offered by the clergy.

Today, it is not obligatory to wear black to a funeral; however, dark clothing is usually the best choice. If the coffin is already at the church or crematorium, the mourners may wait outside until the next of kin and chief mourners take their place. In some families, the women may prefer not to attend the graveside.

ENTERTAINING

Entertaining should be enjoyable, but it inevitably involves a certain amount of planning and work.

INFORMAL ENTERTAINING

Spending a day with friends or inviting friends to an informal meal does not involve formal invitations but the host and hostess should plan the event well and make sure the guests know about what time to arrive. If the invitation is a very loose one, just inviting people to turn up at some point during the day, then it should be clear whether guests are expected to leave after tea or whether they are invited for the evening as well.

The important point to remember about this type of entertaining is that the better organized you are, the more relaxed you will be; and the more relaxed you are, the more welcome and at ease your guests will feel.

FORMAL DINNER PARTIES

These may be organized by telephone, a few weeks ahead of the proposed date, and the arrangements should be confirmed a day or two beforehand. The menu should be planned well in advance, making allowance for any special diets and usually offering a choice of desserts.

Guests usually spend a while relaxing before being seated for the meal. Canapes or other nibbles should be prepared along with a selection of pre-dinner drinks. The host and hostess should introduce guests who do not know each other and open some suitable topic of conversation. Coffee may be served at the table or in the lounge.

LARGE PARTIES

Written invitations are sent about a month ahead. The invitation should indicate the type of gathering and suitable dress, if appropriate. At home, drinks, sherry, lunch, buffet or supper are all terms which indicate the type of event. Combined with the time of day, this will indicate the likely refreshment and when the guests are expected to leave.

GUESTS TO STAY

If guests are made aware of plans and/or routines which affect their stay, they can relax and enjoy themselves without fear of embarrassing mistakes. For example, always tell people roughly when you intend to get up in the morning and approximately when you have breakfast; guests who are already bathed and dressed and trying to help in a strange kitchen at the crack of dawn while the hostess flies around in a dressing-gown, will feel awkward.

Provide clean towels, drinking-water and tissues in the guest room. Fresh flowers are a nice touch, as are magazines or a book or two for anyone who is staying for more than a night.

An early morning drink of tea, coffee or fruit juice always goes down well. You may take a tray to close friends or relatives or, more usually, have everything prepared downstairs for those who are up first, so that they can relax while everyone gathers for breakfast. It is a good idea to show friends where the tea, kettle, milk and other essentials are kept so that they can make an early morning drink if they wish.

Exactly how you prepare for guests who stay depends on how well you know them and on the household routine. If you do find yourself in a formal situation, with guests who do know you well, it is especially important to plan ahead and keep them well informed as to what is expected of them.

BEING A STAYING GUEST

The ideal guest is one who fits into the household routine. If in doubt, ask your host or hostess about any plans they have and what the normal routine is in the morning.

Although taking a gift is not essential on every occasion, some flowers, confectionery, wine or similar are often appreciated, but do not be too lavish.

When you are staying with friends, try to be sensitive about helping and mixing with family and other guests. For example, find out whether the host or hostess is relaxed about having you in the kitchen, helping or chatting, or whether your interest in a tour around the garden is welcome or likely to break up a peaceful after-breakfast interlude reading the papers.

FRIENDS, ACQUAINTANCES AND COMMUNITY CUSTOMS

Meeting people, making friends and becoming part of a community or social group is important but not always easy. During school years or at institutions such as colleges, a ready social framework exists to support individuals; once a young person begins work, particularly if this involves moving to a new area, this framework can disappear completely – and very suddenly. Similarly, when an individual. a couple or family move from one area to another, they may not know anyone and will have to integrate with a new, often quite different, community. This can be particularly difficult for people who live alone.

WORK-RELATED SOCIAL GROUPS

Many large organizations have social clubs or their employees may arrange various out-of-work activities. In smaller companies, people of the same age or interests may develop a friendship but this can be limited to young single people, particularly in large towns and cities.

SPECIAL INTEREST CLUBS AND CLASSES

Joining clubs or attending classes can be good ways of meeting people and, in turn, making friends. This depends on the type of classes; for example, few people attend car-maintenance classes with a view to making friends, whereas individuals joining a squash club usually expect to meet others who share their interest in the sport. The most important point to remember about getting involved with clubs and classes is that you must have a genuine interest in the subject and be prepared to spend your spare time participating in the specific activity. As a consequence, you are likely to get to know people with similar interests and the acquaintanceship may develop into a broader friendship.

NEIGHBOURS

Links with neighbours vary enormously according to area, age and lifestyle. In many large towns and cities the people living next door can be totally anonymous, whereas in small communities neighbours can be life-long friends. As a general rule, it is a good idea to get to know immediate neighbours and to develop a pleasant relationship with them. It is customary for existing residents to introduce themselves to newcomers. The idea of offering neighbours tea on the day they move in, when cups and kettle are not unpacked, is still an excellent way of creating an opportunity for an introduction which may, or may not, develop.

Although neighbours can become friends, keeping a certain distance in the relationship can be important; time should be allowed for a genuine link to be formed once both parties get to know each other. In places where many long-established friendships exist between neighbours, being accepted into the community may be slightly difficult.

COMMUNITY GROUPS AND CHURCH GROUPS

Belonging to a group related to some aspect of everyday life is a common way of meeting people. Many groups of this type actively welcome new members.

COMMITTEES

Committees are the basis for most forms of public life. The members are usually voted on by the organization and the committee has a chairperson (someone to oversee the proceedings) who is usually an experienced committee member. Other members of the committee fulfil different roles in running the organization. Being on a committee means sharing the work involved and accepting the decisions which are reached by the group. An agenda, or order or business, is prepared and circulated before each meeting and all members should be prepared to make relevant contributions.

Being offered a position on a committee is a vote of confidence in your opinion and judgement: meet the honour by working hard to fulfil your role in the organization.

STYLES OF ADDRESS

When speaking to royalty, the address 'Your Majesty' or 'Your Royal Highness' should not be used more than once and, indeed, may be omitted altogether in favour of the simpler 'Ma'am' (pronounced to rhyme with Pam) for the Queen and 'Madam' or 'Sir' for other members of the Royal Family.

The Queen Letters to the Queen should be addressed to the Private Secretary to Her Majesty the Queen. Begin the letter 'Dear Sir', and ask him, for instance, 'to submit for Her Majesty's approval/consideration …' Never refer to the Queen as 'she', but always as 'Her Majesty'. Close the letter 'Yours faithfully'. If you do wish to write to the Queen direct, the opening style is 'Madam, With my humble duty'. Use 'Your Majesty' and 'Your Majesty's' instead of 'you' and 'your', and close the letter 'I have the honour to be/remain, Madam, Your Majesty's most humble and obedient servant' .

Other Royalty Letters to other members of the Royal Family should be addressed to their Equerry, Private Secretary or Lady-in-Waiting. Begin' (Dear) Sir' or '(Dear) Madam'. Refer to the member of the Royal Family first as 'His/ Her Royal Highness' and subsequently as 'Prince/Princess …' or 'The Duke/Duchess of … as appropriate. End the letter 'Yours faithfully'. When writing direct, open the letter 'Sir' or 'Madam', use 'Your Royal Highness' instead of 'you', and end 'I have the honour to be, Sir/ Madam, Your Royal Highness's most humble and obedient servant'.

When writing to royalty or people of title, the envelope should bear their most important title.

Titled Persons When addressing a person of title, either verbally or in writing, the form of address varies according to whether the communication is formal or social. Thus, when writing formally to a Duke, the style of address is 'My Lord Duke', and the formal verbal address is 'Your Grace'; but socially, the written form of address is 'Dear Duke', and the verbal form simply 'Duke'. A Duchess is written to formally as 'Madam' or 'Dear Madam', and spoken to as 'Your Grace', but socially she is addressed in writing as 'Dear Duchess'.

A Marquis, Earl, Viscount or Baron is addressed formally as 'My Lord' and socially as 'Lord …' both verbally and in writing.

The wife of a Peer is addressed formally in writing as '(Dear) Madam' and verbally as 'Madam'; socially she is addressed as 'Lady (surname)'. Style of address for a Peeress in her own right is the same as that for a wife of a Peer, although she may choose to be known as 'Baroness (surname)' rather than 'Lady (surname)'. A Baroness in her own right and the wife of a Baron are also addressed in the same way.

A Baronet or Knight is written to formally '(Dear) Sir', and addressed socially as 'Sir (Christian name)'. The surname should be added if the acquaintance is only slight. Formal and social verbal address is 'Sir (Christian name)'. His wife is written to formally' (Dear) Madam', but for all other purposes the style of address is 'Lady (surname)'.

An Archbishop, like a Duke, is addressed formally as 'Your Grace', and socially as 'Archbishop'. Bishops, Deans and Archdeacons are addressed simply using these titles. Vicars and Rectors are addressed formally as 'The Reverend (Christian name + surname), Vicar/Rector of ...', and socially as 'Mr …' or 'Father …' according to his preference. Wives of all clergymen are addressed simply as 'Mrs …', unless they have a title in their own right.

The formal style of address for a Lord Mayor is 'My Lord Mayor', and his wife is 'My Lady Mayoress'; socially the style is 'Lord Mayor' and 'Lady Mayoress'. A mayor is formally addressed 'Mr Mayor'; a woman mayor may prefer to be addressed 'Madam Mayor'.

Socially the style is 'Dear (Mr/Madam) Mayor'.

ROYAL AND OTHER FORMAL OCCASIONS

An invitation to Buckingham Palace itself, or to one of the official buildings, used for royal or government functions, will include suitable instructions.

Ladies normally wear gloves when shaking hands with the Queen, as a courtesy and no longer as a bounden duty. The gloves should be thin and light but do not need to be white as once was the custom. They are worn for the Queen's comfort since she can get hot and painful hands from too much handshaking. Never grasp her hand firmly for the same reason, merely lay your hand in hers while making a 'bob' curtsey. For men, gloves are optional, but preferred. Again, the handshake should be very light and be accompanied by a slight bow.

When royalty is present at a private function, formalities are more relaxed. If you are to be presented, you will be warned and briefed in advance.

At other formal occasions, banquets, receptions, and so on, be prepared to meet a reception committee. Your name and that of your escort, if you have one, will be taken by an attendant or toastmaster who will announce your arrival. You then shake hands with those who are there to receive you before proceeding to join the party. If the occasion is a formal dinner, it is incorrect to smoke before the loyal toast is drunk.

Index